BREAKING
FAITH

BREAKING FAITH

THE SANDINISTA REVOLUTION AND ITS IMPACT ON FREEDOM AND CHRISTIAN FAITH IN NICARAGUA

Humberto Belli

CROSSWAY BOOKS • WESTCHESTER, ILLINOIS
A DIVISION OF GOOD NEWS PUBLISHERS

THE PUEBLA INSTITUTE

The Puebla Institute, established in 1982, is an independent, non-profit organization concerned with fostering a Christian understanding of theological and socio-political issues affecting Latin America. Through a program of research, writing and publishing, the Institute provides analysis and documentation of key issues and developments.

The Puebla Institute
P.O. Box 520
Garden City, MI 48135

Third printing, 1986

Printed in the United States of America.

Library of Congress Catalog Card Number 85-70475

ISBN 0-89107-359-0

TABLE OF CONTENTS

ACKNOWLEDGMENTS

This book could not have been written without the selfless and constant collaboration of Joseph Davis, my colleague at the Puebla Institute. He edited the whole manuscript and put it in acceptable English form. He also offered me timely and valuable advice on both its content and organization. To him my first and warmest thanks.

I would also like to express my gratitude to the many Christian men and women from the United States and Nicaragua who provided me with documentation for this book. Unfortunately, I cannot mention their names nor the names of others who contributed to the manuscript in various ways—public connection with this book could cause them or their families in Nicaragua real harm. They are known to God and I pray that they may be rewarded by Him for their concern and commitment to see that the difficulties that Christians are facing in Nicaragua become known.

INTRODUCTION

In July 1979, when a bloody revolution swept away the forty-two-year-old Somocista dictatorship in Nicaragua, many eyes looked expectantly to this small Central American nation—especially Christian eyes. An uninspiring, corrupt, and decadent dictatorship had been overthrown by the massive participation of Nicaraguans from all parts of society. Even more notable, the revolution had been won with the collaboration of Marxists and Christians on a scale unsurpassed by any contemporary revolution. Thousands of Christians, including some Catholic priests, had fought with the Marxist guerrillas. The influential Catholic bishops had issued pastoral letters denouncing the government's violations of human rights and spoke about the people's right to rebel in the face of prolonged, unbearable tyranny. In many ways the Nicaraguan revolution seemed to defy skepticism about the possibility of positive social change in Latin America and to challenge previous judgments about the nature of Marxist revolution and the incompatibility of Christianity and Marxism.

Many among the victorious leaders of the revolution, known as Sandinistas, had expressed sympathy for Marxism-Leninism. But four Catholic priests held positions in the government—minister of foreign affairs, minister of culture, minister of social welfare, and leader of the Sandinista youth movement. And the Sandinista government promised to follow policies based on the principles of political pluralism, a mixed state-free market economy, nonalignment with either the United States or the Soviet Union, and full respect for human rights, especially the rights of free expression and religious freedom.

For many people inside and outside Nicaragua the revolution

seemed a long-awaited effect of the winds of political and theological change sweeping through Latin America. At any rate, for all Christians increasingly concerned with the issues of social justice and liberation for the oppressed, the Nicaraguan revolution was a challenging experiment. Could Christians and Marxists drop their historical hostility and mistrust in behalf of a shared effort to serve the poor? Could Christians participating with leftist revolutionaries contribute to the appearance of a new, more humane, Christianized socialism? For years Christian scholars in Europe and the Americas had struggled with these kinds of questions at the theoretical level. Now the Nicaraguan revolution seemed to provide a testing ground for such hopes.

Many Christians who saw Christianity and Marxism as incompatible, and did not harbor hopes of Christian-Marxist partnership in the cause of the poor, nevertheless were optimistic that the massive participation of Christians in the revolution would tend to moderate any hard-line Communist tendencies and would produce a moderate outcome. It was also widely believed that even the hard-core Marxists in the Sandinista movement had been—or could be—influenced by the testimony and values of so many "revolutionary Christians" who had been willing to share their sweat and blood in the struggle for a new Nicaragua.

Furthermore, many observers did not expect a fully Marxist government to emerge, because so many non-Marxists held positions in the new Sandinista government. Many democratic forces had participated in the struggle against Somoza and were officially present in the overall effort to shape Nicaragua's future after July 1979. They included a host of non-Marxist political parties, ranging from Christian and Social Democrats to conservatives, labor organizations, the nation's businessmen's association, and a variety of outstanding democratically minded individuals in the press, the churches, and elsewhere. Surely they would count for something in the upcoming constitutional process. In addition, democratic regimes welcomed the Sandinista revolution. Venezuela, Mexico, Costa Rica, Panama, West Germany, the United States, and others extended a rather open hand, at least at first, to the revolutionary government.

The prevailing domestic and international attitude toward the revolution was faith. Faith in its leaders, faith in its promises, and faith in its potential for Nicaragua. Thus, political conditions seemed ideal for the creation of a new kind of society—a third way between the inequalities and miseries of Third-World capitalism and the stagnation and lack of liberties of Communist regimes. At the very least, the experiment seemed to deserve a chance.

An evaluation of this experiment today is not an easy task. The government claims great advances in the lives of the poor— greater literacy, more widely available health care—and there is evidence to support some of these claims. At the same time, the seemingly unified national effort to reshape Nicaragua that was launched in 1979 has splintered into a contest between rival groups. Relations between the Sandinistas and some former supporters—the United States, Costa Rica, and others—have been strained, sometimes to the breaking point.

Observers who set themselves to understand these contradictory indications of the Nicaraguan revolution's success or failure face a confusing array of plausible claims and counterclaims. For instance, regarding the breakdown of unity among the different domestic forces which fought with the Sandinista National Liberation Front (FSLN—Frente Sandinista de Liberación Nacional), the Sandinistas' former allies claim that the Sandinistas have betrayed their original promises of pluralism and want to impose an increasingly repressive Marxist-Leninist rule. The Sandinistas reply that their opponents' real motivations stem from their reluctance to give up their "bourgeois" privileges on behalf of the urgently needed transformation of social and political structures.

To give another example of conflicting assertions, some Catholic and Protestant leaders claim that the Sandinistas have begun persecuting religious believers and are planning to bring all religious institutions into submission to the state. For their part, the Sandinistas and others point to a considerable degree of religious freedom, and explain the charges of persecution as a politically motivated reaction by conservative church leaders who have allied themselves with the upper and middle classes against the interests of sweeping changes for the poor.

A taste of the perplexity that such contradictory versions can produce was provided by Catholic theologian Henri Nouwen after his visit to Nicaragua:

Some say, "What is happening is nationalism: a country trying to
determine its own future." Others say, "No, it's internationalism: a
country becoming the victim of Cuban-Soviet domination." Some
say, "What you see in Nicaragua is the best example of a revolution in
which Christian values are truly integrated." Others say, "No, it is a
revolution based on atheistic principles and bent on the eradication of
all religious beliefs."[1]

The Nicaraguan experiment is of particular importance for
Christians, and its differing interpretations have been especially
divisive for them. The Nicaraguan Catholic bishops and some
Protestant pastors in Nicaragua (and, outside the country, the
Pope and the organization of Latin American Catholic bishops—
CELAM) have been critical of the Christian advocates of liberation theology who have been supporting the FSLN. But Catholic missionaries such as Maryknollers and Franciscans and Protestants associated with the Center for Promotion and Development (CEPAD), and others outside Nicaragua (such as Pax
Christi International) have spoken in support of the FSLN. They
view it as a noble Christian task to defend the revolution against
its detractors.

The problem of assessing the Nicaraguan revolution requires
sorting out disputes over facts as well as an analysis of differing
interpretations. Nowhere is this task more difficult than in respect to the central issue of this book—the record, current
situation, and prospects of the churches under the Sandinista
government. There is no agreement among observers on the
actual degree of repression that the Sandinistas have imposed.
Reports range from those who claim there is none to those who
claim the FSLN has inaugurated a reign of terror. While most
observers would agree that the government has taken some measures that have been harmful to Christians, some observers see
the Sandinistas' actions as justified by an unstable political situation, while others perceive a totalitarian design.

The very importance of the Nicaraguan revolution makes it
worth trying to find one's way through all these claims and
counterclaims in order to get at the truth. But much of the
confusion about the Nicaraguan experiment flows from the fact
that many people with various political investments understand
the importance of the Nicaraguan experiment and have gone
about promoting their own self-interested views of it. Both the

political right and the political left have their own set of vested interests that are affected by how people perceive what is going on in Nicaragua. Both sides are interested in portraying the Nicaraguan situation, including the religious situation, in a certain light for Christians in the United States, for example, either to foster support for United States-supported military countermeasures or to diminish such support.

More broadly, people who advocate the capitalist system but who may not themselves have deep religious concerns may be strongly motivated to discover and highlight religious repression as evidence to use against leftist revolutions. Marxists who for more than a decade have been promoting what Fidel Castro called "strategic alliance with Christians" have reasons to show that Nicaragua is indeed a good demonstration of how Marxists and Christians can work together for the oppressed and benefit from a harmonious relationship with each other.

Personal factors also enter in when Nicaraguans and others view Nicaragua. Nicaraguans who have been touched in their own families and persons by Somoza, the revolution, and its aftermath may react to the FSLN in passionately favorable or hostile tones. On the other hand, some foreigners are so distant physically and psychologically that they are apt to project onto it their own hopes or terrors.

Difficult as the search for truth about Nicaragua is, it is important for Christians outside Nicaragua to pursue it. Expressions of the opinion of Christians outside the country can strengthen or weaken Nicaraguan Christians' resolve to deal with their situation in certain ways. International opinion also can promote or discourage the Sandinista government's policies toward the Nicaraguan Christian communities. Moreover, the Nicaraguan revolution sheds light on important questions that Christians will be increasingly forced to confront regarding liberation theology, the social mission of Christians, and the possibility of Marxist-Christian cooperation. The present book is an attempt to untangle the issue of the nature and dynamics of the Sandinista regime and its conflict with religious leaders and institutions.

Having referred to the kinds of political and personal interests that can shade an observer's view of Nicaragua, it would be best for me to describe my own background. As a Nicaraguan who participated in the Sandinista movement for several years, and then as a convert to Christianity in 1977 who joined the Catholic Church and worked with some of its bishops, I gained a personal acquaintance with both the FSLN and the Nicaraguan church situation. While I cannot claim to be a dispassionate observer, I believe that my involvements have given me an understanding of the Nicaraguan revolutionary process that is often difficult for someone from another culture to obtain.

After my departure from the FSLN in 1975, I did not participate in any political organization, but played a part in the religious discussions that took place in my country before and after the revolution. In early 1980 I joined the newspaper *La Prensa* as editorial-page editor, with the goal of presenting a daily Christian perspective on the important events that we were living through. The editorial page became a forum for discussion of religious and theological issues, especially touching on the interplay of religion and politics, religion and social action. I was concerned to challenge some of the approaches of liberation theology which seemed to provide a blessing for the unrestricted use of political power and to undermine a complete commitment to Christ and the evangelistic and pastoral mission of the church. My stand earned me the animosity of some of the liberation theologians and members of the FSLN.

In March 1982 total censorship was imposed on the press in Nicaragua. This made it impossible to freely debate the important issues regarding religion and politics. I decided to leave the country, primarily to help Christians outside Nicaragua understand the religious dimension of recent events there. My aim in communicating about Nicaragua has not been to influence the foreign policy of the United States or other countries. Important as it is for citizens of other nations to take responsibility for their nations' policies toward Nicaragua, my attention has been elsewhere.

While my central concern is religious and has to do with the situation of the churches in Nicaragua, I have had to devote considerable attention in this book to the nature of the Sandinista government. An understanding of the Sandinistas is crucial because it is they, after all, who determine the political and social environment that Christians in Nicaragua have to deal with. Thus the book begins with a lengthy examination of the FSLN rather than of the church.

Observers have come to sharply different conclusions about

the goals of the Sandinistas. Unfortunately, outsiders' views are seldom based on a close study of the Sandinistas' own statements, particularly those in which the main leaders have expressed their ideology and sociopolitical goals. I am convinced that the ideological statements of the revolutionary FSLN need to be taken seriously as a real expression of what the Sandinistas think and intend.

Having examined the background and self-understanding of the Sandinista movement in the first chapters, the present book explores the Sandinista government's policies in respect to independent organizations (such as labor unions and agricultural cooperatives) and other political parties, the press, the economy, ethnic minorities (mainly the Miskito Indians of the Atlantic Coast), basic human rights, and its foreign policy. The question I shall attempt to answer is whether the Sandinistas' actions since the revolution have been consistent with their origins and stated purposes.

Finally, the book will analyze the relationship between the FSLN and the churches. Clearly there has been conflict, but what kind of conflict? Has there been actual persecution of Christians? Is the conflict basically religious (an atheistic government versus a largely believing populace) or political (Marxists and Christians who want a revolution on behalf of the poor versus Christians and others who are entrenched in the defense of upper- and middle-class privileges)? Has liberation theology in practice modified the Marxism of the FSLN or secularized the faith of Christians?

I sincerely hope that this book sheds light on these questions. They are important ones. They touch on issues that affect how Christians will conceive of their mission in the world in the years ahead. For Nicaraguan Christians, they are already pressing, real-life issues which touch them deeply and personally. I will be happy if this book provides more than intellectual enlightenment for Christians outside Nicaragua. The Pauline understanding of the church as the body of Christ implies mutual responsibility among all Christians. "If one member suffers, all suffer together; if one member is honored, all rejoice together" (1 Cor. 12:26). How Christians outside Nicaragua can live out this reality of solidarity with their brothers and sisters there, "bearing one another's burdens and so fulfilling the law of Christ," is a matter which needs to be carefully considered. The first step is for

Christians outside the country to develop a realistic understanding of the situation of Christians in Nicaragua, and to pray for them.

NOTES

1. Nouwen, "Christ of the Americas," *America,* April 21, 1984, p. 296.

TWO DECADES OF SANDINISTA STRUGGLE

Who are the Sandinistas? While in the eyes of some observers they are clearly Communists, to others they appear to be revolutionaries who embrace a novel blend of Marxist and Christian values. There are those who concede that the Sandinistas are Marxists—but flexible, pragmatic Marxists, unlike their Eastern European counterparts. Others approach the question from a different angle: they acknowledge that there are hard-core Marxists-Leninists in the Nicaraguan regime, but these are not seen as having the upper hand.

The debate is not merely academic. To know the philosophy or ideological inspirations of a political movement is crucial for understanding its dynamics and direction. Without such a reading it is impossible to interpret a movement's actions and devise appropriate responses to them. Take, for example, the FSLN's alignment with Soviet foreign policy and internal policies such as media censorship. If such actions are alien to the Sandinistas' ideological script, they might be interpreted as responses to outside pressures or provocations, or as mistakes. On the other hand, the actions might be in keeping with the Sandinistas' basic philosophy and goals. The two interpretations would lead to different responses. If the first interpretation was true, more favorable international conditions might be expected to foster the Sandinistas' evolution toward a more democratic, nonaligned type of revolution. If the second interpretation was correct, few hopes could be harbored in this regard.

For Christians, the question of the nature of the Sandinista regime has great practical importance. Interpreting the Sandinista revolution as a Christian-inspired undertaking, or at least one compatible with the Christian faith, many Christians in and outside Nicaragua have called on Christians there to support the revolution. Interpreting the regime as a mixed government not controlled by doctrinaire Marxists, others have called on Christians at least to cooperate with the government lest, by taking an adversarial position, the churches strengthen the Marxist forces within the government. By contrast, others believe that the churches confront a Communist regime, and thus emphasize the need for Christians to exercise caution. At issue in these different interpretations is the question of whether the Sandinistas' goals are compatible with independent churches. Do the Sandinistas' goals place them in the category of bona fide allies, competitors, or enemies?

How can we know what the Sandinistas' basic conceptions and goals are? I believe we need to listen to the Sandinistas themselves. This task, however, is not without complications. As we shall see, the Sandinistas have not always been consistent in their statements. Their statements in the months just preceding and following the revolution do not quite match their declarations during most of the sixties and seventies. Some assertions which they have made clearly in documents aimed at their own membership are veiled—or entirely absent—in documents intended for an international audience. Thus, careful analysis is needed.

A reasonable principle of interpretation is that, regardless of how patriotic the Sandinistas may be, they are also politicians, and their public statements should be treated with a certain degree of reserve. Views they express to their own members should be given greater credibility. At the same time, in evaluating discrepancies, allowance should be made for changes in the Sandinistas' ideological foundations and goals. This is the approach we shall follow in the analysis that follows.

It is also necessary to discover the assumptions that underlie the Sandinistas' concepts. Notions of pluralism or nationalism, for example, may have one set of meanings for North Americans accustomed to representative democracy, but may hold an entirely different meaning for Central American revolutionaries.

Once the ideology, values, and goals of the Sandinista movement come into focus, we should accept that the movement's leaders mean what they say. A common mistake of non-Nicaraguan observers has been to take a patronizing attitude toward the Sandinistas. They are portrayed as young idealists who have wanted to change their society for the better, but have not paid much attention to ideological matters. Perhaps North American observers have assumed that they are not astute enough to understand Marxist philosophy.

I joined the FSLN for the first time in 1965 as a member of the Student Revolutionary Front, where many leaders of the FSLN were bred. Later, from 1973 to 1975, I was a full member. In the FSLN, we took ideology seriously. Ideological commitment was a prerequisite for positions in the higher echelons of the organization. If it is true that there were sympathizers and collaborators who mainly had good intentions and guts, it is also true that members in responsible positions were ideologically conscious and even had a zeal for Marxist-Leninist orthodoxy on the issues that really mattered. While our views were in some ways naive and simple, many of the members held them with the utmost faith.

Above all, the leadership of the FSLN knew what it wanted. Indeed, the leadership's ability to distinguish its long-term goals from its short-term objectives helped the Frente pursue its arduous struggle. It knew how to be uncompromising about the former, but flexible about the latter. This clear political vision strengthened the Sandinista movement with perseverance, a virtue which most political movements in Nicaragua lacked. The Sandinistas fought for nearly twenty years to achieve victory, waiting for the unfolding of circumstances that would make Nicaragua ripe for revolution. Many of them were romantics, in the sense of dreaming of a utopian future; but the Sandinistas were also cool calculators. Because they had a clear sense of purpose, they knew better than their adversaries how to make tactical alliances and avoid being caught off-guard. The very fact that the Sandinistas rather than any of the other forces in the Nicaraguan political environment came to power bears witness to their strategic prowess born of ideological convictions.

NICARAGUA IN THE TWENTIETH CENTURY
The appearance of the Sandinistas must be viewed in the matrix of recent Nicaraguan history. Until about 1950, Nicaragua was a largely agricultural and traditional society, where personal relations and bonds of kinship weighed heavily in all transactions,

including political and economic ones. Urbanization was still incipient. But by the 1950s the pace of economic and cultural change was beginning to accelerate, even while political power remained firmly in the hands of the Somoza family, which had climbed to power after nearly a century of internal strife and several years of United States intervention.

More than clashes of ideologies, or even of opposing economic interests, the civil wars which preceded the Somoza regime had sprung from regional and even family rivalries between the cities of Leon and Granada. The former was the seat of the northwestern-Pacific landowners, whose party took the name of Liberals. The latter was the center of the south-central landowners and was the focus of trade. Its party took the name of Conservatives. Constant strife between the liberals and the conservatives made Nicaragua politically unstable and economically stagnant, and invited foreign intervention.

The United States first sent Marines to back a conservative revolt that sought to overthrow the ruling liberal President José S. Zelaya in 1909. A secularizing nationalist and a despot, Zelaya had antagonized the United States by, among other things, hinting that he might allow another power to build a canal in Nicaragua at the time when the United States was building the Panama Canal. The new conservative regime was in turn challenged by liberal revolts, and the country sank toward chaos. More United States intervention followed, at first in an attempt to prop up the faltering conservatives, later in an attempt to achieve a more stable peace between the warring factions.

U.S.-supervised elections took place in 1928, and were won by the Liberals. To solidify the peace another step also seemed necessary. Traditionally armies in Nicaragua had been either conservative or liberal, rather than national. As such, they could not be relied on to support multiparty rule based on elections. According to United States historian Richard Millet,[1] a goal of the American intervention therefore became the creation of a nonpartisan military force as a key to ensuring stability. The National Guard was created as the first professional, nonpartisan army in Nicaragua's history, and a low-profile Liberal, Anastasio Somoza Garcia, was appointed its director.

The whole arrangement turned sour. A nationalist liberal leader named Augusto César Sandino defied the settlements and rejected foreign intervention. He raised a guerrilla force in the

Nicaraguan highlands and vowed to fight until the last Marine left the country. Somoza, on the other hand, a shrewd and ambitious man, began turning the National Guard into his private army. After the Marines left in 1933, Sandino refused to disarm his troops and engaged in vicious battles with the Somoza-led National Guard.

In 1934 Nicaraguan President Juan B. Sacasa summoned both Sandino and Somoza to a peace conference in Managua. Sandino was murdered in a treacherous ambush set up by officers of the National Guard, and Somoza emerged as Nicaragua's strongman. In 1936 he ousted President Sacasa in a coup and became president himself.

Sandino gradually emerged as a legendary figure—a national hero murdered by an agent of U.S. imperialism. In time, the political left in Nicaragua began to blame all Somoza's misdeeds on the United States and to eulogize Sandino as the altruistic precursor of Marxist revolutionaries. These perceptions were not entirely accurate, nor were they shared widely by the Nicaraguan population. The United States did originally promote Somoza through the ranks of the National Guard in the belief that he would play a role in harmony with U.S. interests. But he was not a puppet of Washington's desires. As John J. Tierney, Jr., characterizes him: "He did what most aspiring politicians in twentieth-century Nicaragua did before him, namely, he used Washington as a political lever to increase and solidify his own internal ambitions."[2] Sandino, on the other hand, was not a man without egotistical ambitions, and he displayed, at times, moral callousness and a violent temper. Sandino's and Somoza's forces matched each other in a willingness to commit atrocities against each other and each other's real or imagined supporters.

Many of Sandino's troops were merely bandits who often used threats and murder to enlist peasant support for their cause. Sandino himself boasted of his army's tortures of captured soldiers, which included the taping of a soldier's severed genitals into his mouth and executions by a method he called "corte de chaleco" ("vest-coat cut")—which, with two cuts at the shoulders, removed the victim's arms and with a third cut through the torso disemboweled the victim.[3] Up to the mid-1960s, the romance with Sandino and the strong anti-U.S. feelings that went along with it were mainly confined to the student subculture where they developed in the 1940s. The population at large, particularly the peasants, did not share this view, but welcomed the end of struggle and the opportunity to return to business as usual.

Once Sandino's army was liquidated, Somoza, following an established Nicaraguan pattern, turned the National Guard into an army for his family and friends. With control of the government and the military, he rewarded his loyal followers with quick and easy enrichment and punished his enemies. Within ten years he was Nicaragua's wealthiest as well as its most powerful man. Somoza cultivated relations with Washington and boasted of his friendship with the U.S. government as a way of finessing his conservative opponents, who did not find many options open to them.

The end of the period of civil war, followed by the economic boom which began in the fifties, greatly helped to consolidate Somoza's hold on Nicaragua. Some observers in the seventies and eighties have suggested that the Somozas were kept in power by the United States. In fact, until the late seventies their political control was never seriously challenged. They managed to survive their first four decades with a rather small and primitive military force (approximately six thousand to eight thousand men), with a less-than-sophisticated secret police force, and with less U.S. funds than comparable Latin American nations.[4]

During the fifties and sixties Nicaragua modernized itself at an amazing rate. Traditional subsistence crops gave way to efficient cotton plantations, and good international prices for this fiber injected foreign currency into Nicaragua as never before. Roads were extended; a new manufacturing and commercial system was developed. The state bureaucracy multiplied—and with it the number of those who regarded Somoza as a benefactor. Cities grew. The educational and health-care systems began to reach out to a wider range of people. Overall, standards of life improved, even for peasants at the margin of the economy.

But the new wealth, which was unevenly distributed, contributed to making the differences between rich and poor more vivid than before, especially in the cities. At the same time, the old personal, somewhat paternalistic relations between the social elites and the masses of poor Nicaraguans were melting away, replaced by more impersonal market relations.

The processes of change were beset by conflict. New values and new economic activities were placing an emphasis on hard work, personal aggressiveness, and efficiency as keys to social advancement, in contrast to older personalistic and family-oriented traditions, still strong in the countryside. But these traditions continued in the state machinery, where favoritism to relatives and friends outweighed other considerations. This situation often made social advancement seem arbitrary, depending on the right connections and smart politicking—and led to resentments.

Nicaragua in this period was also being secularized very rapidly. The liberal governments had put an end to religious instruction in the public schools. Now new intellectual influences began to penetrate the country through the universities, the media, and the social elites, who as never before went abroad to study. The older generation felt challenged by the influx of new values and changing moral standards. Many, in fact, felt rather bewildered and unable to cope with the changes. The younger generation grew uneasy and rebellious. Above all, the younger people were convinced that they, rather than their parents, were destined to find the answers for Nicaragua's future. The political forum, traditionally dominated by the liberals and the conservatives, became the scene of challenges from new political ideas and parties, particularly Christian Democrats and Marxists.

Nevertheless, through the fifties and sixties these new outlooks, values, and ideas were confined to Nicaraguan campuses and educated elites. The masses of Nicaraguans were too concerned with bread-and-butter issues and too enmeshed in traditional politics to pay much attention to the new visionaries.

In 1956 Anastasio Somoza was murdered by a young Liberal Party dissident. His son Luis succeeded him in the presidency. Luis Somoza turned away from his father's authoritarianism to inaugurate a reformist phase in which freedom of the press was restored and room created for a revival of political activity.

THE SANDINISTAS IN THE FIFTIES AND SIXTIES

In the early fifties the founders of the Sandinista movement, Carlos Fonseca (born in 1936) and Tomás Borge (born in 1930) joined the Moscow-line Partido Socialista Nicaragüense (PSN), a tiny organization of Nicaraguan Communists of that era. Their standard textbook for beginners was *The ABC of Communism* by Nikolai Bukharin. Recalling those times a quarter-century later for *Playboy* interviewer Claudia Dreyfus, Tomás Borge told how his mother was so much against communism that she once told him that "the day you become a Communist, I will fall dead." Borge continued, "I told her that I would not be blackmailed by her gentleness and her naiveté, and that I was a Communist. Needless to say, she did not fall dead."[5]

In 1957 the PSN sent Fonseca on a trip to Moscow as its delegate to the Sixth World Youth and Student Festival. When he returned he wrote a book entitled A Nicaraguan in Moscow, a thoroughgoing apology for the Soviet system.

Fonseca and Borge broke with the PSN at the end of the fifties. The decisive event was the Cuban revolution. It challenged the long-standing reservations that Latin American Communists, including the PSN, entertained regarding armed struggle, on the ground that objective conditions were not ripe. It stirred hopes of a more immediate victory. "The victory of the armed struggle in Cuba, more than a joy, was the lifting of innumerable curtains, a flash of light that shone beyond the simple and boring dogmas of the time," Borge wrote afterwards. "Fidel was for us the resurrection of Sandino, the answer to our reservations, the justification of the dreams of heresy of a few hours before."[6]

Fonseca ventured on the first armed resistance in 1959, shortly after Pedro Joaquín Chamorro, editor of the newspaper La Prensa, had failed in a Conservative-led attempt to start a guerrilla war against Luis Somoza. Before Fonseca and nearly fifty guerrillas succeeded in slipping from Honduras into Nicaragua, they were surprised by the Honduran army. Many of them were killed or captured. Fonseca escaped wounded and fled to Havana.

This was the beginning of a lasting association between the would-be leaders of the FSLN and the Cuban revolutionaries. Fonseca, and shortly Borge and other collegues, met with Castro and Che Guevara. Fonseca soon moved his wife and only son to live permanently in Havana. This city was to become a political haven where many leaders of the FSLN would spend long periods for study and training.

Back in Honduras in 1960 and reassured by the support of the Cubans, Fonseca, Borge, and a new comrade, Silvio Mayorga, set themselves to organize the first Marxist armed revolutionary organization in Nicaraguan history. They named themselves after Sandino, who, although he was a nationalist with only a vague ideology, was the great anti-U.S. figure. Fonseca, and later one of the FSLN's other chief ideologians, Humberto Ortega, made efforts to assimilate Sandino to Marxism. They emphasized Sandino's alleged internationalism and portrayed him as an antibourgeois revolutionary locked in relentless struggle with Yankee imperialism.

Officially founded in 1960, the FSLN departed from the views of the comrades in the Partido Socialista Nicaraguense. As had happened between Fidel Castro and the Cuban Communist Party before the revolution, the differences between the FSLN and the PSN concerned strategy. No dispute arose regarding fundamental philosophy and long-term commitment to create a Marxist Nicaragua.

The Frente made sure that all its militants shared the basic Marxist-Leninist beliefs, and this goal was virtually achieved by the midsixties. In a book entitled *Fifty Years of Sandinista Struggle* written in 1976, Commander Humberto Ortega explained how, during the period from 1960 to 1967, the Marxist-Leninist method, which was not grasped by the militants of the preceding period, became the basis for the direction of the struggle.[7]

While studying law at the Central American University in Managua (UCA), I was a member of the Student Revolutionary Front, unofficially a branch of the underground FSLN, from 1965 to 1967. There I had meetings with Casimiro Sotelo, who would later become the FSLN's representative to the Organization of Latin American Solidarity in Cuba; with Oscar Turcios, eventually one of the top commanders of the FSLN, killed in combat in 1973; and with some other members of the organization, including the Ortega brothers. We made extensive use of Bukharin's primer on communism, and adopted George Pulitzer's *Marxism-Leninism for Beginners* as a standard textbook. We had study sessions and listened to comrades with all degree of sophistication. One of our teachers was Oscar Turcios himself. He had spent some years training at the Patrice Lumumba University in Moscow and was very knowledgeable about Mao Tse-tung. I remember him lecturing on the dictatorship of the proletariat, a period that "has got to be very hard in order to get rid of the enemies of the working class."

In our Marxist view of the world, all evil and injustice were rooted in the private ownership of the means of production, namely, in the capitalist system, defended at the local level by Somoza and the Nicaraguan bourgeoisie and at the international level by U.S. imperialism. The system of capitalism and imperialist domination thus divided peoples and countries into roughly two categories: the oppressors and the oppressed; the rich, capitalist nations and the impoverished, underdeveloped ones. To achieve a new world of justice, it was necessary to destroy the system by the revolutionary struggle of the oppressed against the oppressors, of the dependent nations against the wealthy nations. We strongly believed that the destruction of the local bourgeoisie and Yankee imperialism would open the doors to a world of untold possibilities, a utopian future. We saw the FSLN as the vanguard that would lead the people to their full and definitive liberation.

Castro, our hero, had taught us the path for accomplishing the dream. Cuba, our model, showed us the courageous David facing Goliath, the United States, the archenemy of all peoples. Cuba was the inspiring society where people had undertaken to free themselves from oppression by a collective endeavor that left no room for the undecided.

We were quite clear that the corrupt Somoza regime was not the main enemy, as some sectors of what we considered the reformist bourgeoisie were claiming. He was merely a pawn of U.S. imperialism.

The FSLN launched its first military operation in 1963. The idea was to create a guerrilla operations zone in the Bocay region of northern Nicaragua. After some attempts and a few clashes with the National Guard, the experiment collapsed, for the same reason that the attempt of Pedro Chamorro had failed: lack of peasant support. The guerrillas were not peasants but city-bred students, many of them middle- and upper-class young people.

During the sixties and the early seventies the FSLN suffered several setbacks. In 1967 the National Guard nearly obliterated the FSLN's guerrillas in Pancasan in north-central Nicaragua. Fearing for me because of my involvement with the Frente, my father persuaded me to go to Spain to finish my law studies. Some months after I left Nicaragua, a three-man squad of the FSLN led by Daniel Ortega gunned down a member of Somoza's security police in Managua who had the reputation of being a torturer. The government's swift reaction almost broke the Frente. Top Sandinista leaders were captured, tortured, and killed, including Sotelo and my best friend at that time, Roberto Amaya. Borge, Fonseca, and others escaped again to Havana.

During the remaining years before the revolution's success, casualties among FSLN members remained high. Nine of the fourteen men who belonged at different times to the Frente's top leadership body, the national directorate, died before 1979.[8]

THE SOCIAL BASE OF THE FSLN

The bloody defeats of the FSLN, however, become victories. In Nicaragua, where the Somoza regime was perceived by many as a corrupt, endless family dictatorship, the heroism of the Sandinista guerrillas was a ray of hope, a vindication of national dignity. By contrast with the Sandinistas, other opponents of the regime, mostly the democratic opposition, seemed too feeble, too irresolute, too comfortable to wage the struggle. Especially among students, the more defeats and casualties the FSLN suffered, the more its prestige grew. Many Nicaraguans felt reservations about the guerrillas' ideology, but could not help being touched by their heroic witness. I myself, after the killing of my friend Amaya, experienced a hardening of my resolution to commit myself to the revolution.

Middle- and upper-class students, who were easy prey for guilt feelings in a country where differences between rich and poor was abysmal, were particularly vulnerable to the attraction exerted by the FSLN. The hardships and dangers of life with the Frente provided these newcomers with a "way to purge one's soul of the guilt of being bourgeois in the midst of poverty," as one writer put it.[9] An FSLN recruit, the future Sandinista commander Henry Ruiz, explained, "Our origin was predominantly petit bourgeois students."[10]

The social base of the Sandinistas was not the shanty towns where the urban poor of Managua and other Nicaraguan cities lived. Nor was it among the urban workers, nor, least of all, among the religious traditionalist peasants. The social base for the FSLN was the Nicaraguan college campuses and secondary schools. This was a substantial base. Due to the youth of the Nicaraguan population (half the people are under twenty years old) and the vigorous modernizing process begun in the fifties, the Nicaraguan student population was larger than the rather small proletarian class and was increasing at an amazing rate in the sixties. University enrollment more than doubled between 1960 and 1970. The Somoza regime at that time was pursuing some populist policies and, with the increased revenues from export crops, was able to afford subsidies for education. Consequently university fees were very low (less than $4.30 per semester) and most courses were available in the evenings, making it possible for many low-income people, clerks, and full- and part-time employees to attend.

Many of those who swelled the ranks of secondary and college students came from middle- to lower-class backgrounds and harbored resentments against a social order in which the elites tried to minimize social relations with those of lesser status. A Nicaraguan poet provides a glimpse of this resentment: "The daughters of the rich are beautiful, neat, and proud. They go places—auto, yacht, jet—where we are not invited, where we are ignored."[11] The avenues of advancement for those lower in the social order were indeed crowded with difficulties. The paradox was that the more the educational system opened itself up to enroll larger numbers of lower-class youth, the more the potential for revolutionary unrest grew. These young Nicaraguans developed expectations of social improvement far faster than the system was able—or willing—to fulfill them. For some, these expectations found a revolutionary form in the FSLN.

Yet those joining the Frente were not supposed to carry with them any traces of bourgeois aspirations. Usually those who committed themselves to the FSLN shared at least a strong emotional rejection of the status quo. Building on this, the Frente labored to make sure that new members expurgated the values of their bourgeois background and adopted the ideology of the proletariat: Marxism-Leninism. Open advocacy of Marxist ideology, including its atheist elements, was, however, a break with their past that was more than many young people could bring themselves to, especially those with a strong Christian background. Many wrestled with the question, Can I be both a Christian and a revolutionary Marxist at the same time? In the sixties, answers to this question did not come easily.

GROWTH AND DEVELOPMENTS IN THE SEVENTIES
By the early seventies the FSLN was still a very small organization. An estimate for 1970 by Commander René Vivas put their numbers at fifty to seventy official members and ten to fifteen clandestine operatives.[12] There was also a handful of occasional collaborators and student sympathizers.

Despite its smallness, the Frente had developed a messianic idea of itself and was widely regarded as the symbol of armed resistance to the Somoza regime. It had also refined its conceptions of armed struggle and had given explicit expression to its ideological convictions and plan for government.

Their military experiences persuaded the Sandinistas to adopt a policy which they called "Prolonged People's War" (Guerra Popular Prolongada—GPP). This was to be a patient process of building networks of support for a guerrilla army in remote parts of the country. From these base areas the guerrillas would move easily, but would not seek engagements with the enemy until they had achieved tactical superiority.

The FSLN's leaders embraced Che Guevara's view of the guerrilla life as an indispensable part of the process of washing away bourgeois fixations. Thus, in the seventies a new theme entered the movement—the birth of the new Socialist man through revolutionary action. A poem by my sister, who joined the Sandinista movement in 1972, expresses this belief:

> We will be new, love.
> We will wash away with blood
> The old and depraved,
> The vices, the tendencies,
> The putrid petite bourgeoisie.[13]

In the seventies it came to be accepted in the Sandinista movement that to become a guerrilla fighter was to achieve the highest possible moral status. The Frente looked with scorn on legal labor union organizing and on the political activities of the parties that opposed Somoza. In the Sandinistas' eyes, these groups were preoccupied with immediate bread-and-butter issues and with seeking the approval of the masses. The Frente, by contrast, had undertaken a higher task: the creation of revolutionary consciousness among Nicaraguans. The following remark by Tomás Borge reflects this view:

> The "traditional parties of the left" failed when the political organization was put at the service of the union organization, giving the struggle a strictly economistic, reclamationist, and immediate character. Our working class in general is not spontaneously revolutionary, neither here nor anywhere else. It must be led to its role of vanguard of the revolutionary process.[14]

The conception of the Frente as the vanguard of the working class or of the Nicaraguan people was deeply established in the minds of the FSLN's members. In this respect the Frente was neatly Leninist: the working class had to be led to revolution by a vanguard (the party) which knew better than the workers themselves what their true interests were. Humberto Ortega explained the relation of party to workers this way: "Essentially we are the ideological and political representatives of the interest of the exploited, of the class historically destined to bury capitalism and imperialism."[15]

The Frente did not conceive of itself as an organization that would listen to the masses and give voice to their aspirations. Rather, it saw itself in a teaching role in relation to the masses of Nicaraguans, with the duty of enlightening them, despite their reluctance, and leading them to liberation. This theme was often stressed by the FSLN's leaders. In a speech at the Plaza de la Revolución in Managua on November 19, 1980, Commander Jaime Wheelock expressed what the FSLN had claimed for more than a decade: "The FSLN is the consciousness of our people, and it shall be the guardian angel of our people."[16]

According to the Sandinistas, two things enabled the vanguard to play such a role: the vanguard's mastery of the revolutionary theory of the working class (Marxism-Leninism), and the revolutionaries' personal superiority (they were, in a sense, the first and truest proletarians):

> There are a few men and women who at a given moment in history seem to contain within themselves the dignity of all the people. They are examples to all of us. And, through the struggle, the people as a whole reclaim the strength and dignity shown by a few. . . . I don't think revolutionaries are made by totally ordinary people. We revolutionaries are visionaries. . . .[17]

There was something more than a sense of historical consciousness and moral superiority in the Sandinistas' appreciation of itself as the vanguard, for it not only claimed to represent the people, but in a sense it considered itself to *be* the people. The FSLN has consistently defined the people in a way that does not mean the majority of the population or those who are objectively poor. For the Sandinistas, "the people" are those who, regardless of class or background, have developed a revolutionary consciousness. A worker without such consciousness is not one of the people; a middle-class intellectual committed to revolution is. The people, the future Sandinista Vice President Sergio Ramirez explained in 1980, is not an "abstract and cross-class term," it does not mean "everybody," and it cannot be defined in separation from the vanguard of conscious revolutionaries.[18] Commander Jaime Wheelock expressed the same idea in even clearer terms in 1984: "The FSLN is the representative par excellence of the workers and peasants, and power is in the vanguard, the FSLN, and with it in the workers of Nicaragua."[19]

As the Sandinistas considered themselves the incarnation of the working class, they regarded all other political and social forces as representatives or expressions of the bourgeoisie. In the Sandinista view, bourgeois ideas and people were not to be tolerated; they were "putrid," "evil," "treacherous." And just as ideological commitment rather than actual class background made one a part of the vanguard and one of the people, so other ideological commitments made people bourgeois even if they were in fact workers. The Sandinistas called Christian-Democratic or Social-Democratic labor unions "bourgeois trade unions." Workers who followed the leadership of the Marxist Nicaraguan Socialist Party were considered to be infected by petty bourgeois ideas or values. An intellectual or cleric would be with the bourgeoisie or with the proletariat according to his distance from or affinity to the FSLN.

As the supreme interpreter of history, the vanguard saw itself as above moral constraints and judgments. The atheism of Marxist teaching denied any absolute outside and above man who could hold man accountable for his actions. The vanguard was obliged only to be faithful to the revolution. It would be judged by history.

During the early seventies, calls were made for ideological purity among the Sandinistas. Not only were no efforts made to attract non-Marxists; the Sandinistas regarded them as a threat to be guarded against. The Frente, Carlos Fonseca demanded, should watch out for the enemy who might try to infiltrate the movement with "democratic" Sandinistas who lacked Marxist political commitment.[20]

Links between the FSLN and Cuba became ever closer. Fonseca spent most of the period between 1967 and 1975 in Cuba, directing the movement from afar. Borge and Turcios also spent time there with him, as did Humberto and Daniel Ortega. The Frente was reinforced with cadres trained in Cuba and the Soviet Union. Henry Ruiz, later to become one of the nine top commanders of the FSLN, joined the organization in 1967 after a period of political education at the Patrice Lumumba University in Moscow and military training with the PLO and in North Vietnam. Leticia Herrera, who became the national leader of the Sandinista Defense Committees after the revolution, received her training in Moscow in 1968 before joining the FSLN in 1970.

REVOLUTIONARY INTERNATIONALISM

The prevailing outlook in the FSLN in the seventies could be described as sectarian. Fonseca called on revolutionary students to reject hypocritical Christian demagoguery about class conciliation and to realize that "Marxism is now the ideology of the most ardent defenders of Latin American man."[21] Fonseca repeated this call later. The Frente embodied the Marxism of Lenin, Fidel, Che, and Ho Chi Minh, Fonseca claimed from Cuba. "It must not compromise its ideological purity."[22]

The FSLN's Marxist vision for Nicaragua involved a rejection of bourgeois society, reformism, and pluralism in favor of Socialist state control. At the beginning of the Frente's first public program for government, in 1969, the Sandinistas made their first goal

> replacement of the constitutional theory of elected representation (never effectively implemented in Nicaragua) with a revolutionary government that would promote direct popular participation in its structures. Freedom of expression and organization in the interest of the people. Punishment for members of the old regime.[23]

The statement indicated a distaste for multiparty rule and for people electing their leaders, and envisioned a scheme for direct popular participation organized and directed by the government—that is, by the FSLN. Freedom of expression and organization there would be, but in the interest of the people, not against it.

The FSLN's 1969 program also reflected a desire to politicize all education and to produce intellectuals faithful to the revolution. Clause 8 vowed the FSLN to the task of "reclaiming the university from the domination of the exploitive classes . . . teaching students about the spirit of the noblest ideals and against exploitation and oppression. Freedom for the intellectuals who work for the people." The phrase "for the people" is to be understood in light of the Sandinistas' views examined above.

A similar qualifying phrase was to be found in the FSLN's intentions regarding religious freedom. In clause 9, the program promised "respect for religious beliefs and support for clerics who support the working people."

Two other features of the Marxism of the FSLN, also apparent in its 1969 statement, were its anti-imperialism and its internationalism. The Sandinistas' anti-imperialism was exclusively focused on the United States and its allies, the capitalist nations. The Sandinistas had no criticisms of the Soviet Union or its foreign policies. In this regard, the FSLN tended to be more loyal to the Soviet Union than neighboring Communist parties. Sandinista literature, from the birth of the FSLN to the present, is entirely lacking in criticism of the Soviet Union.

Such strict adherence to Soviet views and policies cannot be explained as a reaction to hostile U.S. policies. It can only have been due to a conscious commitment by the Sandinistas. Sandino himself had been a nationalist mortally opposed to U.S. intervention in Nicaragua, but that did not make him a Communist. In fact, he declined the suggestion by the Salvadoran Communist leader Farabundo Martí to join the Comintern (Communist International). The Sandinistas, by contrast, saw their mission as one of joining in the international effort to defeat the enemy of all peoples, the United States, by siding with the vanguard of all liberated nations, the Soviet Union, and supporting Marxist revolutionaries throughout the region. A line of the official Sandinista anthem, sung at all the party's ceremonies, goes: "Let us fight against the Yankee, enemy of mankind." Carlos Fonseca also expressed his opinion that "it is necessary for us to strongly emphasize that our major objective is the socialist revolution, a revolution that aims to defeat Yankee imperialism."[24]

Just as the FSLN saw Nicaragua divided between the oppressors and the oppressed, between the people's vanguard and its enemies, the FSLN saw the world divided between two gigantic forces—the oppressing nations and the liberated ones—in a confrontation of good against evil. This was an extension of Marx's theory of class struggle to the international level. Humberto Ortega, commander-in-chief of the Sandinista army and brother of Sandinista president-to-be Daniel Ortega, expressed this picture of the world in a 1981 address:

The historical development of society finds itself polarized today into two great camps: on one side the camp of the reactionaries and of imperialism, on the other side the camp of the revolutionary and progressive forces . . . on one side the imperialist camp headed by the United States and the rest of the capitalist countries of Europe and the world, and on the other side the socialist camp, composed of different countries of Europe, Asia, and Latin America, with the Soviet Union in the vanguard.[25]

The FSLN's duty in this world confrontation was to join the forces of progress and revolution without regard for borders. More than nationalists in the conventional sense of men and women concerned to defend their own country's traditions, culture, and autonomy, the Sandinistas were internationalist revolutionaries. They recognized a brotherhood with fellow revolutionaries around the world that outweighed national bonds. Their call was not just to work for revolution in Nicaragua, but to labor for the world's Socialist revolution.

The Sandinistas' Marxist-Leninist internationalism was expressed in various ways. In 1965 Fonseca met the leader of the Guatemalan Rebel Armed Forces (FAR), Luis Turcios Lima, and in 1966 a group of Sandinista guerrillas, led by Oscar Turcios, of Managua, went to Guatemala to fight alongside the FAR and gain military experience. Daniel Ortega was among the future Sandinista leaders that spent time with the Guatemalan guerrillas. As perhaps a symbolic tribute to the FSLN's Marxist internationalism, one of Fonseca's closest aides and later a member of the Frente's national directorate was a Mexican Marxist who joined the FSLN in 1963, Victor Tirado Lopez. Casimiro Sotelo, in the year he died, also expressed his conviction that the FSLN's task must be to contribute to the fulfillment of Che Guevara's prophecy of "one, two, many Vietnams."[26]

The Sandinistas' commitment to revolution beyond the borders of Nicaragua was also expressed in the oath taken by new militants at the ceremony of their incorporation into the FSLN. Standing before pictures of both the Nicaraguan nationalist Augusto Sandino and the Marxist international revolutionary Che Guevara, recruits declared, "I place my hand on the red and black banner that signifies 'free fatherland or death' and swear to defend, with arms in hand, the national dignity and to fight for the redemption of the oppressed and exploited of Nicaragua and the world." The movement's intentions were given more explicit expression in a section of the 1969 program of government, already mentioned, in which the Frente vowed to

> struggle for a "true union of the Central American peoples within one country," beginning with support for national liberation movements in neighboring states. Liquidation of the Central American Common Market.[27]

A later edition of this document (described as a reprint but containing more than stylistic revisions) continued this commitment in more rhetorical, less specific terms:

> [The Sandinista people's revolution] will actively support the struggle of the peoples of Asia, Africa, and Latin America against the new and old colonialism and against the common enemy: Yankee imperialism.[28]

INCORPORATING THE REVOLUTIONARY CHRISTIANS
In the course of the seventies, while the FSLN's basic ideological suppositions and goals did not change, the movement became more imaginative and flexible in its tactics. As Commander Henry Ruiz explained,

> It is necessary to have enough flexibility—capacity to change course—to accommodate the line of action to the developing historical circumstances, without ever losing sight of the strategic objectives.[29]

A phenomenon which had an important effect on the FSLN's handling of its public profile was the appearance of Christians oriented to social change. In taking advantage of this opportunity, the Sandinistas shared in a general change in Latin American Marxists' approach to religion beginning at the end of the sixties.

Sparked by developments at Vatican Council II and the Latin American bishops' conference at Medellin, Colombia (1968), many Latin American Catholics became more aware of a responsibility to further social change on behalf of the poor and to denounce injustices. This awakening took place in Nicaragua as elsewhere. For example, the archbishop of Managua, Miguel Obando y Bravo, typified this shift by the way in which, from his assumption of office in 1970, he broke with the tradition of church-state accommodation. His reading of modern Catholic social teachings led him to a position that could be described as progressive-democratic and favored representative government.

Some Catholics began to rely on Marxist theory for an understanding of social ills and remedies for dealing with them. They became advocates of socialism. The most prominent Nicaraguan churchmen who took this approach were Fr. Uriel Molina and Fr. Ernesto Cardenal.

Fr. Molina organized a "base community" in his parish of Fatima, in a very poor barrio of Managua. The members of the community were mostly upper-class students who came to live under Fr. Molina's roof in the first weeks of 1972. The group felt a sympathy for the struggle of the FSLN, but found it difficult to square with their Christian beliefs. A new theological approach, "theology of liberation," as advocated by Fr. Molina, provided a way out of this impasse. According to this approach, love for the oppressed could be lived out through revolutionary action. In fact, only through a radical change of the present order could the poor be rescued from bondage. Therefore, commitment to the revolution was not alien to Christianity but integral to it.

Fr. Cardenal was developing a similar rationale for revolutionary commitment in a community he founded on the Solentiname island in Lake Nicaragua in 1965. Some trips to Cuba which he undertook in the early seventies convinced him that the Communist revolution there had brought a foretaste of the kingdom of God. A poet of international renown, Fr. Cardenal's writings made a striking impression on Nicaraguans at the time.

Marxists studied these developments closely. As early as the midsixties, Guevara had spoken of the tactical need to draw Christians into the revolutionary struggle, given the religiosity of Latin Americans and the difficulty of persuading the poor to embrace the revolutionary creed. Guevara's concern was picked up by Castro. Pablo Richard, a Chilean who became a spokesman of Christians who advocated socialism in Latin America, gave this report of a visit with Castro around 1972:

Fidel invited us to Cuba. We spent three weeks getting to know the Cuban process and, at the end, we spent about ten hours discussing, along with Commander Fidel, the issue of an alliance between Marxists and Christians. We were also helped by the famous words of Che Guevara: "When the revolutionary Christians dare to give an integral testimony, that day the Latin American revolution will be irreversible." Fidel was deeply convinced that there would be no revolution in Latin America without the Christians.[30]

Castro was probably right. Armed revolutionary efforts proved unsuccessful in Venezuela (1963), Peru (1966), and Uruguay (1971), and were stagnant in Colombia and Guatemala. A key factor was the lack of popular support.

In 1969 Tomás Borge approached Fr. Ernesto Cardenal, and in 1971 Fr. Uriel Molina. Carlos Fonseca approved these exploratory moves. The meetings were friendly and led to organizational linkages between the FSLN and the revolutionary Christians. Some Protestant leaders followed suit. In 1972 José Miguel Torres, a Nicaraguan Baptist pastor, went to Cuba, where he spent long hours with Humberto Ortega, who taught him the basics of Marx's dialectical materialism.[31]

For the Sandinistas, the revolutionary Christians were an attractive discovery:

> It was a tempting matter for the FSLN, from the viewpoint of the resources we could get, the social background [of the revolutionary Christians], and the relations we could then handle, the possibilities of getting homes, cars, farms for training, etc.[32]

As mostly upper-class youngsters, the revolutionary Christians were able to provide the FSLN with some key logistical support. But they offered wider opportunities also. Through its association with the revolutionary Christians, the FSLN could give an air of greater legitimacy to its struggle and increase its appeal to the masses of Nicaraguan Christians who were deeply alienated from the unchecked corruption of the Somoza dictatorship.

The moral bankruptcy of the regime was fully demonstrated after the devastating earthquake which destroyed Managua in December 1972. Foreign aid was rushed in to help Nicaragua recover, but Somoza and his associates took the lion's share. The National Guard indulged itself in pillage and profited from relief supplies. As reconstruction plans proceeded, Somoza and his friends benefited from the sale of lands where new roads and settlements were to be built and from his monopoly on cement and concrete blocks. The greed of the Somocistas alienated the business community, which found itself locked into unfair competition with so many booming Somoza enterprises. Many children of bourgeois families in this period sat through countless meals at which they heard their parents bitterly decry Somocista corruption. Yet the adults felt powerless to restrain Somoza and ambivalent regarding the FSLN. They did not want the Frente to gain power (which, in any case, seemed impossible), but they did take delight in the FSLN outsmarting the state machinery or kidnapping Somocistas.

In these circumstances the FSLN decided to allow revolutionary Christians into its ranks without extracting a show of loyalty to Marxist-Leninist doctrine. Commander Monica Baltodano described this step in the following terms:

> All this was decisive for the incorporation of the people. . . . It was hitting the mark for the Frente Sandinista. For the Frente saw the reality of our people—a very Christian people, a very Catholic people. It did not position itself as if it were Marxist and had to convert people to Marxism. It was seen that the key thing was not whether the people were Marxists but whether the people were ready to fight against dictatorship. Within this framework, there was no need of anything else.[33]

CONVERTING TO SANDINISMO

Crucial to the successful development of the strategy of linking up with the revolutionary Christians was the idea of creating a vanguard within the vanguard. The Frente was gradually redesigned as an organization of concentric circles: an outer ring of sympathizers and collaborators, an intermediate structure of ideologized militants, and a directive nucleus of committed Marxist-Leninists. As long as the Sandinista nucleus remained faithfully Marxist, the organization could benefit from the support of all kinds of collaborators without jeopardizing its ideological integrity. The idea was articulated by Commander Humberto Ortega:

> This "avant garde" vanguard Sandinista nucleus should take over and direct the main organizations. This nucleus should use the scientific doctrine of the proletariat, Marxism-Leninism, as an absolute and unquestionable guide in the action undertaken for the transformation of society.[34]

It is worth observing that Ortega applies the term "doctrine" to Marxism-Leninism, and treats it as an "absolute and unquestionable guide."

Besides the Sandinistas' organizational arrangements, another factor which made the incorporation of revolutionary Christians "safe" was that many of the newcomers fell away from their religious beliefs and became orthodox Marxists-Leninists. This process was not forced by hard-core FSLN ideologues. It came about through the dynamics of the social situation which naturally influenced Christians who were already rendered open to Marxism by the radical version of liberation theology.

An outstanding case was that of Commander Luis Carrión. The son of a wealthy family, Carrión joined Fr. Molina's group in 1972. As members of the Movimiento Cristianos Revolucionarios (MCR), Carrión and his companions studied Marxism in order to have a scientific tool for understanding Nicaragua. Carrión ended by becoming an atheist, and in 1975 he became the leader, with Jaime Wheelock, of the most doctrinaire Sandinista stream, which called itself the Proletarian Marxist-Leninist FSLN.

Commander Carrión's case was not unique. The MCR acted as a preliminary stage for many young Christians who were concerned about social change but had reservations about the Marxist line of the FSLN. In the MCR their fears of Communism were resolved; later they went on to join the FSLN, and most of them exchanged their Christian beliefs for Marxism. In fact, most of the nearly dozen founders of the MCR became atheist Marxists. Fr. Fernando Cardenal, S.J., brother of Fr. Ernesto Cardenal and FSLN militant from 1974 on, gave this account of the process:

> From motivations rooted in true Christian faith we made the youngsters step forward to a commitment to work for justice and for the people. This led to a second stage, where they ended up committing themselves to the FSLN. In this second stage many of them abandoned the Christian faith, but not the profound values that motivated them. . . . What is interesting is that from this commitment with the people the youngsters found that the way was the FSLN. This was always successful—perhaps in as many as 97 percent of the cases.[35]

Margaret Randall, herself a Marxist who works with the FSLN, provides evidence of this phenomenon in her book *Cristianos en la Revolución Nicaragüense,* in which she offers first-person stories by most of the leaders of the MCR. Among some of the cases of Christians who abandoned Christianity for Marxism through their involvement in the MCR were Sandinista Commanders Joaquín Cuadra, chief of staff of the Sandinista army; Alvaro Baltodano, director of military training; and Monica Baltodano, head of the FSLN mass organizations. Others included Salvador Mayorga, vice minister of agrarian reform; Roberto Gutiérrez, vice minister of agrarian development; José A. Sanjines and Angel Barrajón, former priests now working for the government; and Francisco Lacayo, an officer in the ministry of agrarian reform.[36]

One outcome of this process was that many people who were regarded inside and outside Nicaragua as Christians in the FSLN were Christians no longer. But the Frente arrived at the tactical decision of encouraging many of its new converts to continue to present themselves as Christians and keep working inside the MCR and other Christian movements. "I was always seen as a religious leader, but the [Christian] communities were, in fact, infiltrated," Fr. Uriel Molina candidly acknowledged to Margaret Randall.[37]

A more detailed account of the same tactic was provided by Commander Monica Baltodano. Converted through the MCR from being a Christian to a Marxist-Leninist who no longer held religious beliefs, Baltodano thought that she would then work only in FSLN. But no; she and others were told by the Frente, "You have a work to do inside the MCR. . . . You stay in the [MCR], go to their masses, go to everything. What we are interested in is that the work that you develop get tied in to the vanguard." "In fact," Baltodano recalls, "all the [MCR] was working under the guidance, in some ways, of the Frente." The tactic had many advantages. "We were definitely less subject to repression," she says. "We would arrive in a barrio and say some things, but we were there 'with an umbrella' because we were Christians."[38]

All this is not to say that the process was only one of hypocrisy and deceit. Many of the Christians involved with the Sandinistas had adopted a definition of Christianity which blurred the distinctions between atheism and belief. To Fr. Ernesto Cardenal, the idea of God was akin to the idea of revolution: "In becoming a Marxist, I considered him to be the force of social changes and revolutions."[39] Were they Christians or Marxists? Many thought they were both. Certainly some of them felt they could present themselves as Christians without lying. At the same time there were some Christians who, while holding to their faith, grew close to the Sandinistas, thinking that they were noble idealists whose atheism could be modified along the way.

The effect of these developments was to give outsiders the

impression that the FSLN was no longer a sectarian Marxist-Leninist organization, but one where many Christians had found a friendly welcome. This helped to make the Frente more acceptable to a wider spectrum of Nicaraguans.

The question arises whether the Sandinistas were affected by their Christian collaborators. Fr. Fernando Cardenal asserted that young people who left behind their Christian beliefs for Marxism in the FSLN nevertheless maintained "the profound beliefs that motivated them." Later he justified Christians' involvement with the FSLN on the grounds that their presence in the revolution is "an important testimony to the value and the role of faith," and that their "presence in the Nicaraguan revolution brings a great transcendence" to the process of social transformation.[40] This suggests that the harsher or more rigid aspects of revolutionary practice would be humanized by the Christians' involvement, or that the tightly secularist outlook and political messianism of the Sandinistas would be modified. Did the presence of such people affect the FSLN's outlook, ideology, or behavior?

An examination of FSLN documents from the seventies would fail to turn up positions that could be considered "Christianized Marxism." The FSLN's 1977 and 1979 public programs showed a modification of some of the Frente's earlier views—as we will see further on. But they continued to reflect the total secular view of Marxist revolutionaries according to which human liberation comes about only by means of a political revolution. The Sandinistas' public statements continued to evidence their commitment to social engineering—that is, the notion that human individuals and society can be released from vices and oppressions by institutional remedies imposed through government power. The vanguard was still seen as the secular messiah that would interpret the social situation and execute the revolution. A comparison of FSLN documents from the seventies with statements by other Marxist organizations around the world would not turn up fundamental differences in regard to outlook, assumptions about human beings and society, and so on.

The Sandinistas did become more subdued in their criticism of religious beliefs during the seventies. They did not attack religion in their public literature, and they even praised Christians who collaborated with them. But their praise was always confined to Christians who were open to the revolution. I myself, in 1969, mimeographed a leaflet for the FSLN praising the revolutionary priest Fr. Camilo Torres, a Colombian who joined the Marxist guerrillas of his country and was killed in combat there in 1966. We liked him because he was a revolutionary like ourselves. He was a Christian able to see the fairness of our struggle—unlike other Christians. Thus he was able to increase our sympathy for Christians who joined the revolution, and to reinforce our disdain for those who did not. During this period I remember reading the New Testament and admiring Jesus in the same light. I liked Him when He seemed to take positions that I interpreted as defying the status quo. At those times He sounded like a fine man, a prophet. At other times I thought His message needed to be revised, "rescued for the revolution," striking out references to the divine and supernatural.

During an interlude in my studies I once visited the revolutionary Christian community at the Fatima parish. There I talked with the future Sandinista commanders Luis Carrión and Alvaro Baltodano and others, as well as with Fr. Uriel Molina. I was pleased to see these Christians coming closer to Marx and revolution. In no way did I experience any encouragement from them to consider the validity of Christian views. It was not we Marxists who had the identity crisis. They did. And the fact that they were moving in the direction of our philosophy was one more piece of evidence of the soundness of our philosophy. We hoped they would mature even more and drop their religious beliefs altogether. We felt these to be a hindrance to full commitment to the revolution. But we were learning to be tactful, as we discovered that we could count on time to aid the process of their conversion to the revolution. We had no fears of the revolutionary Christians converting Sandinista militants to Christian faith—nor did we need to. There was no reciprocal process of conversion. Sandinista atheists were not becoming believers.

CRISIS IN THE FSLN

I returned to Nicaragua after completing graduate studies in sociology in the United States in May 1973. The last time I had collaborated with the FSLN was in 1969 following my graduation as a lawyer. My studies and some experience—which included a couple of brief visits to East Germany and Yugoslavia—had largely undermined my commitment to Marxist theory. I no longer harbored utopian dreams about a future of love and justice brought about through sociopolitical means, nor did I believe any more that Marxism was a true science.

Yet I still felt attached to the FSLN. For so many years it had been for me the symbol of heroism and total commitment, the only force able to deal with Somoza. Some of my best friends were in the Frente, and some of my former best friends had been killed while in the Frente. With some hesitation, I joined the FSLN again in 1973.

The bunch of inexperienced revolutionaries I had met in 1969 were now much more sophisticated. The militants were instructed in hard-learned security measures and trained to develop habits that fostered safety—like driving around the block to look for spies. Much greater emphasis was also placed on ideological training.

At this time I met Tomás Borge and Bayardo Arce, members of the national directorate of the FSLN, Commander Eduardo Contreras, head of the organization in Managua, and other leaders. The head of my cell was William Ramirez, who after the revolution became the Sandinista commander for the Atlantic Coast region.

I remained in the FSLN for two years. At one point during that period, I was entrusted with the task of teaching Marxist theory to some of my fellow members. Naturally I felt very uneasy with this assignment, and after a few attempts I quit. I neared the breaking point with Ramirez when he asked me to teach a group of new recruits from the Jesuit-run Central American University, and I refused. The FSLN was a highly centralized organization with decisions being made at the highest levels and then passed down through the ranks. Obedience was a fundamental duty. Matters worsened when a couple of articles I submitted to the FSLN's underground periodical *Pancasán* were turned down on the grounds that they deviated from the official line of the organization.

By 1974, the FSLN was still small. The focus of its actions was in the Nicaraguan north-central highlands. There FSLN cadres concentrated on developing a peasant support network and on murdering real or potential informers of the Somoza government while avoiding clashes with the army. The killings were called "ajusticiamientos"—bringing someone to justice.

A major kidnapping of nearly twenty high government officials on December 27, 1974, brought the Frente a lot of notoriety. Forced to meet the rebels' demands, Somoza released FSLN prisoners and allowed the broadcast of an FSLN communique which made reference to his mistress and blamed North American imperialism, together with the local bourgeoisie (the "Liberal-Conservative oligarchy"), for "the sacking and exploitation of our victimized country." The communique also contained praise for the "revolutionary Christians" of the MCR.

Somoza's response to this humiliation was to impose a "state of siege," which lasted until 1976, and to step up repression. The Nicaraguan Permanent Commission for Human Rights (CPDH) estimated that between six hundred and two thousand peasants were killed by the National Guard during this period. One of the FSLN's casualties was its most prominent leader, Carlos Fonseca, killed in 1976. My best friend, a member of the cell to which I belonged, was captured in January 1975. He was tortured and held incommunicado for four months. To our great relief, he did not reveal our names to his torturers.

The campaign of repression dealt the FSLN severe blows, both in the countryside and in the cities, where several more leaders were killed or jailed. Eventually it contributed to a division within the FSLN. A "Proletarian Marxist-Leninist" tendency broke with the main body of the movement which followed the GPP (protracted people's war in the countryside) strategy, and, later, in 1977, a further split from the GPP strategy produced the "Terceristas," advocates of urban insurrections and of building a broad, anti-Somoza front with members of the non-Marxist political parties. This division into tendencies emerged over differences of strategy in the struggle against Somoza, but did not involve differences over long-term goals or ideology, as some observers were later to claim. Daniel Ortega, a leader of the Terceristas, in an interview conducted in 1978, explained that "the tendencies express themselves in different strategic conceptions, which in turn imply different tactics as well as organizational forms."[41]

The Proletarian Tendency (TP) called for focusing the Frente's efforts on the urban working class, rather than relying on the peasants as the GPP was doing. They also considered armed struggle premature. Led by Luis Carrión and Jaime Wheelock, both of upper-class background, the TP called for strict adherence to Marxist orthodoxy and even derided the other tendencies as congeries of petty bourgeois backsliders.[42] The MCR (revolutionary Christians), which Carrión had helped to found, adhered to the Proletarian Tendency group.

The GPP faction, on the other hand, defended its strategy of focusing political effort on the peasants of the remotest rural areas. Led by Borge and Moscow-trained Henry Ruiz, the GPP dismissed the Proletarians as a bunch of cowards who wanted, above all, to avoid fighting. Borge further declared in October 1975 that the Proletarians were no longer members of the FSLN due to their failure to adhere to ideological discipline. The GPP even threatened the Proletarians with "ajusticiamiento."

It was around this time that I left the FSLN. My reservations about Marxism had been followed by disillusionment with many individual members of the organization. Reports from my jailed friend, whom I visited on occasion, alerted me to the ease with which self-centeredness and corruption could develop even among the revolutionaries. In prison, he witnessed all manner of intrigue, hatred, and abuses of power going on among the FSLN prisoners. Although not yet a Christian, I was developing the suspicion that unless people experienced an internal transformation or revolution, changes in a political system would only lead to new oppressions. I questioned the wisdom of risking my life for what I increasingly believed to be a set of empty promises.

The following two years saw a decline in the FSLN's overall strength. Fonseca was killed in 1976, and Borge was captured. Under these conditions, a new split developed in early 1977. FSLN veterans Humberto and Daniel Ortega moved away from the GPP's line and argued that conditions for a revolutionary upheaval could be precipitated by armed insurrections in the cities. This tendency, popularly known as "Tercerista," was officially called "FSLN-Insurrectional." Borge's imprisonment and the exile of various other leaders of the GPP left this new group with virtual control of the national directorate.

THE TERCERISTAS' STRATEGY

The Terceristas dismissed the Proletarians' goal of building a worker's party, claiming that neither the objective nor the subjective conditions were present for the Nicaraguan workers to develop "revolutionary consciousness" in the near future. In this regard, the Terceristas followed the FSLN's traditional scorn for trade unionism. They stressed the fundamental importance of a vanguard of revolutionaries guiding the masses toward liberation through their higher awareness of the nature of the historical struggle and their commitment to proletarian goals. Although the notion of the Sandinistas as a vanguard had been a guiding light since the FSLN's inception, the Terceristas raised it to a new level.

In addition to an emphasis on urban-based insurrections, the Terceristas insisted on the need to create a broad anti-Somoza front which would include other political parties and organizations and even the "bourgeoisie." They made a conscious decision to avoid public references to Marxism and to give their program a more social-democratic tone. The experience with the "revolutionary Christians" in the early seventies highlighted the political advantage of widening the circle of allies while a central nucleus of committed revolutionaries maintained ultimate control. The Terceristas made room for the incorporation of Eden Pastora—a Social Democrat who later became famous for leading a spectacular assault on the Nicaraguan National Palace—and invited other democrats and additional Catholic priests to participate. The more the Frente disguised its Marxist-Leninist commitments and included Social Democrats and Christians in its outer circle, the more acceptability it gained with the Nicaraguan people. In this way, the Terceristas proved to have the strategic edge on the Proletarians. They realized sooner than Carrión and Wheelock that the Nicaraguan people could not be won over to a party that made Marxism-Leninism its explicit ideology.

This strategy, however, did not imply that the training of militants in Marxist-Leninist theory would be abandoned. That requirement, declared Humberto Ortega, had to continue, but it had to be limited to the first concentric circle of cadres:

> It is right that we demand in the ranks more regarding standards and party life, more class consciousness, and much more Marxist ideological clarity, but let us not do this on an open and mass level, since we run the risk of becoming sectarian and isolating ourselves from the masses.[43]

Reflecting later in 1979, Humberto Ortega wrote:

> Without slogans of "Marxist orthodoxy," without ultraleftist phrases such as "power only for the workers" (such as the Proletarians used to use), "toward the dictatorship of the proletariat," etc., we have

been able—without losing sight at any time of our revolutionary Marxist-Leninist Sandinista identity—to rally all our people around the FSLN.[44]

This strategy, according to Ortega, enabled the FSLN to attract "not only workers aware of their own class interests (who are few . . .), but mainly all the humble Nicaraguans, workers (although they are not proletarians) who, praying to Jesus Christ because they are believers, are shedding their blood for the freedom of our people."[45]

The strategy took definite shape in 1977 with the creation by the FSLN of a group known as "the Twelve." This was a collection of twelve prominent Nicaraguans, including two priests, who were not known to have Marxist leanings and who were highly regarded within and outside Nicaragua. They threw their moral and political weight behind the FSLN and began to tour the world seeking support for its cause. Four of the Twelve were in fact secret members of the FSLN (Sergio Ramirez, Fr. Miguel D'Escoto, Fr. Fernando Cardenal, and Ernesto Castillo), two had sons in the FSLN (Emilio Baltodano and Joaquín Cuadra), while most of the others were liberal or left-leaning democrats who had been living outside of Nicaragua for some years (such as Arturo Cruz). What appeared to be wide participation of Christians in the FSLN, plus the FSLN's public soft-pedaling of its espousal of Marxism-Leninism, made some of these figures hope that what remained of sectarian Marxism within the Frente could eventually be tamed by their own participation. Conceivably, some of these new allies shared the patronizing attitude toward the Sandinista leadership that has been exhibited by some foreign observers—namely, that the leaders of the Frente are idealists whose Marxism should not be taken very seriously.

An April 1978 bulletin of the FSLN explained how the Sandinistas intended to use the Twelve to gain the support of national and international "bourgeois" bodies:

The group known as "The Twelve" . . . represents a very important element for neutralizing the local and international bourgeoisie which distrust, or distrusted, the guarantees of an objectively democratic process promoted by the FSLN. This does not mean that the FSLN has abandoned its goal of socialism; only that the FSLN must walk a part of the road [to socialism] together with the bourgeoisie [the transition phase]; on that part of the road the bourgeoisie and imperialism will try to crush us and to moderate the Sandinista liberation process, as we shall also try to crush them and dump in the garbage can their reactionary aspirations.

The Twelve and the groups that gather around them, nationally and internationally, carry out some tasks that are directly channeled to them by the FSLN. In this regard, however, the Twelve should continue as a group and a movement without substantial organizational or partisan strength, for their strength would subtract political force from the FSLN. The Twelve should continue, as up to today, as a magnet for groups that come to the FSLN in an indirect way and that reach our movement faster than if we ourselves would try to directly bring them to us. At the same time, the Twelve and the rest of the groups that gather around them should receive from us special, political-ideological attention, in order to rapidly radicalize them in behalf of our revolutionary goals.[46]

The choice of the twelve personalities that would enable the Sandinistas to neutralize the "bourgeoisie," abate its fears, and coax it to walk part of the road toward socialism with them required great care. The decision to include Fr. Fernando Cardenal but not his priest-brother Ernesto is suggestive of the criteria that the Sandinistas used in making their choices. Looking back, Ernesto singled out his public identity as a Marxist as the probable reason for his exclusion:

There were some meetings abroad with all of them [the Twelve]. . . . Fernando, my brother, who was a member of the Twelve, was to participate. I was not participating, I had not been included, possibly because I had been regularly proclaiming myself a Marxist and they [the FSLN] were choosing a group of persons that would not awake, let us say, provoke, an American aggression.[47]

The formation of the Twelve gave the Sandinistas a formidable boost. It gave the Frente a good deal of legitimacy, especially abroad, and fed the growing belief that they were a heterogeneous assemblage of Social Democrats, Christians, Marxists, and apolitical Nicaraguan patriots. But as the history of the Christian Revolutionary Movement had shown, allies of the FSLN were not to share in its control. In the case of the Twelve, they did not even have positions or a vote within the hierarchy. They were never more than goodwill ambassadors, their endorsement helping the FSLN to unite under its umbrella a broad array of political forces rallying against the faltering Somoza dictatorship.

Although the Tercerista strategy of a broad front later proved to be successful, it did not exempt them at first from criticism by the other FSLN factions. Referring to the Proletarians' and GPP's accusations regarding a possible loss of Marxist-Leninist purity, Humberto Ortega scornfully remarked: "We refuse to transform the organization into a political philosophy seminar."[48]

Inter-Tercerista tensions brought about by the broad-front strategy were described by Ortega in a letter to Francisco Rivera. About those in his own ranks who objected to the policy of alliances with the bourgeoisie, Ortega had this to say:

> The disadvantage is that some of our militants, with the characteristics of youthful Marxist theoretical training, do not understand very well the policy of local as well as international tactical alliances. . . . [They] do not know how to relate to anti-Somoza bourgeois sectors, which objectively, in their present attitude, favor our movement. . . . Those comrades still have not understood properly the positive role which, for example, the group of the Twelve played. Therefore, it is our duty to be ready to combat these immature attitudes critically and fraternally, not tiring of persuading those who act this way about the correct line of our National Executive Committee.[49]

Ortega himself was not unaware of the dangers of the strategy he and his brother Daniel were advocating.

> It is necessary to include all in this great crusade, although the pro-Yankee bourgeoisie may attempt to take control of such a movement from us. [But] the secret is in our directing these changes ourselves— products not only of popular and revolutionary participation, but also of the bourgeoisie itself—toward the interest of the popular Sandinista revolution. Let us continue getting the support of the international bourgeoisie which opposes Somoza and let us intelligently use such backing.[50]

His brother Daniel expanded on this theme of alliance with non-Marxists:

> We have urged the creation of a wide anti-Somoza front. It would aim at joining together all the anti-Somoza sectors and mass organizations of the country, including sectors of the opposition bourgeoisie. . . . In doing so, we seek to conserve the political hegemony of the FSLN and in this way, as our platform signifies, we avoid the possibility of the bourgeoisie becoming the political leader of an anti-Somoza front. . . . We assign a tactical and *temporary* character to this front.[51]

The need to convince their own militants, trained in sectarianism and hatred for bourgeois forces, of the wisdom of joining hands with the historical enemies of the proletariat, while at the same time appeasing the fears of those bourgeois elements who knew the background of the Sandinistas, was a difficult juggling act for the Frente.

THE TRANSITION PHASE

On occasion, both the public agenda of broad alliances and the FSLN's private political agenda and convictions surfaced at the same time. At the very point in 1977 that the anti-Somoza alliance was being constructed, the FSLN distributed a political-military platform to its cadres. The document, designed to provide the members of the Frente with a "revolutionary perspective" on past, present, and future political events in Nicaragua, expresses explicitly some of the organization's underlying philosophy, key views, and long-term goals. Chapter 2, which deals with the general causes of the Nicaraguan revolution, begins with the assertion: "The dialectical development of human society leads to the transition from capitalism to Communism."[52] After explaining how the capitalist system is the cause of all oppression, it continues:

> With the installation of the first socialist state in Bolshevik Russia in 1917, world capitalism was deeply shaken. Its historical agony and death began at that moment. Today . . . the cause of the proletariat has triumphed in different parts of Europe, Asia, Africa, and Latin America.[53]

The breaking of the chains of oppression in Nicaragua, the document continues, will be a twofold process: breaking the imperialist yoke and breaking the local yoke of the Nicaraguan reactionary classes. "Both tasks will go together inseparably if there is a Marxist-Leninist cause and a solid vanguard leading the process."[54]

The document states the Terceristas' thesis of the need for a *transition* phase between the triumph of the revolution and the full implementation of revolutionary socialism. But it makes it clear that this "democratic-popular" phase must not be mistaken for a willingness by the FSLN to reconcile itself with the other social forces.

The present struggle against the tyranny should lead to a true people's democracy, which will be an integral part of the struggle for socialism. Our process shall never stop halfway. The democratic-popular phase should be for the Sandinista cause a means whereby the revolutionary position can be consolidated and the process can take off in a secure way toward socialism. . . . This phase should not lead us to capitalist development, reformism, nationalism, or any other such form.[55]

The same idea, in almost the same words, appears in Humberto Ortega's letter to Francisco Rivera.

The fact that we [cannot] establish socialism immediately after overthrowing Somoza does not mean we are proposing a capitalist-type social-democratic or similar development policy; what we propose is a broad, democratic and popular government which, although the bourgeoisie has participation, is a means and not an end, so that in its time it can make the advance towards a more genuinely popular form of government, which guarantees the movement towards socialism.[56]

Chapter 2 of the platform ends with the words: "Our cause lives and develops in our working and patriotic people. It is the sacred and historical cause of Marx, Engels, Lenin, and Sandino."[57]

The following chapter, which deals with the nature of the transition phase in more detail, anticipates that the "bourgeois" forces, with which the Frente was seeking an alliance, would later become a hindrance:

The bourgeoisie in general, including the fraction which today opposes the Somocista regime . . . also constitutes part of the reactionary forces that will try to block to the maximum our general cause of socialism. . . . The key factor in keeping the democratic process aiming at socialism will be the political, moral, and military position of strength that the Sandinista Peoples' Revolution achieves at the downfall of the tyranny.[58]

The document also reveals the FSLN's awareness of its need to avoid being too explicit about its long-range goals:

On the other hand, factors of a tactical and strategic order do not allow us to state, in this phase, either nationally or internationally, [the goal of] socialism in an open manner. [Yet] not to refer in this immediate phase to socialism, does not imply that we are for a bourgeois-democratic revolution.[59]

It is important to read the terminology of the Sandinistas in its Marxist ideological framework. "Bourgeois democracy" is a reference to representative, or "Western," democracy. By a "popular," "democratic," or "revolutionary" government they mean the system outlined in their 1969 program. Essentially this is the form of government that East European Communists call "people's democracies": the revolutionary party assumes full control of the state apparatus, determining the participation of other parties and individuals. Likewise, when the Sandinistas refer to socialism, they do not mean the kind of democratic socialism found in some Western European countries. Social democracy, in their view, is "reformism": a change that reforms or improves a social system but fails to replace it with a radically different system. By socialism the ideologists of the FSLN are referring to the system of collectivism and one-party rule found in countries like Cuba and the Soviet Union. These countries are often referred to by the Ortegas, Fonseca, and other Sandinista leaders as possessing the most advanced forms of socialism.

Two other noteworthy goals of the 1977 platform include establishing a foreign policy of "independence and support for the progressive and revolutionary causes of mankind,"[60] and the creation of "a workers-peasants Sandinista army to replace the National Guard and to defend the interests of the revolution."[61]

THE POPULAR INSURRECTION

Through their 1977 platform and other statements, the FSLN made it clear that it intended to seek a broader alliance with Nicaragua's democratic opposition in order to gain legitimacy and to draw the anti-Somoza forces into their own camp. This was not an easy task. The human rights policy of United States President Jimmy Carter forced Somoza to lift the state of emergency in 1977. This move gave the Nicaraguan opposition more room for action than they had had in years. The most prominent leader of the opposition was the popular Pedro Joaquín Chamorro, owner and editor of Nicaragua's largest newspaper, La Prensa, and leader of a political coalition called the Union Democratica de Liberacion (UDEL). This coalition included a large part of the Nicaraguan Conservative Party, two liberal parties, the Social Christian Party, the Nicaraguan Socialist Party (PSN), the Confederation of Nicaraguan Workers, and the Independent Confederation of Labor, led by the PSN. In many ways UDEL represented the kind of broad alliance between conservatives and leftists that the FSLN wanted to lead. But it was led by a democrat with a long history of opposition to FSLN policies. The new breathing room enjoyed by the country allowed UDEL to hold various public meetings and political campaigns throughout the country, and to position itself as an alternative to Somoza.

The FSLN feared such an alternative. It already suspected that this was what the Carter Administration would try to promote in Nicaragua. If the plan was successful, it would deprive the Frente of its ability to rally people around itself. Without an easy target like the dictator Somoza, the Frente knew that there was little chance that ordinary Nicaraguans would continue to struggle.

Competing with Chamorro for the leadership of a mass movement already gaining steam, however, was no small matter. Chamorro was a strong, charismatic leader whose direct style, acrid pen, and history of courageous opposition to Somoza, including imprisonment, torture, and exile, had earned him the reputation of being the greatest and most unshakable adversary of the dictator. And he did not trust the FSLN. As early as June 1977, he was mobbed by a group of Sandinistas who sabotaged a UDEL meeting in the city of Matagalpa. In his editorials, he often criticized the Sandinistas for their ideology and their pretense of being the interpreters of the people's will. He insisted that Sandino had been a nationalist and not a Communist, as the FSLN sought to portray him. His last editorial, in January 1978, entitled "Bourgeoisie and Revolutionism," scorned the young, Marxist intellectuals who sought to shake their own bourgeois backgrounds by being radical, but who in turn would label as "bourgeois" anyone objecting to their views.

Chamorro was ambushed and murdered on a deserted street in Managua on the morning of January 10, 1978. One of the killers was captured the next day by Somoza security forces. Three more were arrested within a week. The interrogations and early evidence seemed to suggest an intricate conspiracy implicating some friends of Somoza that lived in Miami. Chamorro's eldest son, Pedro, however, called public attention in 1985 to the fact that his family was unhappy with the Sandinistas' investigation of the murder. He mentions that Marcel Pallais, the young guerrilla responsible for the custody of three of the alleged murderers immediately after the triumph of the revolution (the fourth escaped), was himself stabbed to death under very strange circumstances during the first days after the revolutionary triumph. He also says that a file he sent to the Ministry of the Interior in 1982, informing them of the whereabouts of the fourth killer, was mysteriously lost.[62] Violeta Chamorro, the widow, has said that she suspects the FSLN of assassinating her husband.[63]

Most people, however, immediately blamed Somoza, and at that point Nicaragua exploded. Deprived of their leader and symbol of resistance against the dictatorship, the democratic sectors, the business community, the labor unions, and the people at large revolted in anger and frustration. Peace was not to be restored until the downfall of Somoza. A general strike, called by the business community, was followed by weeks and then months of ever increasing rioting in the cities. In February 1978, the Indian community in Monimbó, a barrio of the central-Pacific town of Masaya, staged the first spontaneous mass insurrection.

The intensity of the turmoil caught even the FSLN off-guard. No death of a Sandinista leader had sparked anything like a widespread reaction. Humberto Ortega acknowledged in an interview that "it is in response to the murder of Pedro J. Chamorro that the masses unleash themselves. . . . Our capacity to inject ourselves into the mass movement was still limited . . . for we lacked the cadres for this task."[64] After the Monimbó incident, the Sandinistas rushed to try and infiltrate upcoming insurrections. All the rural guerrillas were ordered to move to the cities and concentrate on leading the armed and unarmed uprisings which would be coming. Two new broad-front organizations emerged during this period: the Frente Amplio Opositor (Broad Opposition Front) and the Movimiento Pueblo Unido (United People's Movement). The first included most of the forces formerly united under UDEL and was led by Alfonso Robelo, a liberal-minded businessman with little political experience. The second included several smaller political and student organizations of the left, and was led by the FSLN.

As the political situation deteriorated, armed struggle began to attract larger segments of the population, particularly students and unemployed urban youth, and the leverage of the Frente grew rapidly. The FSLN was the only political body organized as a military front, and hence was the only outlet for radical Nicaraguans who wished to fight Somoza with bullets. The democratic political parties had been designed to wage civil struggles, but it was an armed struggle that was taking place. Hundreds of new combatants joined the Frente every month. Patrols and individual members of the National Guard were being attacked and killed in ambushes set up by young people in civilian clothes. Some Guardsmen, becoming paranoid, began to shoot youngsters, assuming them to be enemies. This led more young people to join the guerrillas, perhaps as a safer option than remaining idle.

The overall decay of the Somoza regime indeed made its repression blind and counterproductive for its own purposes. In early September 1978, for instance, I was briefly arrested in a massive sweep of political opponents launched by the state's security system. In jail I found some people, innocent of ploting against the government, horribly tortured. But some who were linked with the Sandinistas were spared. I was released unharmed and with no explanation of why I had been detained.

The FSLN, meanwhile, began to receive weapons and logistical support from abroad. Solidarity networks with the Nicaraguan revolution had spread throughout the Western world with the help of the Twelve—particularly the priests, Fr. Cardenal and Fr. D'Escoto—and with the help of leftist intellectuals such as Garcia Marquez and others. As the international image of Somoza sank deeper, other governments, such as the Venezuelan and Panamanian, began to send aid to the FSLN. In June 1978 the Carter Administration refused a military credit to Somoza, casting a shadow of doom on his regime and further encouraging his armed opponents.

The Frente also gained crucial support from the newspaper La Prensa, which, deprived of the leadership of Chamorro, had come under the control of a low-key Marxist named Danilo Aguirre. Fearful of further sanctions from the United States, Somoza allowed La Prensa a remarkable degree of freedom. Aguirre used it to pursue a policy of encouraging the alliances sought by the Sandinistas and of censuring the Nicaraguans who wanted to dialogue with the government and seek a peaceful solution to the conflict.

Thus, what a year before had been a small, elite organization whose success only a visionary could have anticipated, had become, by extraordinary circumstances and tactical skill, a political-military body able to challenge Somoza. But the insurrectional process, Ortega conceded, "was a spontaneous reaction on the part of the masses, which, *in the end,* the Sandinista Front began to direct through its activists and military units. It was not a mass movement responding to a call by the Sandinistas; it was a response to a situation that nobody had foreseen."[65] In 1978 the FSLN achieved what the 1977 platform had sought: hegemony in an alliance with the bourgeoisie. The military nature of the organization, built on a centralized command structure, guaranteed that the reins would remain in the hands of the national directorate. Neither the broad-front alliances nor the massive influx of new militants from all walks of life challenged the Frente's fundamental ideology and leadership.

HARVESTING VICTORY

In August 1978 a Sandinista commando unit led by Eden Pastora seized the Nicaraguan National Palace (equivalent of Capitol Hill) and held the entire Nicaraguan Congress and nearly one thousand public employees hostage. The FSLN threatened to execute the hostages if its conditions were not met. These were: the freedom of Sandinista prisoners, including Borge; ransom money; and the broadcast of a new communique addressed to both a Nicaraguan and an international audience. The conditions were met.

The communique was styled as the expression of a broad, popular movement. In contrast with the 1977 platform, which called for a Sandinista army, the new communique spoke about building a truly national army. It said that "forty years of Somocista tyranny and Yankee interference" had now led to a movement of students "pointing out for the people where their enemies lay."[66] The document contained a reference to the "true Christians, those who have decided to follow the road of sacrifice and combat to achieve a just society. . . . Today the Frente Sandinista counts in its ranks hundreds of revolutionary Christians and rebel priests, such as Ernesto Cardenal and Gaspar Garcia Laviana."[67]

The communique from the National Palace vehemently rejected any dialogue with the government, even criticizing a pastoral letter of the Catholic archbishop of Managua in which he asked Somoza to resign in behalf of peace.[68] The FSLN was not about to support any move which would open the way for its democratic competitors and short-circuit its complete military victory. The FSLN was opposed to elections and to Somoza resigning in a way that would produce a coalition government to the liking of the democratic opposition and the United States. The longer Somoza clung to power and rejected major concessions, the better. The Sandinistas thus warned those who worked for a different outcome: "The Frente Sandinista . . . condemns as a crime of high treason any maneuver that would promote dialogue with Somoza or with his civil or military representatives."[69] The communique issued a call to kill ("ajusticiar") Somocista informers and members of the National Guard who lived in or entered the barrios.[70]

The communique also made reference to the non-Sandinista opposition and to the transition phase. Regarding the former, the FSLN acknowledged that practically all the bourgeois sectors save the "financial bourgeoisie" were participating in the struggle against Somoza. Yet in its reference to the first general strike against the government in 1978, the document complained that these sectors had "planned a national strike on the backs of the people"—a way of saying that they had planned the strike without consulting with the FSLN.[71] In regard to the transition phase, the communique was boldly forthright: "We are clear that the process of this struggle will not stop with a popular-democratic government and that it will be the people who shape their own destiny under conditions in which their will will then be respected."[72]

At this stage of the revolution, the Frente must have looked ahead confidently. Arms shipments for its forces continued to arrive at an accelerating rate, while Somoza was increasingly isolated by most other nations. An international brigade of Latin American revolutionaries was also being formed to join the Sandinistas in the struggle. In September the FSLN took the lead of a major popular insurrection in the main Nicaraguan cities. After two weeks of fighting, the revolt was crushed; but it was only a short-term defeat for the Sandinistas. The blind and often murderous way in which the National Guard persecuted young assailants swelled the ranks of the FSLN even further. At this time, the Socialist International recognized the FSLN.

At the end of 1978 Fidel Castro's interventions finally succeeded in reuniting the three factions of the FSLN into a single front. Castro, who had made the unification of the factions a precondition for stepping up Cuban aid, advised the FSLN on furthering a democratic profile. Castro was experienced at this strategy. While a guerrilla, he had openly denied that he was Marxist-Leninist. He had claimed to be inspired by Cuba's legendary hero José Marti, and vowed to build a revolution "more nationalist than the palm trees"—symbols of the country. After the revolutionary triumph in 1959 he entered Havana wearing a rosary around his neck. Only later did the mask come off.

Once the strategy was set and the FSLN's leaders were in agreement, military supplies in large quantities began to travel from Cuba to Costa Rica and then on to Nicaragua. Somoza complained to the Organization of American States about Cuban and Costa Rican complicity with the Sandinistas, but his prestige was by now so low that no country heeded his protest.

The Sandinistas, for their part, skillfully fended off fears about their radicalism. Tomás Borge declared in Mexico that the charge that the FSLN was Marxist was a Somocista lie to discredit the movement. He said that the FSLN was neither Marxist nor liberal, but Sandinista. Edén Pastora, some of the Twelve, and other friends of the Frente who were Social Democrats went on record as insisting that they did not want a Communist Nicaragua. With control of the Frente firmly in its hands, the new unified national directorate was happy to let them speak. The core of the FSLN consisted of the leaders of the three former factions: the Ortegas and Tirado for the Terceristas; Borge, Arce, and Ruiz for the GPP; and Nuñez and Wheelock for the Proletarians. The very visible and popular Pastora was under their orders. The subtleties and implications of these arrangements were not seen by most foreign reporters. Like the *New York Times*'s Alan Riding, most reported that the Sandinistas were "patriots first, Marxists second." Pastora was regularly interviewed; far less often the more reserved Humberto Ortega. Many foreign Christians, likewise, listened attentively to the moving witness provided for the Sandinistas by Fathers Ernesto and Fernando Cardenal and Miguel D'Escoto.

A similar phenomenon was taking place inside Nicaragua as well, although with its own pecularities. People were so eager to be rid of Somoza that they were quick to disregard the FSLN's Marxist-Leninist commitments. I remember a close relative of mine telling me that it was wrong to worry about what might come after Somoza. "Nothing can be worse than him!" he shouted. His was the prevailing frame of mind in Nicaragua. Most people chose to downplay the importance of Marxists-Leninists in the leadership of the revolutionary movement: they will be different, they will be pragmatic, they will be tamed by the many non-Marxists.

Now with close to three thousand guerrillas armed with automatic weapons, Chinese rockets, and bazookas, the FSLN, with the newly arrived international brigade "Simón Bolívar," launched an all-out offensive against the faltering Somoza army in March 1979. The National Guard was simply not able to control the many uprisings taking place in the major Nicaraguan cities. Many of its now eight thousand to ten thousand members were not even soldiers, but parasites of an organization permeated by corruption at every level. Many of the recruits had little military training, having joined the Guard only months before. The professional army (the infantry battalion) had less than two thousand soldiers. Much of the National Guard was immobilized by the need to defend itself against countless ambushes. Somoza also lacked even a medium-size airforce. Most of his planes were small commercial aircraft hastily modified to carry rocket launchers. His only armored "battalion" consisted of three Sherman tanks donated by Israel in the 1950s. By the middle of 1979, the National Guard was running low on ammunition. An Israeli ship carrying war supplies to Somoza never reached Nicaragua. According to Somoza's own statements, the CIA stopped the ship at Puerto Barrios in Guatemala.

In June 1979, the Sandinistas announced the creation of a provisional five-member government junta made up of FSLN militants Sergio Ramirez, Daniel Ortega, and Moisés Hassan, and democrats Alfonso Robelo and Violeta Chamorro, Pedro Joaquín Chamorro's widow. The arrangement could hardly have been better. Outside observers took this junta to be the real leadership, when in fact control remained with the less visible national directorate. The Frente also issued a program of government which, among other things, promised a return to pluralism with universal suffrage (clause I-1.1) unrestricted freedom of expression (clause I-1.4), a mixed economic model (clause II—2.1.3), respect for human rights (clause I-1.3), freedom of organization (clause I-1.4), religious freedom (clause I-1.4), the creation of a national army (clause I-1.12), and a foreign policy of nonalignment (clause I-1.14).[73] Gone were most of the qualifiers on freedom that had characterized earlier FSLN programs. The only exception, in clause 1, stated that political parties would be free to operate without discrimination of any kind, except those parties seeking a return to "Somocismo."

In itself, the 1979 program of government included most of the essentials of "bourgeois" democracy. It called for a separation of powers, with the Supreme Court being the highest judiciary body. The executive branch would be in the hands of the junta, officially the highest authority, and there would be a Council of State, whose functions, although somewhat vague, resemble those of a modern congress or parliament. The Sandinistas were to have one-third of the seats in the Council of State, while the various other forces, which included a host of political parties, labor unions, and even the business community, would have the remaining two thirds. The program made no references to socialism or the transition phase.

On July 17, 1979, Somoza fled the country. The highly centralized National Guard, whose unifying force had been Somoza, panicked and collapsed the next day. On July 20, the new junta and the Sandinista leadership entered Managua in triumph. "The bones of Carlos Fonseca," said a Sandinista poet, "were rejoicing."

NOTES

1. *Guardians of the Dynasty: A History of the U.S.-Created Guardia Nacional de Nicaragua and the Somoza Family* (Maryknoll, N.Y.: Orbis Books, 1977).

2. *Somozas and Sandinistas: The U.S. and Nicaragua in the Twentieth Century* (Washington, D.C.: Council for Inter-American Security, 1982), p. 44.

3. See Neill Macaulay, *The Sandino Affair* (Chicago: Quadrangle Books, 1967).

4. The mean annual military aid from the United States to Nicaragua during the years 1953 to 1978 (in millions of dollars: corrected for inflation) was:

1953-61	1962-66	1974-76	1977-78
0.21	1.48	3.33	2.76

Source: John A. Booth, *The End and the Beginning: The Nicaraguan Revolution* (Boulder, Colo.: Westview Press, 1982), p. 128.

5. *Playboy,* September 1983, p. 60.

6. Tomás Borge, *Carlos, El Amanecer Ya No Es una Tentación* (Havana: Ediciones Casa de las Américas, 1980), pp. 20, 21. Quoted in David Nolan, *The Ideology of the Sandinistas and the Nicaraguan Revolution* (Coral Gables: Institute of Interamerican Studies, 1984), p. 22.

7. Humberto Ortega, *50 Años de Lucha Sandinista* (Managua, Nicaragua: Ministerio del Interior, 1981), pp. 92, 93.

8. *Op. cit.,* Nolan, p. 36.

9. *Ibid.,* p. 41.

10. Ruiz, "La Montaña era Como un Crisol Donde se Forjaban los Mejores Cuadros," *Nicarauac,* No. 1 [May-June 1980], Managua, p. 18, quoted in *op. cit.,* Nolan, p. 42.

11. Published in *Nicarauac,* No. 2, Managua, 1980.

12. Pilar Arias, ed., *Nicaragua: Revolución—Relatos de Combatientes del Frente Sandinista* (México: Siglo Veintiuno, 1980), p. 85.

13. Giaconda Belli in Bridget Aldaraca, et al., eds., *Nicaragua in Revolution: The Poets Speak* (Minneapolis: Marxist Educational Press, 1980), p. 275.

14. Borge, "La Formación del FSLN," in *La Revolución a Través de Nuestra Dirección Nacional* (Managua: Secretaría Nacional de Propaganda y Educación Política del FSLN, 1980), p. 27. Quoted in *op. cit.,* Nolan, p. 28.

15. Humberto Ortega, "Letter to Francisco Rivera," *Joint Publications Research Service,* January 7, 1979, p. 81.

16. Quoted in *Amanecer* (publication of the Centro Antonio Valdivieso), Managua, May 1981, p. 10.

17. Dora Mariá Tellez in Margaret Randall, *Sandino's Daughters: Testimonies of Nicaraguan Women in Struggle* (Vancouver: New Star Books, 1976), p. 53. Quoted in *op. cit.,* Nolan, p. 120.

18. Ramirez, "Sandinismo, Hegemony and Revolution," *Contemporary Marxism,* No. 3 [Summer 1981], p. 25, from *Barricada,* July 8, 1980, quoted in *op. cit.,* Nolan, p. 112.

19. Wheelock, *FSLN es la Organización de los Trabajadores,* speech of May 1, 1984, published as a leaflet by *Barricada,* n.d., p. 5.

20. Fonseca, "Síntesis de Algunos Problemas Actuales" [1975] in *Bajo la Bandera del Sandinismo: Textos Políticos* (Managua: Editorial Nueva Nicaragua, 1981), p. 303. Cited in *op. cit.,* Nolan, p. 38.

21. Fonseca, "Mensaje del Frente Sandinista de Liberación Nacional [FSLN] a los Estudiantes Revolucionarios" [April 15, 1968], in *Bajo la Bandera,* pp. 144-146. Quoted in *op. cit.,* Nolan, p. 37.

22. Fonseca, "Sandino, Guerrillero Proletario," in *Bajo la Bandera,* p. 279. Quoted in *op. cit.,* Nolan, p. 38.

23. FSLN, "Program of the Sandinista Front of National Liberation," *Tricontinental,* No. 17 (March-April 1970), pp. 61-68.

24. Fonseca, "Nicaragua: Zero Hour," in Bruce Marcus, ed., *Sandinistas Speak* (New York: Pathfinder Press, 1982), p. 40.

25. Humberto Ortega, "Discurso del Ministro de Defensa, Commandante en Jefe del EPS y Jefe Nacional de las Milicias Sandinistas Humberto Ortega S. en la Clausura de la Reunión de Especialistas, 25 Agosto 1981," in *La Principal Tarea del Pueblo es Prepararse Militarmente para Defender su Poder* (Managua: Sección de Formación Política y Cultural del Ejército Popular Sandinista, 1981), p. 9.

26. Sotelo, "In Sandino's Footsteps," *Tricontinental,* No. 3 (November-December 1967), pp. 121, 122. Quoted in *op. cit.,* Nolan, p. 33.

27. FSLN, "Program," p. 68.

28. FSLN Department of Propaganda and Political Education, June 1981, in *Sandinistas Speak,* p. 21.

29. Ruiz, "Montaña," p. 24. Quoted in *op. cit.,* Nolan, p. 108-109.

30. Richard, "The Experience of Christians in Chile during the Popular Unity Period," in *Cristianos Revolucionarios,* No. 4 [publication of the Instituto Historico Centroamericano], Managua, 1980, p. 31.

31. Torres, in Margaret Randall, *Cristianos en la Revolución Nicaraguense* (Caracas: Poseidón, 1983), p. 189.

32. Commander Joaquín Cuadra, in *op. cit.,* Randall, p. 177.

33. Baltodano, in *op. cit.,* Randall, p. 187.

34. Ortega, "Some Strategic Reflections," *Bulletin of the FSLN,* April 1978, reprinted in Gabriel García Márquez, et al., *Los Sandinistas* (Bogotá: La Oveja Negra, 1979).

35. Fernando Cardenal, S.J., in *op. cit.,* Randall, p. 193.

36. See *op. cit.,* Randall, pp. 212-214, 220.

37. *Ibid.,* p. 198.

38. Baltodano, in *ibid.,* Randall, p. 187.

39. Cardenal, in *ibid.,* Randall, p. 128.

40. Fr. Fernando Cardenal, S.J., "Why I Was Forced to Leave the Jesuit Order," *National Catholic Reporter,* January 11, 1985, p. 6.

41. In *op. cit.,* Marquez, et al.

42. FSLN-Proletario, *Documentos Básicos I,* n.p., FSLN-Proletario, 1978, p. 92. Cited in *op. cit.,* Nolan, p. 55.

43. Humberto Ortega, "Letter to Francisco Rivera," p. 83.

44. *Ibid.*, p. 81.

45. *Ibid.*, p. 82.

46. In *op. cit.*, Marquez, et al., pp. 205, 206.

47. Ernesto Cardenal in *op. cit.*, Randall, p. 98.

48. Humberto Ortega, "Interview with a Sandinista," *Liberation* [Paris], August 25, 1978; reprinted in *Newsfront International*, October 1978, p. 13. Quoted in *op. cit.*, Nolan, p. 78.

49. *Op. cit.*, "Letter to Francisco Rivera," p. 83.

50. *Ibid.*, p. 82.

51. Daniel Ortega, Interview by Pedro Miranda, in *Latin American Perspectives*, 20, Winter 1979, p. 117, emphasis added.

52. FSLN Dirección Nacional, *Plataforma General Político-Militar del F.S.L.N. para el Triunfo de la Revolución Popular Sandinista*, "Somewhere in Nicaragua," May 4, 1977, p. 28.

53. *Ibid.*, p. 28.

54. *Ibid.*, p. 29.

55. *Ibid.*, p. 30.

56. *Op. cit.*, "Letter to Francisco Rivera," p. 83.

57. FSLN, *Plataforma*, p. 31.

58. *Ibid.*, p. 32.

59. *Ibid.*, p. 33.

60. *Ibid.*, p. 35.

61. *Ibid.*

62. Pedro J. Chamorro, Jr., in *La Nación*, Costa Rica, January 10, 1985, p. 16A.

63. *Ibid.*

64. Humberto Ortega, "The Strategy of Victory," in *op. cit.*, *Sandinistas Speak*, p. 62.

65. *Ibid.*, emphasis added.

66. Laszlo Pataky, *Llegaron Los que no Estaban Invitados* (Managua: Editorial Pereira, 1975), p. 49.

67. *Ibid.*, p. 53.

68. *Ibid.*, p. 74.

69. *Ibid.*, p. 66.

70. *Ibid.*, p. 56.

71. *Ibid.*, p. 55.

72. *Ibid.*, p. 63.

73. Junta de Gobierno, "Programa de Gobierno," in *Leyes de la República de Nicaragua,* Volumen 1 (Managua: Ministerio de Justicia, 1980), pp. 9-34.

SANDINISMO
IN POWER

After eighteen years of struggle, the revolutionary movement set in motion by a small band of radical students had come to power. The revolution had been the outcome of efforts by countless Nicaraguans from all walks of life. The Terceristas' strategy had worked: broad front alliances proved to be precisely what the Sandinistas needed. They allowed the Sandinistas to make themselves palatable to the people while gaining full control of the revolution. Christians, democrats, conservatives, businessmen, and other groups and interests with the most varied philosophies and political ideals were now to be included in the new government. Real power, however, was in the hands of the leadership of the Frente: the nine-man national directorate.

Now in power, what would their agenda be?

As in the years just prior to the revolution, two basic agendas were discernible—a private one and a public one. The private agenda reflected the original ideology and goals of the movement. Outstanding among these was the belief in Marxism-Leninism as the doctrine of the proletariat and an unquestionable guide for the revolution, and the rejection of "bourgeois" society and its belief in private property and representative democracy, in favor of a Socialist system that would be free of oppression and would give rise to a new, unselfish, revolutionary man. Coupled with these beliefs was a strong internationalism, a call to wage a life-or-death struggle against "Yankee imperialism."

Publicly the Sandinistas continued to maintain a democratic

profile after the revolution. They included citizens in the first cabinet who had democratic credentials, and four Catholic priests were given high positions as cabinet ministers and party leaders (the Cardenal brothers, Fr. Miguel D'Escoto, and Fr. Edgar Parrales).

As before the revolution, having two such disparate agendas caused tensions which were not easily reconciled. On the one hand, the Sandinistas knew that most of the internal and external support that the revolution had brought them hinged on their commitment to democratic goals. They did not have strong or sizable trade unions or peasants organizations of their own. They knew that the international situation would make a Socialist Nicaragua vulnerable to pressures and attack. They also knew the Nicaraguans to be deeply religious. And they were aware of the backwardness of the country and the lack of human resources to administer a state-owned, state-controlled economy.

On the other hand, the Sandinistas knew that they were riding a wave of public approval unprecedented in Nicaraguan politics. They could use this political capital to forward their ends, so long as they did not spend it too soon.

Sandinista commander Dora Téllez, during the victorious entry into Managua on July 19, 1979, declared in a somber television speech that the real struggle was just beginning and that the new phase was going to be harder than the war. In the euphoria of the moment few listeners understood why. The tyrant was defeated, the country was united, foreign nations were friendly— why would harder times be in store? Téllez and her comrades knew why, but at this point they were not about to be more specific.

THE DOCUMENT OF THE 72 HOURS
In October 1979 the FSLN party elite met behind closed doors to analyze their position and to delineate a postvictory strategy. The result of their three days of deliberation was a private document known as the "Document of the 72 Hours." It is a valuable source for gaining an understanding of Sandinista policies during the first phase of the revolution.

The document begins by acknowledging that the Government of Reconstruction—the new five-member junta—was the result of a class alliance which was necessary to isolate Somoza, gain domestic support, and neutralize the danger of Yankee intervention. "In the conditions of 1977," the document stated,

the alliance with the democratic layers of the bourgeoisie had the foremost objective of isolating the Somoza forces and of expanding the forces of the Sandinista Front. It was an alliance for internal neutralization. . . . The alliance expressed by the government of national reconstruction, the cabinet, and, in some important measure, the minimum program of the FSLN . . . respond to the need to neutralize the interventionist policies of the Yankees.[1]

The document candidly acknowledges that the incorporation into the new government of democrats such as Alfonso Robelo and Pedro Joaquín Chamorro's widow, Violeta, the inclusion of some moderates in the cabinet, and many of the clauses of the 1979 program of government were all strategic moves designed to avoid antagonizing potentially hostile outsiders.[2]

The document once again repeats the view that the revolution must go through a "stage of democratic transition."[3] It issues a call to bring all forces "under the leadership of the FSLN."[4] Specifically, the document advises Sandinista militants to keep Nicaragua's small, splinter political parties alive because of the international situation,[5] but it exhorts the militants to infiltrate these parties: "Work within them in order to assimilate for the revolution their more consequent elements."[6]

In reference to the bourgeoisie, the Sandinista leadership recommended that "we should hit it not as a class but through its most representative elements, as soon as they offer the first opportunity."[7]

On the churches, the advice reads:

With the Catholic and evangelical church, we should foster relations at the diplomatic level, observing a careful policy that seeks how to neutralize, as far as possible, the conservative stands and how to increase the links with priests open to the revolution, at the same time that we promote the revolutionary sectors of the church. With the Protestant church . . . we should implement a restrictive policy, developing intelligence surveillance on them, and, if they are caught off guard, expel them at once.[8]

On the economy, the document states that the government-controlled sector should be the axis of the national economy.[9]

On foreign policy, the document expresses the internationalism ever characteristic of the FSLN.

> The Sandinista popular revolution bases its foreign policy on the full exercise of national sovereignty and independence and on the principle of revolutionary internationalism.[10]

As a consequence, the revolution vows to "contribute to the struggle of the peoples of Latin America against fascist dictatorship in behalf of democracy and national liberation."[11]

In another section, the document asks the Frente's partisans to work for the organizing of Sandinista-controlled mass organizations, giving priority to the Sandinista Confederation of Labor (CST), the Agricultural Worker's Organization (ATC), and the Sandinista Defense Committees (CDS's).[12]

The Sandinista leaders also expressed awareness of a need to purify the army of dubious elements. "It is a task of the FSLN to strengthen the political education section of the Sandinista People's Army. The section should be made up of militants of the vanguard with impeccable revolutionary credentials."[13] "The army should be purified at all levels, eliminating those elements not compatible with revolutionary measures."[14]

The document ends with references to the vanguard and to the national directorate as the supreme authority in the country. Borrowing from Lenin, it states that the vanguard

> is the political apparatus that establishes itself as the most notable collective leadership of society . . . able to untangle the contradictions that surface while the [revolutionary] process unfolds, that solves the problems that systematically appear, that directs the class struggle and leads the whole nation on a road marked by victories.[15]

The vanguard is the "highest form of organization of the workers and its most characteristic leader."[16] The party's key task is "to educate our working people in the acknowledgment of its vanguard and of the tasks to which the vanguard has committed itself, based on the fundamental premise that the FSLN is the legitimate organization that leads the revolutionary process."[17] The concrete expression or embodiment of the vanguard is the national directorate. As such, the first organizational task of the FSLN is to achieve the goal of "strengthing the leadership of the national directorate as the supreme organ of the FSLN and of the revolution."[18]

This document again confirms the strategic prowess of the Sandinistas. In order to proceed toward their long-term goal of revolutionary socialism, they had a carefully devised plan for the intermediate period: concealment of their true ideological commitments and goals, temporary alliances with non-Marxist individuals and organizations, and an economic phase in which capitalist remnants, including some private ownership of property, would be tolerated for a time.

Although carefully tailored for the Nicaraguan situation, the "transition phase" strategy the Sandinistas adopted is a common Marxist method and is familiar from the history of other Marxist regimes. One example was the period of the New Economic Policy in the Soviet Union in the 1920s, which in many ways revived aspects of the market economy. Another example is the initial period of Communist government in Czechoslovakia, from 1945 to 1948, when the forms of democratic government were used to mask the elimination of all independent political elements.

For Marxists, the prudence with which the transition phase is handled is a sign of maturity. Fidel Castro himself recommended that the Sandinistas handle their transition phase more carefully than he did.[19] The Marxist priest Fr. Ernesto Cardenal, Sandinista minister of culture, confirmed this piece of advice in an interview when he said that Fidel advised the Sandinistas to go more slowly in the nationalization of industries than the Communist government had in Cuba.[20] These statements are revealing because they distinguish speed from direction: the process of implementing totalitarian control of Nicaragua should go more slowly than the process went in Cuba, but it should end up at the same destination—a society where the individual, whether proletarian or bourgeois, peasant or Indian, is totally under the control of an absolute state.

In the chapters that follow we shall examine how the Sandinistas have gone about trying to bring Nicaragua under their control. This process of moving toward their goals, despite the transition phase cloak, has necessarily involved the breaking of innumerable public promises. In addition to providing factual information as to what has taken place, the following chapters will explore the inner logic of these developments and consider some of the longer term consequences for Nicaragua.

NOTES

1. FSLN National Directorate, "Documento de las 72 Horas," Managua: restricted circulation pamphlet, October, 1979, p. 7.

2. *Ibid.*

3. *Ibid.*, p. 18.

4. *Ibid.*, p. 19.

5. *Ibid.*, p. 20.

6. *Ibid.*

7. *Ibid.*, p. 21.

8. *Ibid.*

9. *Ibid.*, p. 23.

10. *Ibid.*, p. 24.

11. *Ibid.*, p. 25.

12. *Ibid.*, p. 27.

13. *Ibid.*, p. 29.

14. *Ibid.*

15. *Ibid.*, p. 31.

16. *Ibid.*

17. *Ibid.*, p. 33.

18. *Ibid.*, p. 34.

19. Fidel Castro [July 26, 1979 speech in Havana], *Barricada,* July 27, 1979.

20. Ernesto Cardenal [interview], *Playboy,* September 1983, p. 190.

THREE

THE FORECLOSURE OF POLITICAL PLURALISM

From the start, the Sandinistas' goal was to subsume all existing forces and organizations under its leadership. Within weeks of the victory over Somoza, the Sandinistas made decisive moves in this direction. A key development was the deliberate policy of joining state and party.

In a first break with the 1979 program of government, which had promised to replace the National Guard with a truly national army (Clause I-1.12), that is, one free of political affiliation, in September 1979 the Sandinistas established the Sandinista Army, designed as a partisan organization, the armed branch of the FSLN. That this represented the formation of a partisan military force, rather than an honorary renaming of the army after a patriotic hero, was confirmed by an early decree of the junta which declared that the name "Sandinista" could be used only by the FSLN and its branches.[1] The police likewise adopted the name "Sandinista Police" and came under the jurisdiction of the FSLN. Elite members of both the army and the police were issued membership cards in the Sandinista party.

As control over the army and the police was secured, the Frente moved rapidly to build huge mass organizations. They were designed to incorporate most of the population into occupational groups under the leadership of the Sandinista party. For the urban workers the organization was the CST; for the agricultural workers and peasants it was the ATC. For the housewives there was the Luisa Amanda Espinoza Association of Sandinista Women; for the youth the organization was the July 19 Sandinista Youth (after the date of the revolutionary triumph);

and for the kids there was the Carlitos, honoring the name of Carlos Fonseca. Politicized associations were also created for "Sandinista cultural workers" (intellectuals and artists), for college professors and school teachers (the Association of Nicaraguan Teachers), as well as many others. Privileges for joining the Sandinista organizations were coupled with pressures on those who did not.

Another powerful tool for the progressive encroachment of the party-state was the Sandinista Defense Committees (CDS's). Patterned and named after the Cuban Committees for the Defense of the Revolution, the CDS's were partisan paramilitary organizations established by the Sandinistas on residential blocks in the cities and towns. The CDS's, called the "eyes and ears of the revolution," while soliciting the "voluntary" participation of the local residents, were entrusted with the function of spying on the residents of the neighborhood, of reporting any "suspicious activities," and of maintaining a nightwatch. They also assisted the government in health campaigns and in some other social activities. From the first weeks after the revolutionary triumph, the Sandinistas worked hard to install a CDS on every city block.

The first time I attended one of their meetings there was a big poster of Lenin on one of the walls. Another time I visited my local CDS in order to get them to sign my application to renew my driver's license. Starting in January 1982, we had to get our rationing cards for basic foodstuffs from our local CDS.

By their nature the Sandinista Defense Committees were agencies of a political party, the FSLN, which acted with state prerogatives. With the passing of time, the functions and powers of the CDSs continued to grow. People who wished to apply for a job in the ever-expanding state-controlled sector of the economy or in any branch of government had to get a letter of recommendation from their local CDS. Shopkeepers or members of any cooperative or trade supplied by the state needed the seal of approval of their CDS in their applications. As the state increasingly became the main supplier for all industries, commerce, agricultural cooperatives, artisans' shops, and so forth, people increasingly relied for their livelihood on a good relationship with their CDS.

PLURALISM WITHIN THE REVOLUTIONARY FRAMEWORK

Not surprisingly, this process of "Sandinizing" Nicaraguan society led to tensions and contradictions with the goal of political pluralism stated in the 1979 Sandinista program of government. The program had guaranteed "the rights of all Nicaraguans to full political participation, to universal suffrage, to the organizing and functioning of political parties without ideological discrimination, excepting those parties and organizations intending a return to Somocismo" (Clause I.1.1). Nicaraguans read the clause as a commitment to representative democracy. But stumbling-blocks for movement in this direction were created from the outset of Sandinista rule.

Could there be no discrimination between the FSLN and the other political parties when the army, the police, the CDSs, the television, and most of the other media belonged to the Frente? Adding to this confusion was the fact that there was no way to separate the party's budget from the state's (a reason, perhaps, why the government's budget became a secret). In addition to the army and police, many of the other branches of the FSLN, such as its press and television, were funded by the government. The Sandinista party, therefore, was not a party that stood before the law on an equal footing with other parties. Rather, it was an armed party, funded by the state—and thereby by the taxes of all citizens—whose power and privileges far outweighed the leverage of any other political organization.

Nonetheless, the FSLN, not content with virtual political hegemony, sought to eliminate all independent forces. The earliest crackdowns on dissidents were aimed at the independent labor organizations. Attention turned to the political parties in April 1980. The national directorate decided to change the composition of the state council, the semilegislative body which included all forces that had fought against Somoza. The change increased the FSLN's representation from one-third to two-thirds. This was largely accomplished by adding the Frente's mass organizations (CDS's, CST, the July 19 Youth, etc.) to the council and by reducing the number of votes allotted to some of the other rival groupings. This move prompted the resignation from the government junta of moderates Alfonso Robelo and Violeta Chamorro. Robelo vowed to continue fighting for democracy through his party, the Democratic Nicaraguan Movement (MDN). Mrs. Chamorro returned to the board of directors of the newspaper *La Prensa,* which, after an internal break with a Sandinista-controlled union, which had prevented it from publishing news or commentaries critical of the government, began to publish with a good deal of independence.

The FSLN sensed that the crisis was too early and engaged in negotiations with the private sector, including the business community (represented by an organization known as COSEP) and other independent organizations. Two of the demands made on the FSLN were that they announce a date for elections and stop confiscations. The Sandinistas appeared to agree. The elections announcement was to be made by Commander Humberto Ortega, head of the army, at the closing ceremony of the literacy campaign (August 1980).

His speech, however, dissappointed his former allies. Ortega began by reminding the country of where the real power lay—with the FSLN. He then explained what kind of elections the FSLN had in mind.

> Once in power, the Frente Sandinista, as the authentic vanguard and leader of the Nicaraguan people, decided to install a government Junta that would organize and lead the governmental tasks. . . . The national directorate has decided that the government Junta shall continue at the forefront of this task until 1985. . . .[2]

After announcing that the electoral process would not begin until January 1984, Ortega explained:

> The elections that we are referring to are very different from the elections sought by the oligarchs and traitors, conservatives and liberals, the reactionaries and the imperialists, "piles of scoundrels," as Sandino called them. . . . The elections imposed by the gringos will not be ours. . . . Remember well that our elections shall be to strengthen revolutionary power, not to raffle it off, for power is in the hands of the people through its vanguard, the Sandinista National Liberation Front and its national directorate.[3]

Ortega's speech, given just four months after *La Prensa* had become an opposition newspaper, also contained some warnings about freedom of expression:

> There are some who are stirring up economic alarmism—that there are not these things and those things . . . that it is because of the government, that we are incompetent. . . . They take advantage of the freedom of the press, which cost so much blood, to attack the revolution. . . . We are sure that the government will take steps to establish controls, so that a freedom of the press is achieved which does not become prostituted and used to make counterrevolution.[4]

As new voices of dissent began to express concerns about the direction the revolution was taking, the Sandinistas began to refer to them in harsh terms. A standard practice, common in the prewar literature of the FSLN, reappeared: the branding of dissidents as "reactionaries," "bourgeois traitors," "those who sell out their homeland," "counterrevolutionaries." This aggressive rhetoric set the stage for more direct actions. The government denied dissenting organizations access to television and to almost all other mass media. It banned workers' strikes (September 1981) and campaigning by political parties ("proselytizing," the Sandinistas claimed, could not take place in the midst of so many urgent social and economic concerns). The FSLN, meanwhile, continued to stage political rallies, a practice which became one of the most common features of Sandinista Nicaragua.

But perhaps the most effective method of subduing opposition to the government was the use of mobs. They were organized by the FSLN along the lines of the Nazi Brown Shirts to engage in street actions against opponents. The state provided support, including police protection and the use of government vehicles. (In their first violent appearance on February 14, 1981, the mobs were mobilized in trucks of the ministry of public works. *La Prensa* provided photographs showing the license plate numbers of several of the vehicles.) The mobs harassed political dissidents, independent journalists, and church and labor leaders. They were also instrumental in breaking up political rallies that non-Sandinista organizations attempted to hold.

In March 1981, Alfonso Robelo's MDN Party announced that it was going to hold a political rally in the town of Nandaime on the 15th. Sandinista Commander Leticia Herrera, the Moscow-trained leader of the CDS's, issued a call over the state media asking the militants of the FSLN to break up this rally using "any means." Taking to the streets the following night with machetes, sticks, chains, and other such weapons, mobs terrorized the homes of several dissidents (including my own). The headquarters of the MDN party was vandalized, the home of its local Nandaime leader burned down. The installations of the independent radio station Radio Mundial were also destroyed. (In 1954 a Somocista mob had done the same thing to Radio Mundial.)

The official Sandinista newspaper *Barricada*, commenting on the incidents, said that "the revolution holds the view that these actions, regardless of the forms they take under the present circumstances, are the most advanced, educated, and progressive ones."[5] The Sandinista mobs and their actions thus received full legitimization and encouragement from the Sandinista authorities. Commander Daniel Ortega even started calling them "divine mobs."

As a consequence of all these developments, by the first months of 1981 political pluralism and the right of dissent were in serious jeopardy in Nicaragua.

A quick look at the country's hierarchy of government shows the national directorate of the FSLN as virtually an absolute power, and checks and balances between the different branches of government essentially nonexistent. The national directorate had direct control of the army and the militias through Humberto Ortega, and of the ministry of the interior, including the secret police and the regular police, through Tomás Borge. The national directorate also appointed and controlled the members of the government junta, whose leader was Daniel Ortega himself. The national directorate was also the supreme authority over the Sandinista Assembly, which was the highest organizational body of the FSLN party. This body was in turn in charge of appointing and overseeing the leaders of the FSLN's mass organizations, which had effective control over the state council after the restructuring of April 1980. The FSLN's Propaganda and Political Education section, in charge of the mass media, was also under the direction of the Sandinista Assembly. Only the Supreme Court kept a semblance of independence, at least for a time, although it was often undermined—or simply bypassed— by the ministry of justice and by the creation of the FSLN-sponsored People's Courts. These were set up to judge "Somocistas and counterrevolutionaries." The People's Courts themselves decided who fit into these categories, and their verdicts could not be appealed to or challenged by the Supreme Court.

Despite the contradictions, the Sandinistas continued to claim that they were democratic and committed to pluralism. The discrepancy between their claim and their policies is resolved, to some extent, if one considers their point of view. The Sandinistas often point to the presence of delegates of the CST, the ATC, and other of the FSLN's mass organizations in the council of state as a demonstration of pluralism. And their view is correct within their standpoint, since in it their organizations are the

ones which truly represent the people. They understand pluralism to be legitimate only to the degree that it works within the
framework of their own revolution, only insofar as it does not
question the vanguard's claim to absolute supremacy. Every other
view is subversive, "counterrevolutionary," and outside the range
of the allowable plurality of opinions. This is the outlook expressed by Tomás Borge when he said:

> Other social sectors also play a role, but only insofar as they identify
> with the interest of the country, with the interest of the majority. We
> can speak of political pluralism, a mixed economy, and national
> unity—but always within the framework established by the revolu-
> tion, not against the revolution; a mixed economy, pluralism, unity
> not to wipe out or weaken the revolution, but to strengthen it.[6]

Borge's view echoes that of Castro, "Anything inside the revolution, nothing outside the revolution," and of Mussolini, who
earlier penned the totalitarian formula: "Everything within the
state, nothing outside the state, nothing against the state."

FSLN leaders often use the term "direct democracy" to contrast their own understanding of democracy with that of representative or "bourgeois" democracy. An example of direct democracy is the political gatherings called "cara al pueblo" (facing
the nation). At such meetings, government representatives, usually Sandinista commanders, appear in a neighborhood to talk
with the people, listening and responding to their complaints. An
American observer, Ronald Radosh, writing in a periodical
which tends to be sympathetic to leftist political programs, describes well the tone of these meetings:

> The relationship between people and leaders was more feudal than
> revolutionary: the lord dispensing justice in return for loyalty. Nor
> did the intimidating atmosphere encourage dissent. The meetings are
> largely symbolic—theatrical productions designed to dramatize the
> government's concern for and closeness to the people. They are
> hardly a substitute for institutions of representative democracy
> through which a people can freely debate and define their country's
> course.[7]

Radosh's comments highlight an important point: the Sandinistas are not interested in dealing with dissent, but in com-
manding submission. One of their most widely used chants goes:
"National Directorate, order us!" ("Dirección Nacional, Or-

dene!")—a replica of Cuba's most popular chant, "Commander-in-Chief [Castro], order us!" Central to the national directorate's conception of itself as leader of the vanguard is the belief that it possesses superior—and, in a way, absolute—knowledge. Hence, its members deserve obedience. Radosh, quoting the left-wing Honduran writer Rodolfo Pastor, adds that in Nicaragua "the highest civic virtue is submission to discipline, and the worst sin is open political disagreement. This is the antithesis to the revolutionary spirit of criticism."[8]

This intolerance of opposition unavoidably led the Sandinistas into direct conflict with their domestic opponents. By the middle of 1983, in fact, many of those opponents were in exile, their political organizations largely crippled by the policies of the FSLN. Among these leaders were men such as Alfonso Robelo, former member of the government junta and head of the National Democratic Movement (MDN), of center-left orientation; Adolfo Calero, president of the large and traditional Conservative Party, who had been imprisoned by Somoza in 1978; Eden Pastora, the popular hero in the takeover of the National Palace in 1978; Wilfredo Montalvan, head of the Social Democratic party; Stedman Fagoth and Brooklyn Rivera, the top leaders of the Miskito Indians; José Dávila, a Somoza antagonist who headed the Social Christian Party; and Edgard Macías, former vice minister of labor in the Sandinista government and head of the left-leaning People's Social Christian Party. Most of these men—Calero, Robelo, Pastora, Fagoth, and Rivera—have continued their political opposition to the Sandinistas by joining the armed conflict, claiming that channels for civic opposition inside the country do not exist. Tragically for Nicaragua, the foreclosure of political pluralism has once again driven scores of Nicaraguans to the battlefield.

THE 1984 NATIONAL ELECTIONS
Despite the Sandinistas' approach to political pluralism, national elections were nonetheless held in November 1984. Naturally, they raised considerable controversy. What kind of elections took place? Should they be interpreted as a departure from the Sandinistas' basic direction or as another instance of transition phase strategy?

There is, again, no way to properly interpret events in Nicaragua unless they are placed in the perspective of the Sandinistas' stated goals. Free elections, as a reading of the history of the FSLN and its programs and documents makes clear, are not a goal of the Sandinistas. Elections, at least in the Western sense of the term, implying plurality of options and the other features of representative democracy, are alien to the ideology of the Frente. Their program of government calls for a more "direct" form of "people's democracy," where the leadership of the Frente is uncontestable. The Sandinistas' qualifying statements about elections indicated this: "We will not raffle power," "Our people have already voted . . . voted for themselves, for Sandinism," "Elections in Nicaragua will not be to contend for power, they will be to strengthen the Revolution," "Elections will not be like the bourgeois elections of Costa Rica, Venezuela or the United States," and so on. So why then did the Sandinistas hold elections?

Perhaps the timing of the FSLN's decision to move up the elections to November 1984 (they originally scheduled them for 1985) provides a clue. They made this change shortly after the invasion of Grenada took place. That invasion sent shock waves through the Nicaraguan government and may have convinced its leaders that their country would be next on the Marines' agenda. It is conceivable that the Sandinistas moved quickly to beef up their public image with talk of democracy and pluralism. The timing may have been coincidental, but in a private speech that was leaked to the public, a Sandinista leader plainly suggested that the elections were a response to internal and external pressure and nothing else.

In a speech to the central committee of the pro-Soviet Nicaraguan Socialist Party (PSN), Bayardo Arce, one of the nine commanders of the national directorate of the FSLN, tried to explain to his Marxist comrades why the FSLN was embroiled in the almost heretical exercise of holding elections. Arce's speech was intended to reassure his friends in the PSN that the elections were merely a stratagem to confuse the bourgeoisie. He insisted that the long-term goals of the revolution—a one-party state with a collectivized economy—would not be jeopardized but guaranteed by the elections. A member of the audience, for reasons still unclear (he might have been a zealot dissatisfied with Sandinista tactics), discreetly tape recorded the entire speech and then made it public. The Sandinistas could not deny the authenticity of the tape. Daniel Ortega sought a way out by suggesting that the speech represented the private views of Arce. But it would be impossible to disentangle Arce's private views on such an issue from official positions, given that he is responsible for the political propaganda and public relations of the FSLN. At one point in his speech he said:

> Let me remind you that back in 1979 the Organization of American States was trying to find a nonrevolutionary solution [to the Somoza government]. In that context, we [the FSLN] came up with a program that made us acceptable, based on three points that we knew we could manage in a revolutionary way. They were nonalignment, a mixed economy, and political pluralism. Without these negative commitments, it is true that the elections would be absolutely untimely.
> If it were not for the state of war forced on us . . . the electoral problem would be something completely out of step in terms of usefulness. What the revolution [the Sandinista government] truly needs is the expediency [power] to take action. And this power to take action is what constitutes the essence of the dictatorship of the proletariat . . . so the election is, from this point of view, a hindrance.[9]

Note how Arce acknowledges here that commitments to nonalignment, a mixed economy, and political pluralism (obviously including elections) were a tactical step taken by the FSLN in 1979 in order to gain acceptability. Also note that for Arce the election is a hindrance to what the Sandinistas need in order to establish a Marxist dictatorship of the proletariat. They would not be thinking about elections if it were not for the state of war forced upon them. Concerning what to expect in the future, Arce adds that after the elections

> The time will have come to think about a single party. Why should we Communists go on wearing different shirts. . . ? We are discussing . . . first the idea of putting an end to all this artifice of pluralism . . . which has been useful to us up to now.[10]

Against the backdrop of Arce's and other Sandinista commanders' statements, the Nicaraguan elections can thus be seen as a tactical maneuver of the Sandinistas. They did it only after external pressure had become so intense that continued delay was no longer strategically advantageous. In fact, even if the elections could be regarded as a hopeful sign of the Sandinistas' willingness to compromise, their own words and actions lead one to conclude that it was the closed fist and not an open hand from foreign nations which prompted them to engage, however imperfectly, in a political process they ultimately abhor. What is particularly ominous is that even under fear of invasion the Sandinistas gave in so little. With the Western media watching and waiting for signs of a democratic process, they kept press censorship alive, harassed opponents, and failed to meet even the moderate demands for fairness that democratic opponents like Arturo Cruz (a former member of the Sandinista government junta and Sandinista ambassador to the United States) and some leaders of the Socialist International were asking. A brief examination of how the Nicaraguan election was held shows that it falls far short of meeting the minimum requirements for a free political contest.

Although the particularities of each culture and nation may warrant some exceptions, generally speaking elections are not free unless (1) there are real choices available; (2) people are reasonably free from coercion regarding their choice; (3) the competing political forces are reasonably free to reach out to people and enjoy equal rights before the law; and (4) there are workable safeguards against fraud. A country like Nicaragua, with no tradition of true democracy, might not be expected to meet these conditions to the same degree that countries with well-developed democratic institutions and traditions of political pluralism might. But it is difficult to conceive of truly free elections if any of these requisites are seriously violated.

During the Somoza regime, for instance, Nicaragua had several elections, but the absence of some of these conditions cast a shadow on the results. Political opponents of the regime often decided not to participate in races in which, they thought, the dice were loaded. The Somozas got around this difficulty by inducing the participation of lesser political candidates, usually people from the fringes of the major political parties. In Nicaragua we scornfully called such candidates "zancudos," that is, "mosquitoes," a term expressing their smallness and lack of true bite. With their participation, elections were staged in which condition number one was missing: there were no real alternatives, for the "zancudo" candidates were not true alternatives to the Somozas.

In the elections under the Sandinistas also there were no true choices. The Sandinistas succeeded in eliminating by force or voluntary exclusion all real alternatives. Their opponents in the elections were a cluster of tiny, splinter-party candidates, most of whom were Marxists and close allies of the government. The significant political leaders were either outlawed or exiled; or else, due to what they saw as the lack of other of the minimum requirements for free elections, they refused to participate. Those whom the Sandinistas outlawed were excluded from the elections on the grounds that they were criminals who had supported the armed struggle against the present regime. The Sandinistas branded them "Somocistas," a charge clearly at odds with their political past, but which has often been echoed by some segments of the international media.

Political opponents in the groups who were fighting against the Sandinistas offered to lay down their arms if allowed to participate in the elections. But just as the Sandinistas rejected the Catholic bishops' call at Easter 1984 for reconciliation and dialogue, so they also rejected this offer. The FSLN refusal to dialogue and open up the election process led to the boycott of the remaining independent political forces, together represented by Arturo Cruz. Among the forces in Cruz's Coordinadora Democratica coalition were the Social Christian Party, the Conservative Party, the Liberal Constitutionalist Party, and the two independent labor organizations—the CTN and the CUS.

The Sandinistas filled the political vacuum thus created by resorting to the tactic used by the Somoza regime: induce the participation of minor political figures. They came from several small political parties: the Nicaraguan Socialist Party (PSN); the Nicaraguan Communist Party, a party that separated from the PSN; the People's Action Movement, a Maoist organization that worked under the FSLN during the insurrection against Somoza; the People's Christian Social Party, a splinter organization that broke with Edgard Macías's larger party in 1982, when he and other members of his party objected to the road taken by the Sandinistas; and the Conservative Democratic Party, another splinter organization that broke with the major and traditional Conservative Party when the latter decided not to participate in the elections. The splinter organization claimed the name of the parent organization and the Nicaraguan Supreme Court granted the use of the name Conservative Democratic Party to the newly created organization. The final party that entered the race, and probably the one with the most political clout next to the Sandinistas, was the Liberal Independent Party led by former minister of labor in the Sandinista government Virgilio Godoy. Just days before the elections, however, he dropped out on the grounds that the minimum prerequisites for a free election had not been met by the Sandinistas.

Another basic factor in the Nicaraguan elections was the coercion or serious constraint of both the public and the politicians. There was, to begin with, the state of emergency. The Sandinistas had promised to lift it, but they did so only partially. Individuals were thus deprived of most of their rights and personal guarantees. People could be arrested without trial and held incommunicado for lengthy periods. In addition, Nicaraguans were subjected to the omnipresent control exerted by the Sandinista Defense Committees.

The curtailment of freedom of expression under the state of emergency made things even worse. Those subjected to abuse or arbitrary actions by the government had no outlet to voice their grievances. Although during the weeks preceding the elections the Sandinistas relaxed some of their tight censorship on *La Prensa*, it was heavy enough to prevent the printing of some of their daily issues. Radio broadcasts also continued to be censored. The Sandinistas did offer a limited amount of their television time to the competing political parties (fifteen minutes per day total for all the parties), but this was almost negligible when compared with the unrestricted, round-the-clock use of television and other mass media by the FSLN. Opposition parties also questioned the effectiveness of any lift in censorship when so many legal limitations on free expression and so many social controls existed.

A Sandinista law, intended to regulate freedom of the press in the event that the state of emergency is lifted, prohibited the communication of information which "echoes the interests of the imperialists or reproduces the propaganda campaigns that the internal and external enemies of our revolutionary process are promoting."[11] The minister of the interior is to judge which information fits this description. The law that regulates the functioning of political parties states that all parties are duty bound to "defend the revolution,"[12] while another clause, decreed in February 1984, further and specifically adds that their duty is to "especially respect the People's Sandinista Revolution, the supreme achievement of the Nicaraguan people."[13] The same ruling also states that nobody shall be allowed to "defame" the revolution and requires that criticisms of the administration "shall be constructive and duly documented, respectful of the authorities, and offering solutions according to the national reality."[14] Who was to judge when these criteria are met?—the National Council of Political Parties, a newly created body in which the Sandinistas hold five of the seven posts. The council was given the authority to suspend or suppress political parties for misbehaving on these and related matters.

Another key obstacle to true elections in Nicaragua was the melding of state and party. For example, in the Sandinista party's army, youths are exposed to the daily political indoctrination of the FSLN—a reason why the Sandinistas lowered the voting age to sixteen years.

The Inter-American Commission on Human Rights of the OAS, in a report published five weeks before the elections, asked the Sandinistas to remember Clause 23 of the Pan-American Convention on Human Rights, which says that all citizens should have equal opportunities and access to public office. The report then warned the FSLN that "it had been able to verify that throughout the election process the FSLN had amply utilized all the resources of the state, thus placing itself in a position of advantage in regard to the other competitors."[15] The commission also called "unacceptable" the "harassment of political labor leaders."[16]

Finally, when it came to guarantees against fraud, nearly insurmountable obstacles arose. There was no sound preregistration system for voters, and Nicaraguans lack any standard ID. (Anyone could vote at a precinct provided two witnesses could testify that he had not voted elsewhere.) Often they have no ID at all, precluding the possibility of electronic tabulation. The ballots, on the other hand, were counted by committees on which the Sandinista delegates had decisive majorities. The Supreme Electoral Council was headed by three militants of the FSLN: Mariano Fiallos, Leonel Arguello (a former Somocista), and Amada Pineda. Requests by the opposition to have the elections supervised by the Organization of American States or some other respected international organization were turned down by the Sandinistas.

On election day, many polling places were empty. The bishop of Juigalpa, Pablo Vega, testified that in his diocese abstentionism was widespread. In Managua, where most of the international press assembled that day, the Sandinistas closed down some polling places for an hour or two after they had already been open for some time. By the time the polls were reopened lines had formed thus giving the impression that the turnout was substantial.

Reports of irregularities, such as the many instances where the number of people registered did not match the number of people who voted, were strictly censored. Shortly after election day the ministry of the interior decreed that the media could not publish any criticism or news about the elections that in any way implied that there had been fraud.

Daniel Ortega was declared the winner. Official government figures showed him receiving roughly 65 percent of the vote. (Somoza used to win by about the same margin.)

In view of all these considerations it is no wonder that widespread skepticism was voiced regarding the elections. The prestigious—and liberal—French newspaper *Le Monde* said that the Nicaraguan elections "do not deserve to be dignified by that name."[17] Carlos Andrés Pérez, Socialist International leader, and former Venezuelan president who helped the Sandinistas in many ways during the war with Somoza, sent a letter to Daniel Ortega explaining why he would not be attending Ortega's inauguration as president of Nicaragua.

> My last visit to Managua was on Feb. 20, 1984. . . . We heard you state, in terms even more categorical than those expressed in public, your determination to carry out an electoral process with the broadest guarantees. These were pledges that we received enthusiastically, and repeated widely. . . . Those of us who believe we have done so much for the Sandinista Revolution feel cheated, because sufficient guarantees were not provided to assure the participation of all political forces. Sadly, the limiting in this way of true political pluralism weakened the credibility of the elections.[18]

As Andrés Perez's statement suggests, FSLN promises of political pluralism and free elections are another instance of their breaking faith with those who put their trust in them.

NOTES

1. Junta de Gobierno, "Decree No. 67—Uso de la Denominación Sandinista," September 13, 1979, in *Leyes de la República de Nicaragua*, p. 147.

2. Humberto Ortega, speech in *La Cruzada en Marcha,* Bulletin No. 16, Managua: Ministry of Education, 1980, p. 11.

3. *Ibid.*

4. *Ibid.,* p. 10.

5. *Barricada* March 18, 1981, p. 3.

6. Tomas Borge, "The Second Anniversary of the Sandinista Revolution" speech, July 19, 1981, in *op. cit., Sandinistas Speak,* p. 133.

7. Ronald Radosh, "Darkening Nicaragua," *The New Republic,* October 24, 1983, p. 8.

8. Quoted by Radosh, *ibid.,* p. 8.

9. Arce's speech was first published in the Barcelona newspaper *La Vanguardia.* English excerpts in *CLAT REPORT,* No. 2, January 1985, Flushing, N.Y., pp. 8-10.

10. *Ibid.*

11. Law of Political Parties (Section 32-IV-e).

12. *Ibid.,* Section 5.

13. Decree of February 1984, Section 9.

14. *Ibid.,* Section 31.

15. Quoted by CPDH-OEA, in *Nuevo Amanecer,* No. 5, Madrid, 1985, p. 6.

16. *Ibid.*

17. Agence France Presse dispatch, in *Diario Las Américas,* Miami, July 28, 1984, p. 6.

18. Carlos Andrés Pérez, letter to Daniel Ortega, "Socialist International Leader Sends Daniel Ortega His Regrets," *Wall Street Journal,* January 11, 1985, p. 13.

LINING UP WITH THE SOVIETS AND CUBANS

The public agenda of the Sandinistas lacks any explicit reference to Marxist ideology or to Soviet or Cuban policies. Officially the FSLN is not Marxist but "Sandinista," an undefined term which most people understand as synonymous with Nicaraguan nationalist. Officially the FSLN has vowed to follow a foreign policy of nonalignment. As mentioned earlier, on both counts, ideology and foreign policy, the Sandinistas have taken a public approach very much like that of Fidel Castro during the early stages of the Cuban revolution, when he declared himself and the revolution nationalist. After he fully joined the Soviet camp, many people continued to argue that he had done so as a reaction to hostile U.S. policies. The debate over the Sandinistas' ideological international alignments has followed the same pattern.

We have already examined in some detail the development of the FSLN and the convictions and policies of the men and women who lead it. This evidence shows that the Sandinistas have for many years been committed to a Marxism-Leninism that includes an internationalist and pro-Soviet outlook. Statements of the Sandinistas since the revolution, and the way they have been setting their course in coordination with the Soviet and Cuban government, show that the Sandinistas have not diverged from their earlier views.

In August 1981, for example, Humberto Ortega, minister of defense and head of the army and the militias, addressed an army special unit on the role of Marxism-Leninism in the revolution:

Sandinismo, that beautiful tradition of this people that Carlos Fonseca has kept alive, is our source of inspiration. The scientific doctrine of the revolution is our guide: Marxism-Leninism. A Sandinismo without Marxism-Leninism cannot be revolutionary. . . . Sandinismo is our moral and political force. Our doctrine is Marxism-Leninism.[1]

Ortega followed this familiar explanation of FSLN theory with a practical judgment: it is the Soviet Union that is the avant-garde of all progressive nations.[2] (Ortega's statement first appeared in a restricted-circulation pamphlet designed for the army's elite. After it became public, the government quickly printed a new version in which the direct references to Marxism-Leninism were omitted.)

Similar statements, combining praises of Marx and Lenin with praises for the Soviets and other Communist regimes, are regularly aired by the Sandinistas. For example, on the anniversary of the Soviet army, Commander Humberto Ortega sent the following message to the Soviet Union on behalf of the Sandinista army, which was printed in *Barricada:*

Marshall of the Soviet Union
DMITRI USTINOV
Member of the Politburo
Central Committee of the Community Part of the Soviet Union
Minister of Defense of the USSR:

In the name of the People's Sandinista Army, our veteran People's Sandinista Militias, and in my own name, receive our fraternal and revolutionary greetings on this glorious occasion of the 64th anniversary of the formation of the committed and heroic Armed Forces of the Soviet Socialist Republics.

We are sure that the fight for world peace that your people, government, and party continuously maintain shall always find in the armed forces of the USSR a vital pillar for the strengthening of this sacred cause.[3]

When Leonid Brezhnev, premier of the U.S.S.R., died in November 1982, Daniel Ortega, coordinator of the governing junta, with Commander Bayardo Arce, signed a message that went well beyond the condolences required by protocol and exalted what the Soviets were doing around the world. Brezhnev was portrayed as a great defender of humanity "in the great Fatherland" (the U.S.S.R.) while "that heroic Communist party and people of the Great October Revolution of Lenin are presently engaged in the grandest and most just of all battles, which is that of peace."[4]

This homage to the man who crushed the Czechoslovak reform movement and invaded Afghanistan was repeated in the Sandinista newspapers. *Barricada,* the official newspaper, carried these headlines on November 11: "A Great Champion for Peace Has Died," "USSR Will Keep Policy of Peace and Detente," "A Great Loss for the People of Sandino." *El Nuevo Diario* published articles the same day with such headlines as "Leonid Brezhnev Has Died, Glorious Son of the Working Class" and "FSLN Dips Its Banners Before Leonid Brezhnev."

In an editorial the next day, *Barricada* portrayed Brezhnev as the man who "continued the policy of peace formulated by the Communist party, the party which formed him during those historic days when heaven was taken by assault under the guidance of Lenin."[5] Similar statements were uttered by Commander Rene Nuñez, a member of the FSLN national directorate and president of the council of state and of the Nicaraguan Association of Friendship with the Socialist Countries. He expressed his condolences for "the physical loss of a faithful follower of the policies of Lenin."[6]

As significant as the explicit expressions in support of Marxism-Leninism and Soviet policy is the absolute lack of criticism regarding any aspect of either. Not a single issue of *Barricada,* nor a single statement of a high or even medium rank officer of the Sandinista regime that I am aware of has ever expressed criticism of Communist doctrine or Soviet policy, which would be strange if the Sandinistas were fundamentally pragmatic or unorthodox or nationalist Marxists.

Given the regularity with which the view is expressed that Sandinista friendship with the Soviets is a response to U.S. pressure, it is important to point out the timing of the first Sandinista expressions of loyalty to the Soviet Union. As early as September 1979, when Nicaragua was on very good terms with nearly all countries, including the United States, Daniel Ortega delivered a speech in Havana which provides an outline of the general direction of Sandinista foreign policy: uncritical support of the Soviet Union and its allies coupled with unflagging enmity for the United States. "Imperialism," Ortega said, referring to the United States, "cannot conceive of a free people, a sovereign people, an independent people."[7] He then expressed his support for Kampuchea, Viet Nam, Zimbabwe, the Polisario Front in the Western Sahara, other Marxist movements, and the PLO, while demanding the withdrawal of U.S. troops from Korea.[8]

On March 17, 1980, when the United States was still the greatest single provider of funds for the Sandinista government, the Nicaraguan government sent a top-ranking delegation to the Soviet Union to sign a treaty of friendship and collaboration with the Soviet Communist Party. Signed in Moscow on March 22, the document fully endorses all major tenets of Soviet foreign policy and decries the policies of the U.S. The Nicaraguan delegation was headed by Tomás Borge, Humberto Ortega, Henry Ruiz, and Moisés Hassan. Their joint statement reads in part:

> The Soviet Union and Nicaragua resolutely condemn the imperialist policy of interference in the internal affairs of the Latin American peoples.
>
> The Soviet Union and Nicaragua resolutely condemn the campaign that the imperialist and reactionary forces have launched of building up international tension in connection with the events of Afghanistan, a campaign aimed at subverting the inalienable right of the people of the Democratic Republic of Afghanistan and other peoples of the world to follow the path of progressive transformation.
>
> The Soviet Union and Nicaragua resolutely condemn the policy of building up tension in Southeast Asia, and demand an end to the threats . . . against the Socialist Republic of Viet Nam, the Laos People's Democratic Republic, the Peoples' Republic of Kampuchea, and an end to interference in these countries' internal affairs.[9]

Like previous FSLN statements, the joint communique confirmed the ideological nature of the Sandinistas' anti-imperialism: U.S. foreign policy is by definition imperialistic, Soviet and Cuban foreign policies are by definition progressive.

True to the March 1982 agreement, the Sandinistas abstained from condemning the Soviet invasion of Afghanistan when an overwhelming number of nations, including most of the non-aligned nations, passed a condemnatory resolution at the UN. The Sandinistas repeated this voting pattern a year later when the UN again demanded the withdrawal of Soviet troops. Later, Nicaragua also abstained from condemning the Soviet Union for the killing of the 269 passengers on a Korean airliner in September 1983.

It was rightly said of Somoza that his regime was so aligned with the foreign policy of the U.S. that at the UN it never issued a single vote at odds with that of the United States. The Sandinistas have been repeating the pattern of a wholly subservient foreign policy, substituting the U.S.S.R. for the U.S. To date, the only foreign-policy action independent of the Soviet Union taken by the Nicaraguan regime was the sending of a baseball team to the 1984 Olympics which the U.S.S.R. boycotted.

In practically every international forum, Nicaraguan delegates repeat the same litany in support of the oppressed peoples of the earth and of Marxist-inspired national liberation movements, always in a way that lines up with Soviet policies. They never mention among their concerns the struggle of the Polish workers, the Ethiopian rebels, or the condition of other peoples oppressed by Marxist and Soviet-backed regimes.

Revealing in this regard is a memo of the FSLN concerning events in Poland in December 1981. The memo was signed by Federico López, head of the department of mass media of the FSLN and addressed to the managers and editors of the state-controlled media. It was leaked to *La Prensa,* where it was published the following day. The document, whose authorship the FSLN did not deny, gave instructions on how to approach news about Poland as tensions increased over Solidarity. Here are excerpts:

> In view of the delicate social situation that our Polish brothers are going through and the manipulation of information by the imperialist news agencies, we suggest that our coverage of the problem orientate people along the following lines:
>
> —Do not give space to material from news agencies controlled by imperialism. They distort the facts in order to spread their anti-Soviet views and their anti-Communism. . . .
>
> —Reflect the difficult situation that faces the Polish revolutionary movement from an objective viewpoint, reporting only those facts confirmed by Prensa Latina and Tass.
>
> —Stress that the steps taken by the [Communist] party and government in Poland are aimed at rescuing the country from the crisis. . . . It is not the working class which is being repressed but those counterrevolutionaries that wish to hand over Poland to the imperialists. . . . It should not be emphasized that strikes are prohibited, but that a call is being made to face the economic crisis.
>
> —Neutralize the tendency to present the Polish government as "the new military government" or the "Soviet presence."

—If it is not possible to neutralize the anti-Soviet view of the reactionaries regarding Poland, we can at least neutralize the possible analogies that they make between Nicaragua and Poland, above all in regard to the strikes.

—It is necessary to develop a line that stresses the freedom that exists in our country, the democracy, the accomplishments, etc.[10]

Particularly notable in this statement is the way that the Sandinista official in charge of the government media regrets the anti-Soviet view of what he calls imperialist news agencies, and his conviction that the Soviet news agency, Tass, and the Cuban new agency, Prensa Latina, inform from an "objective viewpoint." This official completely accepts all the arguments that the Polish regime and the Soviets were using to crush Poland's Solidarity movement. Further, he regrets that it may not be possible to neutralize the anti-Soviet views of the "reactionaries."

THE FOREIGN PRESENCE

The most telling development in the Sandinistas' alignment with the Soviet bloc has not been in what they have said, but in the way they have invited a massive influx of advisors and personnel from these countries to help them reshape Nicaragua. Cubans, East Germans, Bulgarians, Soviets, and a host of so-called "international compañeros" (comrades) began working in practically all realms of government, particularly the armed forces, the ministry of the interior, the educational system, and the mass media.

As might be expected, the Nicaraguan government does not provide information regarding the number of foreigners working for it. Circumstantial evidence, however, suggests that by 1985 there were about eight thousand Cubans. From 1979 to 1980, two thousand Cubans came as teachers and two thousand as physicians and health workers. Following a flood in May 1982, the Sandinistas publicly acknowledged that two thousand Cuban construction workers had arrived to help rebuild damaged roads and bridges. (A Cuban radio station placed the number at twelve thousand.) The odd thing about this is that Nicaragua already had a very large number of unemployed construction workers who could well have been utilized without having to resort to imported labor. In fact, the Cubans arrived while unemployment in Nicaragua continued to rise. In all likelihood the Cuban "workers" were mostly men with military training who came, as in Grenada, as a military reserve in disguise. (There appear to be at least two thousand more Cubans as military and security advisors.) Eden Pastora, former high commander of the Sandinista militias and now in Costa Rica, declared that one of every six soldiers in the Nicaraguan army was a Cuban. (In August 1982, a Nicaraguan Air Force plane crashed in Managua. Of the fourteen soldiers killed, two were Cubans. If these casualties were a random sample of the Nicaraguan armed forces, Pastora's estimate may be right.) In 1985, after foreign minister D'Escoto had denied that there were Cuban military advisors in Nicaragua, Daniel Ortega, now president, said that there were no more than eight hundred.

In addition to the scores of Cuban teachers, college education has been reformed by a team of five Cuban specialists.

The television system was placed under Cuban managers in 1980.

By 1982 the foreign presence in Managua had become pervasive. Foreigners could be seen outnumbering Nicaraguans on some of the most popular beaches as well as in many of Managua's restaurants. In nearly any government office one could find foreigners performing all sorts of jobs. A sentiment shared by many Nicaraguans is that theirs has become an occupied country. Antonio Farach, for example, defected from the Sandinista government in early 1984 after more than ten years of service with the FSLN. He had worked with the ministry of foreign affairs as a diplomat in Honduras and Venezuela. In an interview conducted in the United States, Farach told of the significant role that Cubans are playing in the ministry for which he worked, including full access to classified information. When asked why he left Nicaragua, Farach said: "It is not easy for me to give a complete answer, but . . . I felt that we had sold our sovereignty to a foreign nation" [Cuba].[11]

On May 2, 1985, the Sandinista government bid farewell to one hundred Cuban military advisors in a unilateral step aimed at easing tensions in Central America. At a ceremony for the departing military specialists, the head of the Sandinista army, Humberto Ortega, made it clear that this move was not to be understood as indicating a change in Cuban-Nicaraguan relations: "We are not retreating one step in relations between Nicaragua and Cuba."[12] Also present at the ceremony was the Cuban general Arnaldo Ochoa, who was head of the counterinsurgency forces in Angola in the 1970s and has been stationed in Nicaragua since 1983.

Ochoa's ominous presence is but one more reminder of the intimacy of links between Cuba and Nicaragua, intimacy that predates the triumph of the revolution and is an integral part of the history of the FSLN and of the biography of its major leaders. The pro-Sovietism of the Frente dates back before its founding to the visit of Carlos Fonseca to the Soviet Union in 1957. It continued and consolidated itself in the following two decades of revolutionary struggle. It has become government policy since the triumph of the revolution.

NOTES

1. Humberto Ortega, "Discurso del Ministro de Defensa," *op. cit.*, p. 8.
2. *Ibid.*, p. 9.
3. February 23, 1982, p. 1.
4. *Barricada,* November 12, 1982, p. 1.
5. *Ibid.*, p. 3.
6. *Ibid.*
7. Daniel Ortega, "Nothing Will Hold Back Our Struggle for Liberation," in *op. cit., Sandinistas Speak,* p. 44.
8. *Ibid.*, pp. 45-48.
9. FSLN-CPSU, "Joint Soviet-Nicaraguan Communique," *Current Digest of the Soviet Press,* 23 April 1980, pp. 10, 11.
10. *La Prensa,* December 23, 1981.
11. Antonio Farach, interview, "The Cuban Presence in Nicaragua," The Puebla Institute, *Occasional Bulletins,* No. 9, April 1985, p. 1.
12. "100 Cuban Advisors Leave Nicaragua," *The Washington Post,* May 3, 1985, p. A22.

ONLY ONE WORKERS' CLASS, ONLY ONE UNION

With the triumph of the revolution in 1979, organized labor looked ahead expectantly to a future characterized by unprecedented freedom. Clause I.1.4 of the Sandinista program of government promised that "legislation shall be enacted and actions taken to guarantee and promote the free organization of labor, trade, and people's unions, both in the city and in the countryside."[1] Article 32 of the Statute of Rights and Guarantees of Nicaraguans stated that "all workers may exercise their right to strike, according to the law."[2] A brief look at how the Sandinistas have dealt with organized labor provides important evidence of the basic direction that the Sandinistas are taking. In fact, the Sandinistas are bringing the social class they claim to represent under their political control.

Before the triumph of the revolution, the Sandinistas had no sizable labor union of their own. The leading union before the revolution was the Nicaraguan Confederation of Labor (CTN), of Christian Democratic orientation, having nearly sixty-five thousand members. After the CTN came the Independent National Confederation of Labor (CGT-I), affiliated with the Nicaraguan Socialist Party; the Syndicalist Action and Unity Central (CAUS), of Maoist leaning; and the Council of Trade Union Unification (CUS), linked to the AFL-CIO labor movement in the United States. All of these labor unions had engaged in the wide fronts organized to fight the Somoza dictatorship. The Secretary General of the CUS, Luis Medrano, was murdered by Somoza forces in 1978.

Once in power the Sandinistas created and promoted their

own trade unions—the aforementioned Sandinista Confederation of Labor (CST—urban workers) and the Association of Agricultural Workers (ATC—agricultural workers). The FSLN claimed that these were the unions which truly represented the urban and rural workers. They even created the slogan, "Only one workers' class, only one trade union." The government expanded the CST—which in 1980 became an affiliate of the World Federation of Trade Unions, the Marxist international organization with headquarters in Prague, Czechoslovakia—very rapidly by barring all other unions from the state-controlled sector of the economy and by making it mandatory for all public employees to join the union. The ATC was expanded by requiring peasants and farm workers to join as a condition for getting credit and technical assistance.

To increase its influence among workers in the private sector, the ministry of labor favored Sandinista unions over the independent unions in all labor disputes. They also created CST-affiliated unions in businesses where workers belonged to a rival organization. The ministry of labor would then recognize the legitimacy of the CST affiliate, sometimes even withdrawing recognition from the others. Members of the CST were given, in addition, exclusive access to the state-owned worker's cooperatives. In these stores the CST workers could buy rationed items that non-CST workers could seldom find elsewhere.

When many workers resisted these maneuvers and stood behind their traditional leaders and organizations, the FSLN began to harass first the CTN and CUS and then all other independent unions. The Sandinistas accused them of being bourgeois trade unions which had betrayed the working class. Later the Sandinistas claimed that the other unions were instruments of U.S. imperialism and took more direct action against them, including the imprisonment of their leaders, the storming of union halls, and other measures.

In December 1979 the CTN's headquarters in Managua were shot up by Sandinista troops. Then, on September 9, 1981, the government issued the Law of Economic and Social Emergency which banned all labor strikes.[3] They also enacted legislation prohibiting private-sector businesses from paying wages or bonuses higher than those paid by the state.

A letter that the CUS's leaders sent to commander Bayardo Arce in early 1982 is descriptive of the kind of pressures that were placed on a sizable segment of the Nicaraguan working class:

> Distinguished compañero: . . . Certainly encouraged by the trust we have placed in you . . . we take this opportunity to point out that our leaders and activists of the department of Chinandega have been humiliated and placed in jail and that our union headquarters in the departments of Esteli and Chinandega have been taken over by local police and the above mentioned mass organizations [CST-ATC]. . . .
> We request that whenever there is one or more vacant positions in the APP [Area Propiedad del Pueblo—literally the People's Property Area, that is, government-owned enterprises], applicants who wish to fill those vacancies should not be required to hold membership in a given confederation. . . . We also request that the APP not lay off workers merely because they are sympathizers with or members of independent confederations.[4]

The requests of these labor leaders went unheeded. In fact, the situation of organized labor in Nicaragua deteriorated with each passing month. In March and April 1982, forty CTN activists were detained by the police. On May 17, armed men entered the headquarters of the CTN and shot up their archives containing mailing lists and accounting records. Alarmed by these developments, the International Confederation of Free Trade Unions (ICFTU) sent a delegation to Nicaragua in November. The Sandinista ministry of labor reassured them that the Nicaraguan government intended to abide by the International Conventions on Labor, of which the country was a signatory. Shortly after the ICFTU left, however, repression continued to escalate. Several labor leaders were arrested in December and held for more than two years.

In March 1983 the dock workers of the port of Corinto dissaffiliated themselves from the Sandinista CST and announced their decision to join the CUS. This move provoked a Sandinista mob attack on the port workers' headquarters, and many of the union leaders were jailed. Arrests, harassment, and other actions against independent labor followed.

By mid-1984 harassment of independent labor was becoming widespread. In May the CUS opened a vocational school in a working-class neighborhood in Managua to train unemployed young people. On opening day, a Sandinista mob attacked the school with rocks and clubs, forcing it to close. When the CUS leaders complained of this action to government officials, the officials' response was that the training center could not open because the government had already planned to open a sewing school in the same neighborhood. The CUS replied that even two schools in the area were not enough to fill the needs of the people there, and went ahead and opened the school. Due to the Sandinistas' hostility, only thirty-five of the 162 students who originally signed up for the course were able to finish. The Sandinistas' sewing school never materialized.

The CUS headquarters were forcibly occupied, following threats from Tomás Borge, from August 25 to September 6, 1984. Upon resuming control of their headquarters on September 7, CUS officials found their offices had largely been destroyed, the files ransacked, and membership lists confiscated.

Ronald Radosh, commenting on the Sandinistas' stance toward free labor, said that

> The regime sees independent unions as potentially dangerous, and strikes as part of a CIA attempt to destabilize Nicaragua. . . . Legitimate grievances by Nicaraguan workers are almost automatically viewed as suspect, and patriotic union leaders find themselves considered potentially subversive.[5]

William Doherty of the AFL-CIO, said in a 1985 article entered into the *Congressional Record* that

> The same pattern that prevailed from the first days of Sandinista power in 1979 is still being applied: pressure on all workers and local officers of unions which remain affiliated to the Christian Democratic Confederation (CTN) or the ICFTU affiliate in Nicaragua (CUS). The various forms of threats, arrests, beatings, interrogations, slanders, and economic reprisals used in this campaign of repression have been described in a number of articles . . . Sam Leiken, "Labor Under Siege," *The New Republic,* October 8, 1984 . . . [etc.].[6]

An event, perhaps symbolic of the circumstances that now face organized labor in Nicaragua, was a march that the workers affiliated with the CTN and CUS labor organizations intended to hold on May Day 1985 in Managua. A Catholic liturgy celebrated by Archbishop Obando was to be followed by a march to the spot where CUS leader Luis Medrano had been murdered. May Day marches have been a tradition of the Nicaraguan labor unions since the mid-1950s. Somoza always respected these massive parades. On this occasion, however, the Sandinista police broke up the march, pushing the marchers out of the street with the butts of their rifles. The government said that the workers had not received permission to march. Instead they ordered workers in Managua to use May Day to clean up the many trash-filled canals that carry rainwater from the mountains through the capital to Lake Managua.

The frustration these actions brought to the Nicaraguan workers who had challenged the previous Somoza regime in defense of their rights was best summarized by a Nicaraguan labor leader in exile:

> Four-and-a-half years after the takeover by the Frente Sandinista . . . the democratic labor movement finds itself in a very serious predicament. We never dreamed that our labor leaders and workers would be put in jail again in great numbers; we never dreamed that the campaign by the government against our movement would be so vicious; we never dreamed that our workers and their families would be brought to ridicule by some long-time friends and neighbors, who now serve on block committees for the defense of the revolution [CDSs], and it was beyond our wildest dreams that we would be asking once again about the "desaparecidos" [the missing].[7]

NOTES

1. Junta de Gobierno, "Programa de Gobierno," p. 12.

2. Junta de Gobierno, "Estatuto Sobre Derechos y Garantías de los Nicaragüenses," in op. cit., Leyes de la República de Nicaragua, p. 118.

3. Junta de Gobierno, "Decree No. 812—Law of Economic and Social Emergency," cited in CPDH, "Decrees and Provisions of the Present Nicaraguan Legislation that Threaten Human Rights," report, Managua, 1983, p. 28.

4. Bayardo López P., José Espinoza N., Javier Altamirano, et. al., "Carta al Cte. Bayardo Arce," February 1982, mimeographed translation by the International Confederation of Free Trade Unions.

5. Ronald Radosh, op. cit., "Darkening Nicaragua," p. 11.

6. William Doherty, "The Sandinistas and the Workers—The Betrayal Continues," Congressional Record-Senate, February 28, 1985, p. S2352.

7. Quoted in William Doherty, "A Revolution Betrayed; Free Labor Persecuted," in ibid., p. S2355.

THE PRESS:
CONFISCATED AND CENSORED

Given the Frente's disposition toward criticism, the press was a likely candidate for conflict with the young regime. The 1979 program of government promised unrestricted freedom of the press in very clear terms: "A special guarantee shall be granted to the freedom of issuing information and the publishing of information. . . . All laws that repress the free expression and communication of thought and the freedom of information shall be abolished" (Clause I.1.4).[1] The Fundamental Statute of the Republic, decreed on July 20, 1979, stated that the new revolutionary junta would guarantee "unrestricted freedom of thought, written or spoken" (Article 8).[2] The Statute on the Rights and Guarantees of Nicaraguans further guaranteed "the right of all people to freedom of opinion and speech; this right includes the right to seek, obtain, and publish information or opinion of all sorts, without limitations, be it spoken, written, printed, or in artistic form" (Article 21).[3] The Fundamental Statute also stated that the exercise of these rights could not be subjected to prior censorship.

The promises regarding freedom of expression could not have been more straightforward. In 1979 they were particularly instrumental in reassuring the Nicaraguan people and the international community about the democratic intentions of the FSLN.

Nevertheless, when some Nicaraguan moderates wanted to call attention to the contradictions between the stated policies of the revolutionary government and its imposition of various social controls, they found themselves blocked at every turn. Immediately after the revolution, *La Prensa* was checked from publishing views critical of the government by a Sandinista union. The other existing newspaper, along with all television stations and most of the radio stations, were confiscated by the government and turned into the property of the Sandinista party. It was not only enterprises formerly held by Somoza and his friends which were liable to confiscation; the government also expropriated a couple of television channels owned by another family. In December 1979, when a private radio entrepreneur, Fabio Gadea, whose radio company had been a stalwart in the struggle against Somoza, asked for a permit to open a new, independent television station, Daniel Ortega turned the request down, loudly proclaiming in a televised speech that from now on the television in Nicaragua would belong to the people and not to "millionaries of the bourgeoisie." The powerful Sandinista media thus took shape as a branch of the party.

My work as an editorial writer for La Prensa provided me with firsthand experience of the conflict that developed. I joined the paper in April 1980, just after the internal conflict between some of the paper's owners, represented by Violeta Chamorro, and the Marxist-controlled union, headed by Danilo Aguirre, resulted in the latter founding a new newspaper, El Nuevo Diario, and in La Prensa becoming free to criticize the government. I had become a Christian in 1977 and joined the staff to write on issues concerning the interface of Christianity and politics. La Prensa's editor-in-chief, Pablo Antonio Cuadra, a well-known poet and strong Christian who had been an intimate friend of the murdered Pedro J. Chamorro, told me upon my arrival at the paper: "Poet"—that was the way he addressed his friends—"I have called you so that together we might struggle for the preservation of Christianity in this revolution."

Our intent was not to antagonize the Sandinistas, but to offer constructive criticism and commentary aimed at keeping the revolution within the limits of the 1979 program of government. We even instituted a set of policies designed to prevent our own journalists from being overly critical of the government. We were not always successful, but we made an honest effort to avoid a confrontational approach. We had meeting after meeting of the editorial staff discussing how to moderate our criticisms, devising ways to avoid provoking the government's anger, and figuring out how we could offer positive alternatives.

Nothing worked. The Sandinistas interpreted our mildest

criticisms as treacherous lies calculated to subvert the revolution. They typecast us as the "voice of the bourgeoisie." Nothing we said or suggested had value; it could not be sincere; we were, by definition, enemies. Even if we were particularly restrained or had some commendation for a government action, the Sandinistas labeled our behavior hypocrisy. Sooner than later, they began referring to us as "counterrevolutionary schemers," "the hidden hand of the CIA," "those who were willing to sell out their homeland."

The FSLN and the state-controlled media became obsessed with *La Prensa.* We were a constant issue, the target of incessant attacks. In their view, we were devilishly skillful. They said we were following the strategy of the Chilean newspaper *El Mercurio,* which allegedly aided the overthrow of Marxist president Allende (I have never managed to see a copy of that newspaper). They also claimed that we used "subliminal" tactics in order to convey unconscious messages to people by way of associations. This theory was created for the Sandinistas by an American journalist who worked for the official newspaper *Barricada.* I do not know how we could have been so skillful when, in the already hectic pace of newspaper life, we were constantly making all manner of last-minute changes in our headlines, captions, and articles in order not to jeopardize our existence.

We were regularly accused of manufacturing stories for counterrevolutionary purposes. But if, on the other hand, we gave much attention to sports or events that were not necessarily related to the current concerns of the FSLN, the Sandinistas claimed that we were indulging in "ideological diversionism," that is, distracting people from their revolutionary priorities.

A pattern we observed from our first weeks as an independent newspaper was that the Sandinistas, rather than debate or refute our arguments or ideas, responded by accusing us of being agents of the enemy, the capitalists. In a way, they did not have many options. Committed as they were to a hidden agenda, our attempts to disclose it upset them deeply. They could do nothing but repress us. And so they did.

La Prensa was a painful thorn for the Sandinistas. We published the 1979 program of government and asked questions about deviations from it. We questioned the identification of state and party and asked the government to provide information regarding the performance of the APP—the confiscated sector of the economy. We asked the government to publish its secret budget, and questioned the FSLN's unanimous support of the USSR's foreign policy. We debated the pro-Sandinista theologians who claimed that it was a Christian duty to support the FSLN. And in a cartoon strip we made some occasional references to the comandantes' love for Mercedes Benzs and luxurious mansions.

La Prensa's growing circulation was another source of irritation for the Sandinistas. La Prensa jumped from a circulation of forty-five thousand copies daily before the break with the Marxist-controlled union to seventy thousand a year later. By contrast, the FSLN-owned Barricada and the government-subsidized El Nuevo Diario lagged well behind, with average circulations of no higher than twenty thousand to thirty thousand each (only La Prensa certifies its circulation).

The FSLN began to place limits on freedom of expression during the earliest postrevolutionary phase. The first measure, as stated already, was the confiscation of the mass media and the banning of the right to have private television stations. In defense of the ban the Sandinistas pointed to countries like France, where television is state-owned. We at La Prensa replied that in France, unlike Nicaragua, the television is indeed national, but not the monopoly of a political party.

In January 1980 the government ordered the suspension of a radio program directed by Oscar L. Montalvan, a journalist who had been an outstanding opponent of the Somoza dictatorship. In April 1980 a radio newsmen, Guillermo Treminio, was arrested and sentenced to six months imprisonment on the grounds that he had broadcast information "detrimental to the revolution." Shortly thereafter the Sandinistas stormed the headquarters of an ultraleft Trotskyite newspaper, El Pueblo, jailing its editor and putting it out of business.

Following the first, massive, antigovernment demonstration on the Nicaraguan Atlantic Coast, the government ordered La Prensa to abstain from reporting about the region without prior government approval. This was followed by a succession of decrees, each more inclusive than the last. The first was Decree No. 511 (Law to Control Information About Internal Security and National Defense), enacted on September 10, 1980. It established that "the news media of the republic may not release news of information that jeopardizes the internal security of the country or national defense."⁴ The Minister of the Interior, Tomás Borge, was responsible for determining which information fell into this category. An additional Clause No. 2, enacted and added the same day, further directed that

> the news media of the republic, whatever their nature, may not release or publish regular news and information regarding shortages of staple products for popular consumption or news that may bring about price speculation on these products or news or information which in any way may threaten or endanger the economic stability of the nation.⁵

Later, in 1984, when another act to regulate the press was presented to the Council of State, the Sandinista-subsidized newspaper *El Nuevo Diario* voiced the Sandinistas' essential philosophy behind this and similar legislation:

> It should be accepted that within the framework of the situation of Nicaragua, the mass media should basically be at the service of the people and should transform itself into an instrument that effectively contributes to improve the educational, political and cultural levels [of the people].⁶

With these decrees in hand, and the right to interpret them without appeal, the government began ordering temporary closings of *La Prensa*. The first took place on July 8, 1981, after *La Prensa* published photographs of some religious billboards destroyed by unknown vandals. The second closing of *La Prensa* took place after Fr. Miguel D'Escoto's statement to a Mexican newspaper, accusing the Archbishop of Managua of being the leading "counterrevolutionary" in Nicaragua, was quoted. D'Escoto denied that he had made the statement. Charging that *La Prensa* had lied, the government ordered a seventy-two-hour closedown. A member of the *La Prensa* staff was sent to Mexico to inquire about the statement. He returned with a copy of the newspaper *El Tiempo,* with the full interview of D'Escoto, including the controversial quote about the Archbishop. We published it the next day, the government making no further denials. Four more shutdowns of *La Prensa* followed in less than a year.

On March 15, 1982, the government imposed a state of emergency that required *La Prensa* to submit its entire issue for prior censorship. Each day we would take the preliminary copy of the paper to the Ministry of the Interior, where we would wait for one to two hours for their decisions. They would then give us a memorandum with the list of news articles or commentaries to be eliminated or changed. We would take the censored issue back to *La Prensa* and replace the eliminated items with new pieces. As soon as the new issue was put together, we would return to the Ministry of the Interior to repeat the process. Censorship, at times, would eliminate up to two-thirds of the material submitted. The procedure was so time-consuming that on many occasions the newspaper was unable to publish an edition due to the impossibility of replacing in time the articles banned from publication.

The censorship involved the whole scope of news coverage—from political commentaries and news, to sports (from the middle of 1983 *La Prensa* was forbidden even to mention the name of Alexis Arguello, world boxing champion in exile), to statements by the Catholic Church. The most outstanding example of the latter was a letter that the Pope sent to the Nicaraguan bishops in 1982.

A letter of August 19, 1982, from the editors of *La Prensa* to the Nicaraguan government junta is indicative of the scope of Sandinista censorship. It points out that some news barred from publication in *La Prensa* appeared in the Sandinistas' own newspapers. Many of the items censored had no possible relation to the security of the Sandinista government—for example, commentaries critical of the Soviet Union or of Marxism, church news (the government banned all news or commentary related to the 1981 assassination attempt on the Pope), even public statements of officials of the government (as happened with some statements by junta member Cordoba Rivas in late 1982).

At the end of August 1982 Violeta Chamorro wrote an open letter to the Nicaraguan people in which she expressed her anguish at the drastic curtailment of civil liberties that had taken place:

> With each passing day freedom of the press is found to be more limited in our country, not only preventing us from reporting on those events which happen daily in our social, political, and economic life, but also prohibiting us from making known our opinions and, with that, from presenting and defending the ideals which served as the banner of *La Prensa* and of the Nicaraguan people in the overthrow of the Somoza dictatorship.[7]

Media censorship extended well beyond *La Prensa*. Another important target was the Catholic Church. The Catholic archbishop of Managua for several years had had his Sunday mass broadcast by a private television station, but he was put off the air in early July 1981. Catholic Radio, the Catholic broadcasting station, was closed down for the month of March 1982 on the grounds that it had broadcast "inaccurate information" regarding a mob takeover of a church. In April 1983, the government announced that all sermons of church leaders had to be censored by the Ministry of the Interior prior to broadcast.

Several commercial radio programs also disappeared due to government restrictions. In 1978, under Somoza, there were forty-three radio news programs in Nicaragua, while in 1983 there remained only thirteen. It is also interesting to note that under the Somozas' rule (1936-1979: forty-three years) *La Prensa* was curtailed (shut down or censored) nine times. The Sandinista regime surpassed that mark before it was three years old.

In addition to decrees, closures, and censorship, the Sandinistas used government-organized mobs and terror tactics to repress free expression. On February 13, 1981, the owner of the largest independent radio station, Fabio G. Mantilla, a former outspoken opponent of Somoza, was, together with his wife, beaten by a Sandinista mob. In February 1981, following the mob attacks on the MDN's attempted rally in Nandaime, two radio stations were destroyed. At *La Prensa* we closed for two days to protect the safety of our street vendors—mostly children.

On January 17, 1982, the radio newsman Manuel Jiron, director of the Mi Preferida radio station, was attacked by three gunmen who attempted to kidnap him. On June 24, Horacio Ruiz, co-editor of *La Prensa*, was kidnapped by three armed men, who beat him and left him unconscious by the side of the road. Both times, in spite of the fact that the assailants identified themselves as Sandinistas (and in the case of Ruiz carried automatic weapons of the FSLN army), the government denied any responsibility, holding that these events were due to the impassioned venting of grudges. In August 1982 the director of Catholic Radio, Fr. Bismarck Carballo, was made the object of a manufactured scandal.

Since then more journalists have been detained, harassed, and threatened. On April 29, 1984, Luis Mora Sanchez, a journalist for *La Prensa*, was arrested, following harsh accusations made against him by Daniel Ortega, on April 14. Eighteen days after his arrest Mora Sanchez appeared on television (before being brought to court) "confessing" that he had been conspiring against the revolution together with some well-known politicians, members of the Catholic hierarchy (Archbishop Obando), and labor leaders of the CTN and CUS. Tight media censorship, however, has generally made it less necessary for the government to keep up the pressure on individuals. Many other journalists, including myself, have gone into exile.

The FSLN's censorship of the press has not been uniformly tight; there have been periods when censorship has been relaxed somewhat. There was a more relaxed period, for example, during the month preceding the 1984 elections—although even then *La Prensa* was unable to publish news related to the "Coordinadora Democratica," an opposition political coalition led by former junta member Arturo Cruz, as well as other news. Immediately after the elections were over, censorship tightened again, although from time to time, and following an unpredictable pattern, the Sandinistas have allowed some criticism to be aired. This allows the government to show foreign visitors "vigorous opposition," and provides them with evidence for their disclaimer to charges of strict press censorship. On other days, however, censorship has been so heavy as to make it impossible for *La Prensa* to publish its daily issue—twenty-three times between March 15, 1982 and March 15, 1985. Stating that he could stand the situation no longer, Pedro Joaquin Chamorro, Jr., the editor of *La Prensa*, left Nicaragua in early 1985.

When press freedom in Nicaragua is discussed outside the country, supporters of the FSLN usually admit that press censorship has continued under the revolutionary government. But they minimize the importance of the issue. For example, they inform readers in the United States that there is "some" censorship, but that *La Prensa* functions as a "vigorous opposition newspaper." Others have justified government restrictions on the grounds that the press has been "irresponsible" or "inaccurate" in its reporting. Still others have suggested that press censorship is not an important issue. As one American nun in Nicaragua said: "People here are not so sophisticated, and no one minds if the government shuts down a newspaper occasionally."

The Sandinistas themselves have likewise downplayed the severity of their censorship or have explained that "they are protecting the right of people not to be misinformed." More often, they blame curtailments of freedom on the counterrevolutionaries and the CIA: a revolutionary government under attack cannot afford a critical press.

In light of this last excuse, it is important to underline the fact that the Nicaraguan government's actions against freedom of expression did not begin as a response to any increase in counterrevolutionary warfare. In fact, they preceded it. Curtailment of freedom began to take place when the United States, under the Carter administration, was still on good terms with the Sandinistas, when there were no significant counterrevolutionary activities anywhere in the country, and when the Sandinistas still enjoyed overwhelming internal and external support.

The true reasons for the Sandinista government's treatment of the press lie in the government's program for reshaping Nicaraguan society under its political hegemony. A free press provides a forum for those who wish to probe and question basic assumptions, for those who wish to challenge government actions and demand an explanation when those actions are judged to be wrong or ill-advised. In other words, a free press is a forum through which a people can question the government that claims to represent them. Such questioning is illegal in Nicaragua because the Frente is the vanguard of a new social order, not a representative government that must answer to its people. Its assumptions and judgments are to be believed and obeyed, not questioned or held up to some higher standard—including even the Sandinistas own promises.

NOTES

1. Junta de Gobierno, "Programa de Gobierno," p. 12.

2. Junta de Gobierno, "Estatuto Fundamental de la República," p. 36.

3. Junta de Gobierno, "Estatuto sobre Derechos y Garantías de los Nicaragüenses," p. 115.

4. Quoted in CPDH, "Decrees and Provisions of the Present Nicaraguan Legislation that Threaten Human Rights," p. 19.

5. Ibid.

6. Editorial, El Nuevo Diario, May 7, 1984.

7. Violeta Chamorro, "Freedom of the Press Does Not Exist in Nicaragua," Catholicism in Crisis, January 1983, pp. 13-15.

SEVEN

A SANDINISTA ECONOMY

The state's growing role in economic life was yet another aspect of the Sandinistas' drive for complete social control. The FSLN's program of government had promised in 1979 to establish a "mixed economy," a term implying the coexistence of private property and state ownership in some segments of the economy. Although many requests were made to the Sandinistas to define the criteria governing this term, they did not do so. Their 1979 program of government had anticipated the confiscation of all holdings of the Somoza family and immediate friends and associates. The government quickly did this, turning most of the property seized into state-owned property.

It could be argued that given the scarcity of qualified administrative personnel in the country, it would have been more practical to have placed much of the confiscated property in private hands. Many under-used agricultural holdings of the Somozas could have been redistributed to individual peasants. The Sandinistas, however, preferred direct ownership of the confiscated farms and businesses. This decision proved to be a heavy burden on the state. Many of these enterprises went bankrupt, and from late 1980 the government ceased to disclose figures on the performance of the units it held. The government named the confiscated sector Area Propiedad del Pueblo (APP), "Property Area of the People," but in truth it was simply property of the state.

As many workers were petitioning the government for direct ownership of the confiscated property, the government union, the CST, felt the need to instruct its members on what "people's ownership" meant. In one of its educational leaflets entitled

"Analysis of the Slogan: 'We Defend the Revolution for the Construction of Socialism,' " the CST explained:

> When the workers take power—as has happened in Nicaragua—temptation arises . . . to take all the goods of society, all the means of production, and distribute them among the workers. This is the Trotskyist thesis; they claim that socialism should mean distributing the factories and the farms to the workers. . . . But [in our view] . . . to create social justice means to confiscate, to expropriate, everything. The worker-peasant state coming to be the owner of the means of production. . . .[1]

The Sandinistas' agrarian reform also yielded greater state control. The government gave away some "agrarian reform titles" to peasants. But they yoked the peasants to the state in a kind of Socialist feudalism by forcing them to sell their harvest to the government and not allowing them to pass the land on to their heirs. The government also ruled that only the peasant cooperatives affiliated with the ATC were entitled to receive credit. The rationale behind this scheme was philosophical and political. It was not based on criteria of efficiency or even primarily on a concern for overall social benefits. The overruling principle was political control.

I had a little experience of this shortly after the triumph of the revolution. Looking for a new job, I approached the newly created ministry of social welfare. I joined the staff and for a few days participated in some planning discussions. One day we were debating how to promote the lot of the street merchants, who in Nicaragua represent a very large proportion of the economically active population. Borrowing from E. F. Schumacher's *Small Is Beautiful,* I pointed out the convenience of promoting this network of small, independent units and suggested setting up a system of easy credits and technical assistance aimed at enhancing the economic self-reliance of these people. A couple of Sandinistas, one of them the wife of my oldest daughter's godfather, looked at each other with a mixture of embarrassment and caution. "No," she murmured, "that would be politically counterproductive." When I requested that she explain what she meant, she changed the subject and we dropped the whole discussion.

Independence was precisely what Sandinista policies aimed to limit or eliminate. Their plan was to create large, centralized conglomerates. They thus spoke of a "Unified Health System," a "Unified Commerical System," and so forth. An outgrowth of this approach was the creation of the Nicaraguan Basic Foodstuffs Enterprise (ENABAS).

From the outset of their rule, the Sandinistas began working to centralize control over basic grains and food products, and to function as the only agency mediating between the farmers and the consumers. Traditionally this middleman role had been played by several thousand small and medium-sized merchants, who supplied over one hundred thousand street vendors and small shopkeepers. The system had its inefficiencies; yet it provided for the livelihood of close to one third of the economically active population (there is a larger class of poor, independent merchants in Nicaragua than there is a classical proletarian class).

The Sandinistas' efforts to take over this sector through ENABAS proved disastrous. Farmers refused to sell their products only to the state. Scarcities developed, and with them a huge black market, leaving both producers and consumers worse off than before. ENABAS, however, kept trying. At issue was the economic independence of the large commercial sector.

The APP did not work either. Nonetheless, the Sandinistas continued to confiscate lands and businesses. They issued vague and inclusive decrees aimed at enlarging the state-owned sector. Properties deemed by the authorities as "mismanaged" or "decapitalized" or "underexploited" became the subject of confiscation. Later, properties considered by the state as being of "public utility" or "national patrimony" were added to the list. These policies became a tool for penalizing political dissent.

Many leaders of the Nicaraguan business community with fairly productive holdings suffered confiscations. After some time many of these formerly prosperous farms and enterprises experienced drops in production and profits. This led to diminished tax revenues, the laying off of workers, and higher government expenditures.

"Frankly," claimed Arturo Cruz, president of the Nicaraguan Central Bank during the first years after the revolutionary triumph,

we virtually emptied the well of fiscal revenue with the establishment of the so-called People's Property Area (APP). . . . The much ballyhooed 60 percent private/40 percent public ownership is no longer accurate. The APP is a guzzler of resources. The government refuses to recognize that what is really significant for the state is the control of the surplus. Instead, it is obsessed with state ownership of the means of production.[2]

The next president of the Nicaraguan Central Bank, Alfredo César, who resigned in disappointment in 1983, said that the "artificial radicalization of the Nicaraguan economy" was impoverishing the country.[3] But what these liberal economists see as the irrational propensity of the revolutionary leaders toward state ownership is, in fact, from the viewpoint of the Sandinistas' gradual accumulation of power, a highly rational matter, although the Nicaraguan people have had to pay dearly for it.

Many people have observed, however, when studying the Nicaraguan situation, that the private sector is still significantly larger than would normally be the case under a Marxist regime. The Sandinistas themselves have used this fact in their propaganda to disclaim the charge that they intend to follow the classical Marxist pattern of state ownership of the means of production. But as the document from the CST quoted above—about the meaning of the slogan on the construction of socialism—makes clear once again, this is precisely the direction the Sandinistas intend to go. "In three years," junta member Sergio Ramírez said in 1983, "the state has acquired the capacity to manage the economy . . . between 38 and 40 percent of the GNP is now generated by the state—but that does not mean that when the state generates 80 percent of the GNP our problems will be solved."[4]

Overall, it appears that pragmatic considerations may be the single biggest factor in setting the pace for nationalization. The state-owned sector has been a heavy drag on finances, and Nicaragua lacks sufficient managers to run a largely confiscated economy. Victor Tirado, one of the nine top Sandinista comandantes, speaking in February 1985 on behalf of the national directorate of the FSLN, said:

> [Our] revolution stands well-defined. But it would be madness to try to force reality and jump over stages when we have not constructed the advanced material base of our economy. . . . Sometimes for economic reasons, sometimes for lack of human resources or for the material backwardness of the country, the state can not assume all the economic activity. . . . The mixed economy and the private sector

are necessary in the present stage of the revolution, a stage that will be left behind once the country reaches other economic conditions.[5]

It is also important to point out that due to stringent state controls, the terms "private ownership" and "private sector" have little real meaning. They can not set prices, wages, or choose their markets, and even their production is often subject to quotas. In February 1984 the Sandinistas began enforcing so-called Commercialization Agreements, whereby the privately owned factories agree to sell fixed quotas of products at a fixed price to the Nicaraguan ministry of internal commerce. According to the minister of this agency, "Factories ought to produce but not market."[6]

SEVERE ECONOMIC DECLINE

The mixture of state ownership, stringent controls on prices, wages, and marketing, the disruption of traditional commercial channels, and other economic policies of the Sandinistas have brought about a steady and sharp decline in overall production. Many peasants, unhappy at being forced to sell their harvest to the state, planted less beans, corn, and other basic staples. After years of being a net exporter of these foodstuffs, Nicaragua began to import them in ever greater amounts.

The Sandinista government suggested that the reason for the imbalance was dramatic increases in consumption, which according to some of their economists took place when the regime decided to subsidize the purchase of these food staples. Official government statistics show, however, that production declined. Production of beans, in thousands of quintals, declined from 1,339.6 in 1976/1978 to 1,030.1 in 1982/1983. Production of corn fell from 4,193.5 to 4,003.5 during the same period. The population, in the meantime, grew by about 25 percent.[7] The production of cotton, one of the main export crops of Nicaragua, has also fallen considerably (8,159.9 in 1976/78 to 5,070 in 1982/83), along with bananas and other products.[8] Industrial production has also lagged behind prewar levels. Thus, in contrast with the $646 million U.S. (about $750 million in 1984 dollars) that Nicaragua was exporting overall in 1978, in 1984 it was exporting only $461 million.[9]

At the same time that production was falling, government expenditures increased dramatically. The Sandinistas more than tripled the state bureaucracy during the first year in power, imports rose from $600 million in 1978 to $940 million in 1984, and the state considerably expanded its budget in many other areas. Part of this expansion was military and part was for increases in social services—health, education, and housing. The latter were increased dramatically without a corresponding increase in national revenue. The Sandinistas, according to banker Arturo Cruz, "seemed to ignore that social programs must be financed out of public revenue."[10] Military expenditures increased from 419 million córdobas in 1978 ($41.9 million at the 1978 rate of exchange) to 1,701 in 1981 ($85 million at the 1981 rate of exchange).[11] After 1983 the Nicaraguan government ceased to publish its budget.

Decreases in production coupled with increases in government expenditures and imports drained the Nicaraguan economy, with the biggest bite coming from the very people that the revolution was supposed to help the most: the poor. According to the United Nations (Comision Economica para America Latina— CEPAL), real wages experienced a net decline of 12.9 percent in 1982 and of 25.4 percent in 1983.[12] The level of production and consumption per person was at the same level in 1984 that it was in 1962. Inflation has been skyrocketing since the Sandinistas came to power, while salaries remained frozen up to early 1985.

As a result, the hardships and frustrations of the poor grow. A *New York Times* journalist, Stephen Kinzer, spent an afternoon listening to poor Nicaraguans in a small retail shop who complained about the effects of Sandinista economic policies. Kinzer reported that of the nearly fifty visitors, every one had something nasty to say about the Sandinistas.[13]

This situation has been exacerbated by the Sandinistas' insistence on maintaining tight government control of foreign exchange. The government has set an artificially low exchange rate for U.S. dollars, but controls the supply so tightly that dollars are obtainable only under severely restricted circumstances. Because Nicaragua relies so heavily on imports, a massive black market has developed to supply the need for dollars. An ordinary citizen who, for no particular reason, simply wished to buy a U.S. dollar in 1978 could have done so for 10 córdobas; by mid-1985, 700 córdobas were needed on the black market, the only place where dollars can be obtained freely. An import item, like a pair of blue jeans, that cost 200 córdobas in 1978, cost 14,000 in 1985.

Scarcities have developed in almost everything, including products that Nicaragua exports. The official price of rice, for example, a grain grown in Nicaragua and an important part of the national diet, rose in the period from 1978 to 1985 from 0.65 to 2.90 córdobas per pound. However, rice is difficult to find in the state-owned supermarkets; many people must turn to the black market, where a pound costs between 8 and 12 córdobas. At a Managua supermarket on February 28, 1984, the following items were found to be missing: oil, milk, butter, bread (not a single loaf), flour, ham, chicken, jam, jello, fruit juices, batteries, fluorescent lamps, detergent, toilet tissue, shampoo, towels, diapers, razor blades, baby bottles, toothpaste, and so on.[14]

The Sandinistas have cited three major factors for the growing economic disaster: the destruction brought about by the war to overthrow Somoza, the overall world economic crisis, and U.S. hostility—its support of the contras and its cutting of loans to Nicaragua. There is some evidence to support all three of these contentions. But these factors can not by themselves explain the economic decline of the past six years. Overall, foreign nations have been relatively generous to the Sandinistas. Development aid and foreign loans have been made available in amounts that dwarf those received by the former regime. Somoza contracted foreign loans for 1976, 1977, and 1978, of $140.2, $234.7 and $126.8 million, respectively. When Somoza was overthrown, the Sandinistas inherited a real foreign debt of $1.1 billion. The Sandinistas, by contrast, contracted loans for $271.7 million during their first five months in power, $527.6 in 1980, $687.1 in 1981, $526.7 in 1982, $500.0 in 1983. By 1984 their foreign debt had risen to $4.2 billion. It should be added that the Sandinistas were able to renegotiate the debt inherited from the former regime on very favorable terms. Most of the loans they received (59%) were also on very "soft" conditions, while another 16% were on "medium soft" terms. As the former Nicaraguan director of planning for the International Fund for Reconstruction of the Nicaraguan Government, Jorge Alaníz, has testified, "How many governments of the Third World could boast of having doubled in just a few months, the amount of development aid to their country?"[15]

Regarding the damage done by the war being fought against the contras, Alaníz, using statistics provided by Comandander Daniel Ortega, has shown that even taking Ortega's claims at face value, these losses did not become significant until March 1983. In 1981 the war cost $272,000 and in 1982 $8.4 million—when serious economic decline was already in full swing.[16]

The trade embargo decreed by the Reagan Administration in May 1985 will undoubtedly hurt the Nicaraguan economy. But it is not easy to assess its impact in real terms. In 1984, trade with the United States represented less than 10 percent of Nicaragua's imports ($57 million) and about 25 percent of its exports ($115.5 million). The embargo's effect will depend on Nicaragua's success at finding alternative markets. The Sandinistas, however, will use the embargo—they already call it "blockade"—as another explanation for their economic ills, and will probably exaggerate its consequences.

As mentioned earlier, the Sandinistas' approach to the economy derives from ideological and political goals, not criteria of efficiency or a primary concern for raising the standard of living of the majority. Junta member Sergio Ramirez, referring to the nationalization of the banks, for example, explained that

> the revolution [the FSLN] was not looking at the nationalization of the banks as just a step for financial health; rather it sought in it to achieve a strategic move, to advance politically, a step forward.[17]

For the Sandinista government, the ideal economic program is one which benefits the poor while at the same time increasing the control of the state. But financial benefits are no more than one of many elements in an analysis that ultimately decides every issue on power considerations. The Nicaraguan economy has experienced a steady and sharp decline since the Sandinistas came to power. The Sandinistas have experienced a steady and sharp increase in their political control.

NOTES

1. CST, "Análisis del Slogan: Defendemos la Revolución, por la Construcción del Socialismo," Managua, August 1982, pp. 1, 2.

2. Dr. Arturo Cruz, "Nicaragua's Imperiled Revolution," *Foreign Affairs,* Summer 1983, p. 1036.

3. Alfredo Cesar, "Carta a Daniel Ortega," Costa Rica, unpublished letter, 1983.

4. Sergio Ramírez, "El Estado ya Controla y Dirige la Economía," *Barricada,* February 28, 1983, pp. 1, 5.

5. Victor Tirado L., speech published in *Barricada,* Monday, February 11, 1985, pp. 1, 5.

6. Quoted in *Dario Las Américas,* Miami, February 15, 1985, p. 6.

7. Source: MIDINRA, in *El Nuevo Diario,* July 18, 1983, p. 6.

8. *Ibid.*

9. Enrique Bolaños, "Nicaraguan Sandinista Economy," excerpts from an interview in Managua, March 1, 1984, St. Charles, Mo.: Nicaraguan Information Center, 1984, p. 3.

10. *Op. cit.,* Cruz, "Nicaragua's Imperiled Revolution," p. 1036.

11. Source: Nicaraguan Central Bank, Report, March 1983.

12. Quoted in *Pensamiento Propio* No. 14, May-June 1984, a publication of the Instituto de Investigaciones Económicas y Sociales, Managua, p. 23.

13. Stephen Kinzer, "Nicaragua: The Beleaguered Revolution," *The New York Times Magazine,* August 28, 1983, p. 28.

14. *Op. cit.,* Bolaños, "Nicaraguan Sandinista Economy," p. 2.

15. *Op. cit.,* Alaniz, p. 235.

16. *Ibid.,* pp. 232, 233.

17. Ramírez, in *Nicarauac,* Managua, July-August 1980, p. 12.

EIGHT

THE LITERACY CAMPAIGN
AND OTHER IMPROVEMENTS

During the first phase of the revolution the Sandinistas launched a national literacy campaign. Aimed at substantially lowering the country's high degree of illiteracy (50 to 60 percent according to most estimates), the campaign provided a great boost to the Sandinistas' prestige by showing their commitment to the poor. The campaign does appear to have increased literacy levels, although certainly not as much as the official statistics indicate (postcampaign surveys are nonexistent).

It is important to note that the Sandinistas designed the campaign, as the Cuban government had, with well thought-out political goals in mind. The FSLN used the campaign as a major tool for political indoctrination and as a means to draw the young educators into the party's orbit. The political intent of the campaign was candidly confessed by the Sandinista leaders themselves:

> The literacy campaign will take to each corner of the country the experience of the Sandinista struggle and will enable our people to know the thoughts of Carlos Fonseca and all the other heroes and leaders who made the revolution possible.[1]

The general coordinator of the campaign, Fr. Fernando Cardenal, expressed a similar view:

> We do not pretend to teach only how to read, write, and handle basic math; we also have as key goals the consciousness raising and politicization of the illiterates. . . . The youngsters who will join the "People's Literacy Army" will also undergo a very intense process of consciousness raising.[2]

To achieve these goals, the Frente printed thousands of copies of didactic materials (pamphlets, first reading lessons, etc.) promoting the FSLN as the vanguard of all Nicaraguans, exhorting people to join the FSLN's mass organizations, and extolling the memory of Fonseca and the revolutionary martyrs. Thousands of Nicaraguans, including nearly all high school students, were mobilized and trained to act as educators. Most did it willingly, since the campaign received the backing of the Catholic and Protestant churches, the private schools, and practically every other sector of Nicaraguan society. Yet the FSLN's leaders, including the coordinator of the campaign, Fr. Fernando Cardenal, did not forget to warn students about the meaning of not participating.

> At the beginning of the literacy campaign we said that those youngsters who would not join this great crusade in a conscious way could not be Nicaraguans.[3]

In the same speech at the end of the campaign, Commander Ortega announced that the national directorate had decided that all youngsters who had participated in the campaign

> become, from this very moment, members of the July 19 Sandinista Youth . . . to fulfill, in an organized manner, different tasks in the economy, the culture, the administration, the party, the struggle against the reactionaries.[4]

Of the strategic value of this involuntary honorific enrollment in the FSLN's youth organization, Ortega explained:

> You are the main cord tying the revolution to the peasants. It is the responsibility of each one of you that each peasant continues to be a Sandinista—or else you will loose the title of Sandinistas and of revolutionaries.[5]

A paradox of the campaign was that it was the FSLN that reaped all the political fruit; yet most of the human and financial resources came from other sectors of Nicaraguan society, which, as during the war against Somoza, joined themselves with the FSLN in an endeavor that everyone considered noble. Likewise, funding for the campaign was mostly provided by sources from the U.S. and Western Europe. The USSR, with a donation of $525, gave less than one tenth of one percent of the total.[6]

Regarding social improvements in public health, housing, and agrarian reform, problems of assessment arise concerning facts and interpretation. The first task is to discern propaganda from empirical evidence. Reliable statistics are not available, and the secrecy and control under which the Nicaraguan administration operates preclude an objective assessment of the situation.

It is at least true in the area of public health that massive vaccination campaigns have been conducted. (I took my own children to my local CDS for antipolio vaccination.) Free medical attention, which in the past had been restricted to those who were part of the social security system, was opened to everyone. This threefold or more increase in the number of people entitled to public medicine was not accompanied, however, by a corresponding increase in medical resources—personnel, facilities, medicine, etc.—and therefore, the overall quality of services rendered was greatly reduced. Some patients have to wait for several months to get medical attention.

The Sandinistas have claimed significant advances for the poor in Nicaragua due to their social programs. Whether this is true or not is hard to say without hard data, which the Sandinistas are unwilling to allow to be gathered. But whether it is true or not, one observation seems in order given the widespread use of data on Sandinista social programs as "evidence" that the Sandinistas are transforming Nicaragua on behalf of the poor. Even if Sandinista social programs were having some success, they are not the key criteria upon which to judge the direction of the FSLN in regard to the poor. Both Nazi Germany and the U.S.S.R. (even under Stalin) have been able to claim some success for their social programs. The key question is whether the poor are being aided in a way that respects their fundamental dignity and freedom. The next chapter, which deals with the Miskito Indians, indicates the direction that the Sandinistas are taking in regard to those they purport to aid.

NOTES

1. Bayardo Arce, "Levantemos la Conciencia de Nuestro Pueblo," in *La Cruzada en Marcha,* Bulletin No. 1, 1980, p. 8.

2. Fr. Fernando Cardenal, "Objetivos de la Cruzada Nacional de Alfabetización," in *ibid.,* p. 7.

3. Humberto Ortega, speech, in *La Cruzada en Marcha*, Bulletin No. 16, 1980, p. 6.

4. *Ibid.*, p. 9.

5. *Ibid.*, p. 10.

6. "Advances de la Cruzada," in *La Cruzada en Marcha*, Bulletin No. 15, 1980, p. 3.

NINE

THE MISKITOS: AN ETHNIC TRAGEDY

The FSLN's ideology and program called for radical restructuring of the social order to produce a new revolutionary man and new revolutionary community. For this restructuring, they needed uncontested power and the freedom to alter the fabric of society as they deemed necessary. Not surprisingly, this social engineering, when actually implemented with specific groups of Nicaraguans, met with substantial resistance. The Miskito Indians are perhaps the most dramatic example.

The Miskito Indians, inhabitants of the isolated rain forest of the Atlantic Coast, are perhaps the oldest and most culturally distinct ethnic group in Nicaragua. Numbering roughly one hundred thousand, they have a long tradition of communal land ownership and govern themselves through a council of elders. They were evangelized by Moravian missionaries in the middle of the nineteenth century, and today they are a strongly religious people. Most of their elders are local deacons of the Christian church.

Under the Somoza regime, as well as under all previous Nicaraguan administrations, the Miskitos were largely ignored. They received little assistance from the government—or interference. The bulk of their religious, educational, and health facilities were provided by the Moravians and to a lesser extent by some other Protestant bodies. The Miskitos welcomed the few foreign (U.S. and Canadian) companies that worked in the area extracting gold and other minerals. "Many of the groups of the coast, and especially the Miskitos, were 100 percent with the American companies," acknowledged a pro-Sandinista priest, Fr. Agustin

Sambola, "because from these companies they received not only work and wages but also other things they wanted: salt, tools, and many exotic products that they had never had before."[1]

The Miskitos had a tradition of peace. The last act of collective violence involving the Miskitos had taken place in 1782. They spoke their own language and, in some places, a kind of English dialect. They also had a distaste for national politics. During the civil war against Somoza, the Miskitos remained mostly aloof.

When the Sandinistas came to power, they announced that the revolution would rescue the Atlantic Coast from its centuries of "imperialist exploitation," that the Miskitos would be free for the first time, and that the whole region would be incorporated into the nation.[2] The problem was not necessarily with these goals, but with the fact that the Sandinistas believed that they knew better than the Indians themselves what was good for them. In effect, the Sandinista leaders shared the common middle-class prejudice against the Indians—that they were no more than a collection of ignorant wanderers.

The Miskitos, however, had clear ideas about who they were and what they wanted. Over the decades a quite democratic decision-making system had grown up which taught individual Indians how to think for themselves and how to make their own decisions. With the advent of the FSLN government and the promises of freedom, the Miskitos' hope was to achieve a greater degree of cultural and political autonomy. They also hoped to lay claim for their communities on vast expanses of land that the Somoza regime had refused to grant them. But above all, the Miskitos were zealous for their Christian schools and their religious freedom. In this regard, particularly, they wished no interference from the state.

One of the Sandinistas' first actions in the Atlantic Coast region after coming to power was to deny the Miskitos their traditional network of indigenous leadership—including the elders council, which represented 256 communities—and replace it with a network of Sandinista Defense Committees. Aware that there were not many Sandinista Indians, the FSLN sent numerous revolutionary cadres from the Pacific region to fill positions of public authority.

As early as 1979, the Sandinistas also began replacing the Miskitos' centuries-old tradition of communal land ownership with a system of state-operated farms. Land which had been claimed and used by Miskito communities was now declared state-owned. In addition, the FSLN barred the Indians from cutting wood in many of these areas, since they had plans to build a nationwide forest reserve. The government also put pressure on Indians engaged in agriculture to join the ATC, and on the Miskito fishermen to join the CST. Those who refused were deprived of credit and technical assistance, and of a market in which they could sell their products.

The Sandinistas' most explosive move, however, was to begin replacing Moravian and other Protestant schoolteachers with Cubans. The Sandinistas, who knew the Miskitos' uneasiness about the changes they were making, attributed their reluctance to be incorporated into the revolution to their Christian educators' influence. They thought that Cuban teachers would make a difference. The Cubans came, and so did trouble.

The first demonstrations against the Cubans—and indirectly against the Sandinistas—took place just three months after the triumph of the revolution. The government response was ruthless. It insisted that the Miskitos were being led astray by the artful manipulation of the counterrevolutionary leaders and launched a hunt for dissidents. Cadres of the FSLN and of the Ministry of the Interior stormed the headquarters of several Indian organizations and Moravian churches and offices, made mass arrests, and killed some of the captured Miskito leaders. One of the leaders was a member of the elders council, Lyster Athders. Imprisoned in September 1979, Athders disappeared without a trace.

The situation worsened in 1980, the year in which the state expropriated the lands of the Indian communities of Yulo, Taswapowne, and Wulkiamp. The largest demonstration took place in September, with the Miskitos demanding the removal of the Cuban teachers. To give themselves a free hand for dealing with the resistance, the government imposed a ban on all news regarding the Atlantic Coast and began requiring a special permit to travel to the region. Behind the curtain of silence, repression worsened.

Mass arrests and murder of Indian leaders continued in the following year (1981). In February, Roger Suárez, leader of the Puerto Cabezas workers union was murdered, and thirty-three leaders of the Indian organization representing a coalition of

Miskito, Sumo, and Rama Indians (MISURASATA) were jailed. The Indians' anger and frustration toward the Sandinistas flared up the same month in the town of Prinzapolka. There a group of Sandinista soldiers interrupted a religious service to arrest some Miskitos. A bitter battle ensued between the soldiers and the congregation, leaving four Indians and four Sandinistas dead.

Peace between the FSLN and the Miskitos was never restored. There were some attempts at negotiating a settlement, but without success. The Miskito leaders claimed that the Sandinistas were using the negotiations to buy time and that they consistently failed to honor their promises. The Sandinistas claimed that the CIA was behind the Miskitos' resistance, exacerbating their differences and making the Indians afraid of the government. A key obstacle to a peaceful resolution was the Sandinistas' insistence that most of the Indians' demands for more autonomy and for a restoration of their communal system of land ownership were "counterrevolutionary."

In late 1980, *La Prensa* sponsored a meeting between some Sandinista and Miskito leaders. Representing the FSLN was Commander Lumberto Campbell. I recall how proud he was of the social services that the FSLN was providing to the Atlantic Coast region. He did not seem to understand why the Indians were dissatisfied. "We have increased vaccinations twofold," he said. "We have opened so many new health centers, we have increased the number of schoolteachers," and so on. What he did not grasp was that what the Indians wanted was the right to determine their own lives and to maintain their traditions and cultural identity.

In mid-1981 the government issued a Statement of Principles in Regard to the Indian Communities on the Atlantic Coast. While this was an attempt to deal with some of the Indians' concerns, as the International League on Human Rights, one of the oldest international human rights bodies, observed, this set of policies was issued unilaterally, without any consultation with the Indian leadership.[3] The government position in regard to the troublesome issue of land ownership was laid down in Clause 6: "The natural resources of our territory are the property of the Nicaraguan people. The revolutionary state, the representative of the peoples' will, is the only entity capable of establishing an efficient and rational system for the utilization of said resources."[4] The edict was a final blow to the Indians. By the end of 1981 the Miskitos were in open rebellion. In a private interview with *La Prensa* editor Pablo Antonio Cuadra in early 1982, Interior Minister Tomás Borge confessed, "No Miskito loves us."

The Miskitos, a peaceful people, could only have been driven into armed conflict by extreme provocation. In what they perceived to be a last resort, thousands of them took up arms. Several thousand others left the country in a painful exodus to Honduras.

Once a Miskito army began taking shape, with weapons largely provided by the then CIA-funded Nicaraguan Democratic Force (FDN), the Sandinistas responded ruthlessly. According to a report released by the Organization of American States' Inter-American Commission on Human Rights (OAS-CIDH), hundreds of Miskitos were detained by the Sandinistas without due process on vague accusations of "counterrevolutionary activities." "Many of these detentions," according to the report, "have been followed by prolonged periods of incommunicado imprisonment, and in some cases the OAS-CIDH verified that torture and abuse took place." Trials were conducted in Spanish, which less than one-third of the Indians knew, and "confessions" were signed with full signatures, despite the fact most of the Miskitos were illiterate. The report also stated that "the Commission has sufficient information to hold that the government of Nicaragua illegally killed a considerable number of Miskitos in Leimus, in retaliation for the killings in San Carlos"—where anti-Sandinista guerrillas killed six Sandinista soldiers.[5]

As the revolt grew stronger, the Sandinistas resorted to more drastic measures. They decided to forcibly relocate the Miskito villagers scattered along Nicaragua's northern boundary into concentrated and guarded settlements in the south. In a surprise offensive, in January 1982, Sandinista regulars appeared in several Miskito villages, forcing the townspeople to leave. They burned their houses, cut down their fruit trees, and killed their livestock. Forty-nine communities were completely destroyed by fire. An unknown number of Miskitos were killed in the process, as thousands either resisted or fled to Honduras. In the town of Tulinbila, for instance, according to a report signed by the Miskitos' elders council, the Sandinista soldiers trapped thirteen persons inside a church and set the building on fire, killing them all.[6]

The Sandinistas forced approximately ten thousand Miskitos to march through the jungles for eleven to fifteen days, to be confined in relocation camps many miles to the south. In these camps, the Miskitos were guarded by soldiers, who restricted the visits of strangers and enforced an 8 P.M. curfew. Ironically, the Sandinistas christened the first relocation camp with the Miskito name "Tasba Pri," which means "Free Land."

The way the Sandinistas have handled the Miskito situation has brought them criticism from many quarters—from the Nicaraguan Catholic bishops, from the Nicaraguan Permanent Commission for Human Rights, from the OAS-CIDH, Cultural Survival, Americas Watch, and the Denmark-based International Work Group for Indigenous Affairs. Even publications that have otherwise sympathized with the Sandinistas, such as the *National Catholic Reporter,* have concluded that the Sandinistas have violated the human rights of the Miskitos and lied when trying to justify their actions.[7]

On February 18, 1982, the Nicaraguan Catholic bishops issued a communique which said in part:

> We must state with painful surprise that in concrete cases there have been grave violations of the human rights of individuals, families, and entire groups of people. These include:
>
> —Relocations of individuals by military force without warning and without genuine discussion;
>
> —Forced marches, carried out without sufficient consideration for the weak, aged, women, and children;
>
> —Accusations of collaboration with the counterrevolution against entire towns;
>
> —The destruction of houses, belongings, and livestock;
>
> —The killing of individuals.

In response, the Sandinistas accused the Catholic bishops of being instruments of the CIA and American imperialism. Commander Daniel Ortega even asserted that the bishops "were not Christians."[8]

The Nicaraguan Permanent Commission for Human Rights, whose denunciations of Somoza's violations of human rights the Sandinistas never questioned, sent a mission to the Atlantic Coast which confirmed many of the bishops' charges and added some additional ones. The team could not finish its work, however, because the Sandinistas expelled them from the area after a few days.

The OAS-CIDH, which visited Nicaragua later, was unable to document loss of life during the relocations. However, it made the following statement:

> The relocation in Tasba Pri of some Miskitos, and the flight to Honduras of others, uprooted the Miskitos from the banks of the Rio Coco River, where they had lived from time immemorial, resulting in the division of numerous towns and entire families, the destruction of their homes, the loss of their livestock, and in some cases, all of their belongings. The Miskito structure of authority was undermined and later dissolved *de facto* as a result of the repression of the Misurasata leaders, who were accused of "counterrevolutionary" activities. Later, as Nicaragua began to receive greater threats to its external security and as the conflict in the Atlantic zone intensified, the Miskito villages were increasingly harassed, and the deprivation of or limitations on the liberty of the Miskitos became more frequent, culminating on November 4, 1982, with the establishment of a military emergency zone which affected 24 municipalities along the border with Honduras, several of which were almost entirely inhabited by Miskitos.[9]

The forced relocation of the Miskito Indians was a brutal attempt to neutralize the rebellion of a scattered population by concentrating the people in heavily guarded areas. The Sandinistas called these areas "free lands"; the Miskitos called them "concentration camps." The names are suggestive of which side of the barbed wire each party stood on. Jim Anaya, an American Apache who works with the Indian Law Resource Center, in the U.S., and who visited one of the Jinotega resettlement camps, said the Miskitos were housed in old plantation barracks; "20 to 30 people lived in three-meter by seven-meter units," with no sanitation, and in "terrible condition," cut off from fellow Miskitos on the Atlantic side of Nicaragua.[10]

During the remainder of 1982, attacks on Miskito villages continued. A history of the attacks is provided in the report signed by the leaders of the Miskito elders council who managed to escape to Honduras. They reported the military occupation of several towns in which the population was confined to their villages, even causing some children to starve. The report names specific villages—Clarindan, Cuanwatla, Kuahbul, Tuara, Sinsin, and a dozen others. The Miskito elders council also reports the burning of other towns, with the ensuing exodus of their inhabitants—Siben Benk, Prata, Kilgna, Raity, Arandakna, Wailahka, and others. The report provides lists of Indians murdered by Sandinista troops. For instance, in the town of Musawas, in late June, twenty people, including four young girls, were killed, and thirty-three were reported missing. The Miskito elders complained that all the churches in the Zelaya province (encompassing the entire east cost of Nicaragua) have been required since May 1982 to submit all sermons and publications to the state security office for approval.[11]

In December 1982 the Sandinistas forcibly relocated another contingent of five thousand to ten thousand Miskitos who lived in the Jinotega province. During this process an overcrowded, Soviet-made helicopter crashed, killing about fifty Miskito children, mostly teenagers. Somehow all four crew members escaped unharmed. Characteristically, the Sandinista government blamed the "contras" for the tragedy. Fr. Ernesto Cardenal, among others, stated that the aircraft had been shot down. The OAS-CIDH thought otherwise. Decrying the complete secrecy of the evacuation (the Sandinistas had promised the OAS that they would allow observers after the OAS complained about earlier evacuations), the Commission found that the testimony of the only Miskito survivor contradicted the version of the story given by the government.[12]

In fact, the Sandinistas systematically lied to cover up its Miskito policy. On December 20, 1983, for instance, the Nicaraguan government announced that a counterrevolutionary task force of the FDN had taken control of a relocation camp called "Francia Sirpre." The contras, the government claimed, kidnapped the entire population and took them by force to Honduras. A Catholic bishop, Salvador Schlaefer, an American of the Capuchin Order who has lived for over thirty years in Nicaragua, was with the Indians. Two days later, Sandinista leader Daniel Ortega announced that the bishop had been killed by the "contras." When the "kidnapped" Miskitos arrived in Honduras, they declared that they had been rescued, not kidnapped, by the FDN. They did not want to return to Nicaragua. Bishop Schlaefer was also with them and acknowledged that they had left the Francia Sirpre camp freely and without coercion. The Sandinistas had announced Schlaefer's death, anticipating that the bishop would be killed by the aerial attacks the government had planned against the escaping Miskitos.

Another example of Sandinista cover-up took place in January

1984. Forty Sandinista soldiers crossed over the Honduran border into the village of Kiwastare and killed eight defenseless civilian refugees in cold blood, as reported by an eyewitness, Fr. John F. Samsa.[13] The next day, however Fr. Miguel D'Escoto, the Nicaraguan Minister of Foreign Affairs, announced that the Honduran army had massacred two hundred Miskito Indians as they were trying to return to Nicaragua. According to Fr. Samsa, who lives in the area where the killings took place, D'Escoto's statements may have confused outsiders, but for the Miskitos all it accomplished was to make them distrust even further the sincerity of the Sandinistas and to reject an amnesty that Managua was offering.[14]

By 1984 the Miskitos had suffered the worst dislocation in their history. Nearly one-third had sought refuge in Honduras, living under the most precarious conditions. They had left their possessions and in many cases were separated from spouses and children. Yet, according to the sober words of Fr. Samsa, who lives with them, they do not want to return to Nicaragua.

> The 23,000 Miskito Indian refugees that are here, are here of their own free choice and remain free to return to Nicaragua. In my last three years of constant contact with thousands of refugees I have not found one who expresses any opinion to the contrary.[15]

Of the Miskitos who remained in Nicaragua, one-quarter to one-third now live in guarded areas with curfews and other restrictions. The rest live in villages where, in many instances, they are forbidden to leave or to go hunting or fishing. As a result, many Indians are starving. Details about their mistreatment at the hands of the Sandinistas were provided in October 1983 by geographer Bernard Nietschmann, a leading authority on the Miskitos and a professor at the University of California at Berkeley. Nietschmann, who has authored several books on the Indians during the past decade, spent two-and-a-half months in Miskito territories inside Nicaragua in 1983. He reported

> widespread, systematic, and arbitrary human rights violations in Miskito Indian communities. These violations by the Sandinista government include arbitrary killings, arrests, and interrogations; rapes; torture; continuing forced relocations of village populations; destruction of villages; restriction and prohibition of freedom of travel; prohibition of village food production; restriction and denial of ac-

cess to basic and necessary store foods; the complete absence of *any* medicine, health care, or educational services in many villages; the denial of religious freedom; and the looting of households and the sacking of villages.[16]

When confronted with these testimonies, observers sympathetic to the Sandinistas have tended to downplay their importance and have offered explanations as to why the Sandinistas have committed so many "mistakes." In an unpublished letter to Congress and religious leaders in 1983, Ron Sider, head of an organization called Evangelicals for Social Action, expressed the view that the Sandinistas have been well-intentioned social reformers who unfortunately have lacked certain anthropological skills in their dealings with the Miskitos. Their desire has been to better the lot of the Indians, but they have been deficient in cross-cultural know-how. When the Sandinistas met with resistance, they overreacted on occasion and became overly forceful. According to Sider, some Miskitos have been killed by the Sandinistas due to the Sandinistas' "ignorance and inexperience," and not because of any bad intentions. Furthermore, if anyone deserves condemnation for acting against the Miskitos' welfare, Sider suggests, it is the U.S. Sider cites Norman Bent, a Moravian missioner now residing in Managua, who believes that if the U.S. would stop interfering, the Miskitos could solve their problems; but if the U.S. continues to manipulate them for larger geopolitical designs, large numbers of Miskitos will continue to suffer and die.

Lack of anthropological sensitivity may indeed be a source of misunderstanding and even serious problems for reformers dealing with an alien culture. But by itself insensitivity could never have precipitated the chain of events that has disrupted the Miskitos' entire way of life. It took something much greater than mere ignorance and insensitivity to so deeply upset the Miskitos as to produce a massive exodus and turn peaceful fishermen into guerrilla fighters. Penny Lernoux, an American who for years took a sympathetic stand toward the Sandinistas—and in many respects still does—confessed in 1985:

> Until recently I tended to think that the Sandinista leadership was genuinely sincere in acknowledging its mistaken treatment of the Indians and that, in any case, the government probably had some justification in its suspicion of them because of their relationship with

contra forces. I now think that is propaganda to hide a genuine indigenous uprising against the Sandinistas' determination to "integrate" the Indians into an unwanted process of development organized and directed by the white/Mestizo government in Managua.[17]

The Miskito tragedy can be traced to the earliest days after the triumph of the revolution, when most other governments, including that of the U.S., were still on friendly terms with the Sandinista regime, and therefore the government's behavior did not stem from a need to combat outside pressures. The Miskitos' tribulations are, in fact, another example of the Sandinistas' determination to reshape Nicaragua according to a preconceived model which does not leave room for independence or cultural autonomy. The Miskitos have perceived in the Sandinistas a mortal threat to their traditional way of life and beliefs. The systematic way in which the Sandinistas have mistreated the Miskitos only bears this fear out.

NOTES

1. Sambola, interview in "The Miskitos and the Bishop Schlaefer Case," *Envío,* publication of the Instituto Histórico Centroamericano, Managua, 1984, p. 6c.

2. Junta de Gobierno, "Programa de Gobierno," p. 24.

3. Felice D. Gaer, executive director of the International League on Human Rights, "Situation of Human Rights in Nicaragua," testimony before the Subcommittee on Human Rights and International Organizations, United States House of Representatives, September 15, 1983.

4. Quoted by Felice D. Gaer, *ibid.*

5. OAS-CIDH, "Report on the Situation of Human Rights of a Segment of the Nicaraguan Population of Miskito Origin," Washington, D.C.: OAS, 1984, pp. 129, 130.

6. Council of Elders, mimeographed statement, Puerto Lempira, Honduras, November 9, 1982.

7. See J. H. Evans and Jack Epstein, "Nicaragua's Miskito Move Based on False Allegations," *National Catholic Reporter,* December 24, 1982, pp. 1, 22.

8. *El Nuevo Diario,* February 1982.

9. *Op. cit.,* OAS-CIDH, "Report on the Situation of Human Rights," pp. 129, 130.

10. Quoted by Penny Lernoux, "Sandinista Treatment of Miskitos a Betrayal of Revolution Ideals," *National Catholic Reporter,* April 26, 1985, pp. 14, 39.

11. Council of Elders, statement.

12. *Op. cit.,* OAS-CIDH, "Report on the Situation of Human Rights," p. 124.

13. Fr. Samsa, "An Open Letter to Agustin Sambola and Francis Solanus Fary," *Inforum,* Detroit, Michigan, May 1984, p. 4.

14. *Ibid.*

15. *Ibid.,* p. 4.

16. Bernard Nietschmann, "Statement Before the Organization of American States Inter-American Commission on Human Rights, On the Situation of the Indians in Nicaragua, October 3, 1983," *Social Justice Review,* January-February 1984, pp. 9, 10, emphasis in original.

17. *Op. cit.,* Penny Lernoux, "Sandinista Treatment of Miskitos."

TEN

THE SANDINISTAS AND HUMAN RIGHTS

As the Miskito tragedy made painfully clear, there is an insurmountable contradiction between the aspirations of a totalitarian
political project and the aspirations of groups trying to assert
their autonomy and cultural identity. The same can be said for
individual rights more generally. An examination of the Sandinistas' human rights record highlight the tension between these
fundamental rights and the demands for absolute power inherent
in FSLN ideology.

A widespread impression concerning the Sandinistas' human
rights record is that, aside from minor exceptions, they have
conducted themselves in a humanitarian way since coming to
power. This opinion has been especially promoted by those who
portray the Sandinistas as men and women strongly influenced
by Christian values. A common contention is that the Sandinistas
were "generous" after the war: they abolished the death penalty
and did not take political revenge, as is often the case after
bloody revolutions. If there were killings, it has been claimed,
they were few in number, isolated and unauthorized instances of
personal revenge. It has also been asserted that most of the
former members of the National Guard who came to trial were
judged fairly and received light sentences for their crimes. As a
sign of the Sandinistas' conciliatory approach, some visitors to
Nicaragua have referred to the existence of billboards speaking
of peace and mercy toward enemies. Still others have been im-
pressed by Tomás Borge's testimony that he forgave the men
who tortured him. On the other hand, there are those who
portray Nicaragua as a Stalinistic reign of terror and who speak
about the "genocidal" practices of the Sandinistas.

Human rights violations are invariabily difficult to document. Torture and murder of political prisoners is seldom done in public. Sensitive to public opinion, governments usually make every effort to conceal violence against their own people. The Sandinistas' handling of the Miskito affair is a case in point. The killing of American journalist Bill Steward by the National Guard in 1979, on the other hand, before the camera of a colleague, illustrates the political cost of public government violence: the outrage of the American public almost certainly weakened U.S. support, contributing to Somoza's downfall.

When human rights violations do become public, there is the thorny issue of interpretation—what really happened and why. Government deception and observers' emotions and prior ideological and partisan commitments are significant obstacles to clear-headed understanding. In spite of the obstacles, there is a substantial body of evidence, much of it gathered by recognized human rights agencies, which allows for an examination of human rights in Sandinista Nicaragua.

Upon assuming power, the FSLN announced that it would not impose the death penalty on convicted criminals. (It has been widely reported that the Sandinistas abolished the death penalty, but this is technically incorrect—the death penalty has never been legal in Nicaragua.) Yet, according to information furnished by the Nicaraguan Permanent Commission on Human Rights (CPDH) and by the Nicaraguan Commission of Jurists (NCJ), scores of killings have been perpetrated by the Sandinista authorities.

Data from the CPDH is quite reliable. Founded in 1977 by José Esteban González, the CPDH became famous by its denunciations of the crimes committed by the Somoza regime. Its work was instrumental in saving the lives of several jailed Sandinista leaders and in undermining Somoza's international support. The CPDH received praise and recognition from the OAS's Inter-American Commission for Human Rights (CIDH), the United Nations' Committee for Human Rights, Amnesty International, and others.

Many of the findings of the CPDH contradict reports by the Nicaraguan Ministry of the Interior in regard to killings after the revolution. Contrary to government assertions, these killings were not few in number, nor were they confined to the very first days of the new government's rule, when the authorities had yet to gain control. The killings were many—probably more than one thousand—and continued for several months.

After the 1979 revolutionary victory hundreds of prisoners, mostly members of the National Guard or supporters of the former regime, disappeared after capture and were later found dead. Of the dead, many were found in mass graves, as in the case of the prisoners of La Pólvora. La Pólvora was the former headquarters of the National Guard in the town of Granada. In the weeks following the triumph of the revolution, the Sandinistas captured an estimated three hundred persons and placed them under custody at La Pólvora. One night, a truck with ten Sandinista soldiers arrived. An officer stepped down and ordered a list of prisoners to get in the truck. They were told that they were being deported. On the road to Los Malacos the truck stopped and the prisoners were unloaded. The first to get off was Dr. César Rivas, a lawyer. After a savage beating he was shot in full view of the others. All others, among them two more lawyers and a high school teacher, suffered the same fate. One of the Sandinista soldiers, Horacio Escobar, protested the killings. Imprisoned for two months and then sent to serve in an army outpost in the interior of Nicaragua, Escobar managed to escape to Honduras and told the macabre story to Ismael Reyes, Jr., son of the president of Nicaraguan Red Cross, who made it public. On-site findings confirmed Escobar's and other earlier reports of the massacre. At the request of relatives of some of the victims, on October 3, 1979, José Esteban González, of the CPDH, traveled with several witnesses to the site and discovered human bones and remnants of clothing in a covered-over ditch.

Similar reports led to the discovery of another site in La Arrocera, near Lake Nicaragua, where several more bodies were found. At the bottom of the crater of the Santiago volcano, near Managua, ten to fifteen bodies were sighted. Thirteen more were discovered in a mass grave in Catarina, a small town near Masaya. Approximately two hundred were found in a deep well near Leon.

How many people were killed following this manner? Estimates based on names of prisoners who were captured and then declared missing or found dead vary. The CPDH has documented the disappearance and most likely death of 785 persons who were captured by Sandinista authorities from July 1979 through September 1980.[1] For each person the CPDH has a notarized

and detailed claim made by relatives, indicating name, circumstances of capture, and other information.

Confronted by the growing evidence of these killings, Tomás
Borge acknowledged many of them in October 1980.

> We said . . . to the members of State Security, to the comrades in the
> army: Don't commit abuses, don't be disrespectful to anyone, don't
> hit prisoners. Because often they did hit prisoners or kill prisoners.[2]

Borge and other Sandinista leaders portrayed the killings as a
phenomenon they tried to stop. At times they probably did. It
might also be said that the task was difficult, since the guerrillas
had had such a bitter hatred of the National Guard. But the fact
that no public disciplinary action was taken at the time against
any member of the FSLN armed forces, and the fact that many
of the killings took place in barracks under the direct supervi-
sion of higher military authorities of the Frente, suggests that
there was a good deal of complicity with such actions. A remark
from Borge himself, comparing the killings to "Fuenteovejuna,"
is suggestive. Fuenteovejuna, a town in Spain, is the title of a
seventeenth-century Spanish drama about the murder of an oppressive tax collector. When the king asks the villagers who
killed him, they all answer: "Fuenteovejuna, sire: all of us at
once."

Some of the killings of the most notorious Somocistas followed a pattern. All were killed at night while trying to escape
from military vehicles on desolate roads. Notorious Somocistas
killed in this way include "Chele Aguilera" from Leon; "Macho
Negro" from Managua; "El Quirri" from Estelí; the murderer of
Georgino Andrade, a Sandinista educator; and a couple of Sandinista defectors who attempted to hijack an airplane.

The killing of prisoners and other victims did not cease soon
after the revolution, nor did it affect only Somocistas. A particularly notorious political murder was that of Jorge Salazar, leader
of the largest and most influential cooperative of coffee growers
in the country, as well as several other organizations of mostly
small and medium-sized farmers. A disenchanted former Sandinista who had helped the FSLN to ambush Somoza National
Guardsmen near his farm in 1979, Salazar was very active in the
unionizing of several thousand independent farmers. The Sandinistas feared him. In the "Document of the 72 Hours," the FSLN
expressed its dismay at his success:

Paradoxically, the reactionary sectors of the bourgeoisie find great opportunity to confuse the masses, and even organize them in blocks to defend themselves from the state's measures. Such is the case of the Grand Cooperative of Coffee Growers, where the reactionary sectors succeeded in uniting thousands of small producers—vigorously manipulated today by reactionary pressure.[3]

On November 20, 1980, Salazar was killed unarmed by State Security. The reports from the government claimed that Salazar was involved in a counterrevolutionary plot. Although Interior Minister Borge acknowledged that Salazar was unarmed at the time of his killing, *Barricada* claimed that he was armed. The official government story that finally emerged was that a police patrol, led by Commander Omar Cabezas, attempted to take Salazar into custody. A companion of Salazar's, however, Captain Moncada Lau of the Sandinista army, who according to the story was conspiring with Salazar, opened fire on the patrol. The police returned the fire, killing Salazar. Captain Moncada Lau was not injured and, strangely enough, his public testimony was not aired. Nor were any charges brought against Lau, who continued on active duty without demotion. We published an article in *La Prensa* which drew attention to these incongruities. Tomás Borge called Pablo A. Cuadra, the editor-in-chief, and ordered him to publish nothing further about this affair. "Whether we killed him or not, your article infuriated the government," Borge told him.

In most cases of political murders, however, the victims have been peasants. For example, a report sent on January 6, 1982, by the directors of the CPDH to the Nicaraguan governing junta gives a detailed account of the killings of seventeen peasants who had been captured by the Sandinista army in the provinces of Jinotega and Zelaya. It also lists eleven more who disappeared after arrest.[4] A case already referred to is that of Miskito leader Lyster Athders. His disappearance was followed by the arrest and subsequent death of several other Miskito and Moravian leaders.

By the end of 1983, the CPDH had fully documented the disappearance of 119 persons after arrest in 1982, and of 209 in 1983. There were thirty and nineteen cases of confirmed murders in the respective years.[5] In November 1983, the Catholic bishop of Juigalpa denounced the capture and killing of four lay leaders of his diocese. Scattered reports for 1984 reflect a continuation of the trend.[6]

It should be noted that many of these crimes against Nicaraguan peasants go unreported. Agencies like the CPDH obtain their information when relatives of the victims dare to question their disappearances or killings—something many prefer not to do, fearing reprisals from the government. It also happens that civilians killed by the authorities are later reported by the army as "killed in combat."

The problem of disappearing persons is certainly large but more difficult to assess in the Atlantic Coast region, where travel has been banned and no independent observers or journalists are allowed without a government escort.

Perhaps equally as disturbing as the figures on killings is the report of the CPDH on the state of the prisoners who have disappeared but are later found:

> In the majority of cases of missing prisoners who have later been found, we have been able to verify that these inmates have been subjected to mistreatment and sometimes to grave instances of torture.[7]

In fact, the Sandinista regime is replicating some of the most vicious features of Somoza's dictatorship: torture of prisoners and what Nicaraguans call "ley fuga" (the escape law), whereby prisoners are forced to escape before the guns of the guards just to legitimize their murder. In a CPDH report, photographs of the body of a young inmate are shown; bruises and lacerations caused by torture are visible. He was presented by the government as one of sixteen prisoners killed in an attempted escape at the Zona Franca prison in June 1981.[8] Photographs in another report show the body of Nicholas Perez, taxi driver taken into custody by the Ministry of the Interior on June 4, 1982, and killed on June 8 when he allegedly attempted to escape. The coroner's report on the condition of the corpse details unmistakable signs of torture.[9] Another documented story provided by the CPDH names a renowned Nicaraguan boxer, Alex Santamaría, who was captured and killed in September 1980.[10] The story shocked many Nicaraguans (at the time the press was still able to publish this sort of story).

Many other instances of the brutal torture and killing of

prisoners have been documented. One of the most reliable is the testimony presented by American geographer Bernard Nietschmann on the Sandinistas' treatment of the Miskito Indians. Nietschmann, who talked to and photographed people who had been tortured, gives this account:

> I was shown scars from what they said were bayonet wounds (a man of 60 years), fingernails pulled out (a man of 48 years), deep scars under fingernails from nails driven in (a man of 52 years). Several men reported that they had been held under water for long periods to extract confessions. Another man had been tied by his feet and hung upside down and beaten repeatedly with sticks. His body still showed evidence of bruises and his shoulders were deformed.[11]

The OAS-CIDH has also reported on the practice of torture. "In its conversation with the detainees, the special commission received various testimonies of torture and other violations of personal security." On interviewing some Miskito prisoners in Managua, the CIDH stated that a considerable number of them (the CIDH was able to count four hundred) declared that they had been tortured and threatened with death. They were warned that they would have their tongues cut out if they told anyone of these abuses. Some of them showed the commissioners bruises and scars that they claimed resulted from this physical mistreatment.[12] The CPDH received seventy-two reports of tortures in 1980, forty in 1981, eighty-five in 1982, and 106 in 1983.[13]

REVOLUTIONARY JUSTICE

In order to prosecute former members of the National Guard and officials of the Somoza regime, the FSLN created what it called Special Courts. These courts alone were responsible for judging these defendants and were not under the jurisdiction of the Nicaraguan Supreme Court.

In August 1980 the International Commission of Jurists of the United Nations, based in Geneva, sent a document to the Sandinista government assessing the work of the Special Courts. The commission was emphatic about the unfairness and faulty procedures of the courts. It pointed out that sentences had been handed down without proof of the defendants' involvement in the crimes, that collective sentences—"mass sentencing" disregarding the specific cases of each defendant—were issued; that basic and universal principles of justice were abandoned (for example, the principle that penal law must not be retroactive); that the Sandinistas were violating international commitments (United Nations members are committed to allow defendants a fair trial and not to discriminate against them on grounds of race, nationality, or creed); and that the time allowed defendants for trial preparation was intolerably short (about twenty-four hours).[14]

Furthermore, the UN International Commission of Jurists warned about the consequences of "having condemned a great number of persons to very long sentences of imprisonment."[15] The following are excerpts from their report:

> Between April 9 and 23, 1980, a team from the International Commission of Jurists visited Nicaragua to observe the state of human rights in the country and, in particular, the work of the Special Courts in charge of prosecuting former members of the National Guard. . . .[16]
>
> An impartial observer must reach the conclusion that the Special Courts constitute exceptional tribunals handing down purely political justice. . . .[17]
>
> We cannot report finding that the Special Courts are concerned for fairness. . . . It can be said that vague accusations are a common problem. We saw various cases of sentences handed down for crimes that did not appear in the accusation.[18]

As a former lawyer, I was assigned by the state in early 1981 to defend five former National Guardsman. In not one of the cases could the court bring any specific evidence of involvement of the defendant in either murder or torture. Yet they were all condemned for such crimes to sentences ranging from ten to thirty years.

One case was particularly striking. It concerned Lorenzo Robleto, a fifty-one-year-old man with severe vision impairment who had been an airforce cook and who had never been involved in combat activities. I presented to the judge personal witnesses and extensive documentation which showed that he had always been in kitchen-related activities. Despite these facts and the absence of evidence regarding his involvement in any crime, he was condemned to twenty-three years imprisonment. My appeal to the court was rejected. Robleto is now spending the remainder of his life behind bars while his wife and children live in extreme poverty.

Despite the protestations of the United Nations' Commission of Jurists in regard to the Special Courts, on April 11, 1983, the government created new courts which duplicated the Special Courts' worst features. They were called Anti-Somocista People's Courts (APC). Commenting on how these new courts would function, the Sandinista Minister of Justice, Ernesto Castillo, said that they would prosecute, for example, those inside the country who speculate on goods, sabotage the economy, and "spread counterrevolutionary rumors." "This justice," he added, "shall not be in the hands of a formal apparatus but in the hands of our people as represented by the Anti-Somocista People's Courts."[19]

The judges of these tribunals are militants of the FSLN, usually those who also work with the CDS's. As with the Special Courts, these courts are outside the jurisdiction of the Supreme Court; their verdicts can not be appealed to a higher court. Perhaps the most ominous feature of these tribunals is that it is up to the General Directorate of State Security to decide which detainees will be judged by these courts. If State Security decrees that the detainee is a counterrevolutionary, his trial will be conducted before a People's Court.

These measures have stripped the judicial process of any semblance of impartiality. Justice is administered more than ever by a political party, the FSLN. The UN International Commission of Jurists has found that the People's Courts do not meet the requirements of impartiality because

> they depend on the Ministry of Justice, which is the accuser in the process; their members belong to and are militants of the FSLN and, thereby, they are political adversaries of the defendant; they [the courts] have been created not only to judge the Somocistas but all others who oppose in any form the policies of the present government.[20]

The OAS-CIDH reached the same conclusion:

> Far from being judicial courts, they are administrative tribunals that are subject to the Ministry of Justice and are composed of the militia, reservists, and militants or supporters of the Sandinistas; in other words, the political enemies of the accused. As a result, their impartiality, fairness, and independence of judgment are seriously compromised.[21]

Amnesty International has asked the Nicaraguan government to repeal the law establishing these courts since it was being used to imprison opponents of the regime.[22]

In 1984 about 620 prisoners were brought before People's Courts, with about 90 percent being found guilty. Sentences were as high as thirty years.[23]

Many visitors to Nicaragua are misled in regard to human rights by a model prison, the "Open Farm," fourteen miles from Managua, where the inmates can be seen working the one hundred and twenty-five acres of farmland and enjoying a most benign penal regimen, which involves no security of any kind. Although this prison, a prison "without walls," only houses a fraction of the total inmate population (chosen on the basis of good behavior), many visitors mistake it for a representative sample of the entire correctional system. They are seldom taken to the "Zona Franca," the huge master prison where thousands of inmates are crammed in filthy cells. The novelist Mario Vargas Llosa, for instance, on a trip to Nicaragua, remembers, "I ask Borge for permission to visit Zona Franca; although he promises he will send it, I never receive the permit."[24]

Besides the Zona Franca (also called the Héroes y Mártires de Nueva Guinea), thousands of other political prisoners are kept at the prison at Tipitapa, in a detention camp at Puerto Cabezas, and in about one hundred and forty "clandestine" jails, which according to former CPDH president José E. González, are scattered throughout the country.[25] The Sandinistas do not normally provide names of the political prisoners, nor statistics about the inmate population, but the government, according to González, did acknowledge in a 1983 report that it still detains between thirty-eight hundred and four thousand former members of the National Guard. González also said that in 1984 between fifteen hundred and two thousand prisoners were detained in the clandestine jails and consequently deprived of any recourse to legal assistance.[26] Furthermore, he estimated that there were between one thousand and fifteen hundred Indian prisoners held on the Atlantic Coast.[27] According to evidence collected by the CPHD, the Sandinista government took at least 2,974 persons political prisoner in 1980, 885 in 1981, 989 in 1982, and 1,169 in 1983 for a total of 6,017. During the same period 588 were reported released.[28]

Since 1980, prisoners in Nicaragua, except those at the "Open Farm," have received a single ration of rice a day as their only meal. Their families must provide the rest of their nourishment—something they often cannot do. The government claims that it does not have the resources to provide better prisoner care.

Reports of mistreatment also abound. In June 1981 a group of desperate prisoners staged a protest inside the Zona Franca prison. In a swift response by the authorities, sixteen prisoners were killed and twenty-seven wounded (there were no government casualties).

On-site observations by the OAS-CIDH in 1980 and 1982 yielded reports that no improvements in prison conditions had taken place during that period.[29] The commission mentioned two particular features of prison life: first, what "appears to be a frequent punishment, consists of being stripped and left naked in groups for prolonged periods"; second, "restriction of visits— they [the inmates] are kept almost entirely incommunicado."[30] In May 1984, Amnesty International condemned the torture and mistreatment of political prisoners in Nicaragua.[31]

FORCED RELOCATIONS
The forced relocations of entire segments of the population, has been another sober aspect of the Sandinistas' human rights record. The first relocations took place in January 1982 when whole communities of Miskito Indians were uprooted from the banks of the Rio Coco River in northern Nicaragua, causing an outcry of domestic and international protests (see Chapter 9). They continued through 1983; in all, fifteen thousand to twenty thousand Miskito Indians were moved.

In 1985 forced relocations were resumed on even a greater scale in five northern Nicaraguan provinces. From January to March, the Sandinistas moved fifty thousand peasants to forty-seven resettlement camps. By May the number of peasants affected was almost one hundred and eighty thousand, according to government minister Reynaldo Tefel, president of the Nicaraguan Committee of National Emergency.[32] Some of the evacuees were given a few days notice, some only twenty-four hours. After the evacuation, Sandinista troops destroyed everything left behind that could possibly be used by the "contras" that were active in the area. The relocations were described by the official newspaper *Barricada* as "the rescue of thousands of peasants from the isolation that allowed the counterrevolution to utilize them."[33] The statement, in fact, is an oblique reference to the reason why the peasants—as the Miskitos before them—were moved: many were helping the guerrillas. According to *Time,* the Sandinistas were attempting "to systematically deprive the contras of a popular base that provides food, refuge and, occasionally, recruits."[34] They also wanted to create a free-fire zone for the unrestricted use of weapons the Sandinistas received from the Soviet Union in 1984: armored Mi-24 helicopters, successfully tested by the Soviets against the Afghan rebels.

The uprooting of people, whatever the palliatives may be, is a brutal procedure. Families witness the destruction of homes and farms to which they have been attached, sometimes for generations. Their neighborhood and village relationships are severed. They are forced to adapt to new work and residence situations which are often highly unfamiliar to them. The people so displaced in Nicaragua amount thus far to close to 8 percent of the total population. Neither Somoza, nor, for comparison, the Salvadoran regime, when confronted with guerrilla war, have resorted to forced relocations. The fact that the Sandinistas have done so is another indication that when their power is at stake, they will place no limits on what they will do.

This absence of moral restraints when "defending the revolution" can also be seen in a document of the Ministry of the Interior, stamped "confidential," which was leaked and published in part by *The Wall Street Journal.*[35] Written in preparation for the 1984 elections, the document gives instructions on how to deal with the press in the event the government sees itself forced to grant more freedom (because of international pressure), and on how to stage a rumor campaign to discredit political opponents. Entitled "Rumor Strategies," the author of the document says that

> It is necessary to articulate a strategy of rumors and gossip that can be transmitted strictly by way of interpersonal communication, to discredit people and ideas of the right.

The document points out the need to create and fabricate rumors that are credible. This involves,

Designing them on the basis of a very detailed study of the basic
requirements a rumor must meet in order to be repeated and believed . . . they should include some elements that are true or believ-
able.

One of the targets of this campaign is Enrique Bolanos, the
president of COSEP, the private businessmen's organization. The
document instructs on how to create a rumor about an incident
that took place in the early sixties, when Mr. Bolanos' father was
fatally poisoned by an employee of his hardware store. The
document suggests that it was Mr. Bolanos (or his family) who
poisoned his father in order to lay hands on the family's money.
This rumor is to be used "to reveal the moral quality, the greed,
and the exploitative nature of COSEP." Another target of the
campaign is

The ecclesiastical hierarchy, particularly the duet Obando-Carballo,
and Bishop Vega; Mr. Arturo Cruz, whose halo of honesty, semi-
sanctity, and great intellectual capacity must be analyzed in detail so
as not to launch counterproductive rumors; Enrique Bolanos. . . ; the
right, which should be blamed for the de-supply [shortages]; the
right-wing political parties (rumor: they have been holding private
meetings with the U.S. Embassy, the National Guard, the CIA, etc.).

This readiness to use any means deemed necessary in the
political and military struggle to consolidate their power lies at
the root of the Sandinistas' approach to human rights.

RECONCILIATION?
As mentioned earlier, during their ascent to power the Sandinistas publicized the slogan, "Relentless in struggle, generous in
victory." Within weeks after they triumphed, however, the slogan
was replaced by a new one: "Relentless in struggle, relentless in
victory." The original slogan ceased to be used. It was removed
from posters, official literature, and broadcasts. (I mentioned this
change in the report from which the present book developed,
Nicaragua: Christians under Fire, published in March 1984.
Interestingly enough, some months later—and five years after
the original slogan had disappeared from public use—the Nicaraguan government built a new billboard proclaiming, "Our slogan has been and continues to be, Relentless in Struggle and
Generous in Victory." The government also took down a giant

poster of Sandino affixed to the facade of Managua's old cathedral that was pictured on the cover of my report and on the cover of a book by a Colombian, Carlos Corsi. I suspect that these changes were the result of the Sandinistas' keen awareness of the importance of maintaining an image of peace and reconciliation abroad.)

Far from promoting reconciliation at home, from the first months after the war with Somoza ended and even more aggressively since April 1980, the government conducted a campaign to foster class struggle and hatred of "the enemies"—"enemies" being not only those who express dissatisfaction with the FSLN's policies, but also those who fail to express support for the regime. The verbal barrage against non-Sandinista Nicaraguans laid the groundwork for mob attacks and physical abuse. The Catholic Church became so alarmed with this campaign that it issued several warnings about the corrosive effects of hatred. The archbishop of Managua wrote,

> What can we say of a practice of imposing on those who do not share our views the label of "enemies" and "suspects," attributing to them hostile intentions and stigmatizing them as aggressors with skillful and continuous propaganda?[36]

It is likewise difficult to discern a conciliatory or humanitarian attitude toward adversaries in the Sandinista media. When the Sandinista newspapers *Barricada* and *El Nuevo Diario* report on the Sandinistas' enemies or "contras" killed in battle, they usually speak of the number of "beasts" or "dogs" killed.

Billboards erected in Managua by individual Christians have mistakenly been cited by foreign visitors as an example of the conciliatory attitude that the Sandinistas are trying to promote. The July 1982 issue of *Maryknoll* magazine, for instance, carried a photograph of a billboard reading, "If your enemy is hungry, feed him," and attributed its placement to the FSLN. In fact, it was placed by a Teresian nun, Mother Ana Zavala, who since 1981 has had many of her billboards defaced and destroyed by Sandinista gangs.

In the context of a discussion of the Sandinista government's desire to promote national reconciliation, it is appropriate to clarify the widely repeated story of Tomás Borge granting an amnesty to the man who tortured him in a Somoza jail. A major difficulty with the story is that Somoza's security forces carefully followed the practice of completely covering the heads of prisoners with a dark cloth whenever they were questioned or tortured. They did this to prevent personal identification by the guerrillas and thus protected themselves from possible reprisals. Borge himself acknowledged this practice. "I was brutally tortured, kept with a hood over my head for nine months, and handcuffed for seven months."[37] It is thus highly improbable that Borge ever saw the man who tortured him. In fact, no torturer has ever been produced.

Furthermore, pardoning National Guardsmen has simply not been Sandinista practice. If the man who tortured Borge was pardoned, why was the airforce cook that I defended condemned to twenty-three years imprisonment without any evidence that he was guilty of a crime? If Borge is so animated by Christian values, why did he and the other directors of the FSLN publicly celebrate Somoza's murder? When news of the assassination reached Managua, the national directorate joyfully paraded through the city. Later their motorcade stopped at Revolution Square, where they staged a giant public party. Somoza may be judged a contemptible man in many respects. But celebrating his murder is hardly an example of Christian forgiveness and love of enemies.

A DOUBLE STANDARD

A curious aspect of Sandinista human rights violations is the degree to which they have been shielded from the international public eye. As stated earlier, human rights violations are inherently difficult to substantiate; allegations must be approached with proper caution. But while reliable human rights organizations have produced a significant body of gruesome evidence, some human rights organizations and segments of the media have chosen not to publicize this evidence.

The document of the United Nations' International Commission of Jurists regarding the gross unfairness of the Special Courts is an instance of this approach. It was not released to the public, but was sent to the Nicaraguan government as a private document. A similar tack was taken by the OAS Inter-American Commission for Human Rights regarding actions against the Miskito Indians. In order not to embarrass the Sandinistas, the commission kept its findings confidential until 1984.

The rationale in these cases has been that addressing the Sandinistas in private, diplomatic ways would offer them a better chance to amend their behavior than outright denunciations. Although at first this might have been a reasonable way to proceed, it proved ineffective. Clear and private as it was, the exhortation of the International Commission of Jurists was to no avail and was completely disregarded by the Managua authorities. The private approach has ultimately covered up government abuses rather than spurred their correction.

A double standard has played a role in obscuring some hard facts about the Sandinista revolution. One who can testify to this is José Esteban González. As president of the Nicaraguan Permanent Commission on Human Rights during the Somoza period, González gained a very responsive audience abroad for reports about human rights violations committed by Somoza. After the revolution, however, he expressed his frustration at the cool reception he sometimes harvested when denouncing the crimes of the Sandinistas. In an article entitled "The Disappeared Who Disappeared," González detailed the tendency of some international human rights organizations to "disappear" reports of Nicaraguans "disappeared" by the Sandinistas. González concluded with the statement that Nicaragua is the most intense country in the Americas: "Even our missing are the ones who disappear the most."[38]

"When Somoza was in power," González told me in a private conversation, "I would only need to call the Washington Post or some other influential newspaper to receive immediate attention. Now they keep telling me that the person I want to talk to is in a meeting." He told David Sperling, of the news agency Free Press International, that "Amnesty International currently acts with extraordinary speed and efficiency in all cases related to, for example, El Salvador, Guatemala, and Chile. But in the case of Nicaragua today, for reasons of which I am still not aware, its attitude is not very cooperative."

How should the Sandinista government's human rights record be understood in the context of the government's overall direction? It is true that the Sandinistas do not have death squads such as can be found in some neighboring countries, although their control of the population, being much tighter than elsewhere, allows for a legal facade for assassinations—victims are arrested first. Nevertheless, so far the Sandinistas have not imposed a fully totalitarian system such as exists in Cuba and other

Communist countries. Opponents of the regime can still enter and leave the country (although with some restrictions); there is press censorship, but the Catholic Church still publishes a little Sunday flyer; dozens of leaders of the CTN labor union are in jail, but the union still operates; most political opponents of the regime are in exile or in jail, but there are others who have braved the storm and remain active, criticizing the regime in mimeographed newsletters.

The explanation for these limited freedoms lies in the Sandinistas' realistic call for a period of transition, warning its militants that the full Socialist state cannot be achieved immediately. The FSLN knows its internal weaknesses—namely, an acute shortage of personnel able to administer the economy, and its external dangers. It is aware that international opinion can affect its rule in a decisive way. "The battle for Nicaragua is not being waged in Nicaragua. It is being fought in the United States," Tomás Borge was quoted as saying by *Newsweek* magazine.[39] The need to avoid stirring up the hostility of foreign observers of the revolutionary process has no doubt slowed the pace of the Sandinistas and acted as a restraint on their human rights abuses. But it is important to keep in mind that it is strategy and not fundamental policy that is providing the breathing room that still exists.

NOTES

1. CPDH, "Los Desaparecidos: Unabominable Crimen Somocista que Debemos Desterrar de la Patria Sandinista," *CPDH Informe Oficial,* Managua, October 3, 1980, p. 2.

2. Tomás Borge, "On Human Rights," presentation before the Inter-American Commission for Human Rights, October 10, 1980, in *op. cit., Sandinistas Speak,* p. 90.

3. FSLN, *op. cit.,* "Documento de las 72 Hóras," p. 14.

4. CPDH, "Carta Abierta a la Junta de Gobierno de Reconstrucción Nacional," letter, Managua, January 6, 1982, pp. 1-3.

5. CPDH, "Denuncias Presentadas a la CPDH de Agosto 1979 a Diciembre 1983," report, Managua: CPDH, January 6, 1984, p. 1.

6. Cf. "Freedom Appeals," *Freedom at Issue,* January-February 1985, No. 82, pp. 51-53.

7. *Op. cit.,* CPDH, "Los Desaparecidos," p. 4.

8. Comité Europa-Nicaragua, "Situación de los Derechos Humanos," *Dossier Nicaragua*, No. 2, a publication of the Comite Europa-Nicaragua, Brussels, January 14, 1985, p. 10.

9. CPDH, "Orto Reo Muere en Intento de Fuga," report, Managua: CPDH, July 1982, p. 1.

10. CPDH, "¿Quiénes Asesinaron a Alex Santana y su Amigo?," report, Managua: CPDH, March 21, 1981.

11. Bernard Nietschmann, "Statement Before the Organization of American States," p. 10.

12. OAS-CIDH, "Report on the Situation of Human Rights," p. 102.

13. CPDH, "Denuncias Presentadas a la CPDH," p. 1.

14. UN International Commission of Jurists, "Tribunales Especiales que Juzgan a Somocistas y Colaboradores del Somocismo," report, Geneva: UN-ICJ, August 1980, pp. 16, 17, 14, 18, 18.

15. *Ibid.*, p. 18.

16. *Ibid.*, p. 1.

17. *Ibid.*, p. 17.

18. *Ibid.*, p. 15.

19. Ernesto Castillo at the inauguration of the Heroes and Martyrs Seminar, quoted by the CPDH in *CPDH Informa*, Managua, May 25, 1983, p. 3.

20. *Op. cit.*, UN International Commission of Jurists, "Tribunales," p. 15.

21. Quoted in *CPDH Informa*.

22. Amnesty International, August 1982 report, quoted in *CPDH Informa*, Managua, May 25, 1983, p. 3.

23. Cited in "Country Reports on Human Rights Policies for 1984," U.S. Department of State, February 1985, p. 614.

24. Mario Vargas Llosa, "In Nicaragua," p. 92.

25. Comité Nicaragüense de Derechos Humanos, "Acusación Contra el Gobierno de Nicaragua Presentada ante el Tribunal Permanente de los Pueblos," report, Brussels: CNDH, October 1, 1984, p. 9.

26. *Ibid.*

27. *Ibid.*

28. *Op. cit.*, CPDH, "Denuncias Presentadas a la CPDH," p. 1.

29. OAS-CIDH, "Report on the Situation of Human Rights," p. 101.

30. *Ibid.*, p. 30.

31. Cited in *op. cit.*, "Country Reports on Human Rights Policies for 1984."

32. *Diario Las Americas,* May 12, 1985, p. 6-A.

33. Quoted by Janice Castro, "No Man's Land," *Time,* April 8, 1985, p. 46.

34. *Ibid.*

35. Claudia Rosset, "Sandinistas Forsake the Truth in Favor of Newspeak," *The Wall Street Journal,* March 29, 1985, p. 29. All English quotes are from this article.

36. Archbishop Miguel Obando, 1981 Christmas message, *La Prensa,* December 23, 1981, p. 1.

37. Tomás Borge, "On Human Rights in Nicaragua," p. 87.

38. Mimeographed copy given to the author, dated June 1982.

39. Larry Martz, "Next Target: Nicaragua?" *Newsweek,* November 14, 1983, p. 44.

ELEVEN

SANDINISMO AND CHRISTIANITY

In the preceding chapters we have examined how the ideology and goals of the Sandinistas have brought them into conflict with various sectors of Nicaraguan society. But nowhere is the conflict more intense and the controversy more fundamental than in the Sandinistas' relationship with the Christian churches.

Many observers, to begin with, have found it difficult to assess the Sandinistas' true intentions regarding religion. Marxist regimes are typically hostile to religion and religious believers; yet there have been four priests in high posts in the Sandinista government. Marxists typically preach atheism and curtail the spread of religious beliefs; yet after the Sandinista revolution there was considerable evangelistic activity in Nicaragua.

Developments such as these have led some observers to conclude that the Sandinista government is not fundamentally opposed to religious freedom. Ron Sider, for instance, has written: "If the Sandinistas intend eventually to promote totalitarianism, atheistic Marxism-Leninism, then they are proceeding in an unusual way. A number of Christians are in government posts crucial for ideological indoctrination."[1] A similar opinion was formed by another Christian visitor who wrote in *Christianity Today* magazine. In the last few years, he noted, the number of Bibles distributed in Nicaragua has doubled or tripled in the wake of efforts by Protestants and Catholics alike. The visitor's conclusion was that "such things do not happen in Marxist countries."[2]

On the other hand, there have been both verbal and physical clashes between the Sandinista government and some Christians.

Are these mainly the result of political tensions between politically conservative Christians and a revolutionary leadership which is perhaps prone to overreact? Or are these instances of religious persecution?

As with human rights, interpreting government conflict with religion is invariably clouded in difficulty. One reason has to do with understanding the term *persecution*. When one speaks of religious persecution, what usually comes to mind is churches being closed, Bibles being confiscated, Christians being mistreated to force them to repudiate their faith. In recent years, however, regimes committed to antireligious policies often refrain from overt and dramatic forms of persecution. More often, such governments adopt strategies aimed at curtailing the influence of religion in society and at undermining people's commitment to their religious beliefs, leaders, and institutions. This shift in strategies has been noted by John Paul II, who has had intimate experience with it:

> We are living in an age in which the whole world proclaims freedom of conscience and religious freedom. We are also in an age in which the struggle against religion . . . is waged as far as possible in such a way as not to create new martyrs. Thus the program of the age is persecution, but, appearances being saved, "persecution does not exist and there is full religious freedom."[3]

The fact that so many self-confessed Christians, including priests and ministers, have joined the Sandinista revolution is an additional complication for interpreting the Sandinista regime's real attitude toward religion. These Christians' involvement can be interpreted in opposite ways. It could be the result of Marxists moving closer to Christian positions, or of Christians moving toward Marxism—or it could be a process of convergence.

To examine the issue of the Sandinista government's relation to Christianity and the prospects for Christians in Sandinista Nicaragua, we shall first explore the Sandinistas' attitude toward religion, move to a consideration of those Christians who have supported the Sandinistas and those who have not, and finally examine the record of conflict between the FSLN and some segments of the churches.

THE SANDINISTAS AND RELIGION
As described in the first chapter, during the past two decades Marxists in Latin America have changed their strategy toward

religion. By the late sixties some Marxist leaders were becoming aware of the need for a new way of handling the religious issue due to the deep-rooted religiosity prevailing in the large traditional sectors of Latin American societies. In Nicaragua, this new approach was especially appropriate for the Marxists. Nicaragua, according to many observers, is one of the most religious countries in Latin America. Religious devotion is deeply rooted, particularly among the Catholic peasantry, and priests, bishops, and the Pope are held in great respect. In some ways, Nicaragua resembles Poland, where the Catholic faith is also deeply rooted in the lives and traditions of the people. Protestants are relatively few in Nicaragua (perhaps 18 percent), and, as elsewhere in Latin America, are mostly adherents of an evangelical, Bible-oriented faith which emphasizes personal conversion rather than political action as the road to social transformation.

When the Sandinistas came to power in 1979, they were conscious of the depth of faith among the majority of Nicaraguans. Not wishing to antagonize believers, their 1979 program of government guaranteed full freedom of religious practice without any qualifications (Clause I.1.4). Assurance of religious freedom was also offered individually at various times, albeit ambiguously, by many of the Sandinista leaders, who not only boasted of being tolerant of religion, but of being personal friends and allies of numerous Nicaraguan Christians. To substantiate their claim of being upholders of religious freedom, the Sandinistas pointed to the participation of Catholic priests and other revolutionary Christians in their government, and the Christians involved were themselves eager to support this claim.

However, a careful reading of FSLN statements shows that there was an important qualification in the FSLN's tolerance of religion. The Sandinistas consistently expounded an approach which evaluated religious beliefs, institutions, and leaders on the basis of *whether they supported the revolution.* The 1969 FSLN program offered to respect religious beliefs and support "clerics who supported the working people" (Clause 9). The program of 1977 repeated this promise: "The Sandinista Peoples' Revolution . . . will support the work of the priests and other religious preachers who defend the working people" (Clause 8B). In the government's manual for the literacy campaign, lesson 22 reads: "There will be freedom of religion for all those churches that defend the interest of the people."[4] The FSLN was thus indicating that it would treat Christian leaders and other members of

churches according to whether they fell into one of two categories: those who supported the working people (by FSLN logic,
the FSLN), and those who refrained from supporting the revolution.

In its 1981 New Year's message, the Nicaraguan government
junta made this terse statement:

> The true Christians, the sincere Christians, embrace the option of the
> Sandinista revolution which today constitutes . . . the option for the
> poor.[5]

In other words, Christians unwilling to embrace the revolution—that is, the politics of the FSLN—are not sincere Christians. They may pretend to be loving and virtuous, but how
could they be if they fail to embrace the embodiment of justice
for the poor which is the revolution? As the "Document of the
72 Hours" had stated unambiguously, these Christians must be
watched carefully and, whenever possible, neutralized.[6]

It is important to note that failure to "embrace the option of
the Sandinista revolution" need not involve explicit rejection or
criticism of the revolution. It might mean merely the failure to
explicitly support the revolution.

This demand of the Sandinista government was shaped by the
Marxist belief that no act is politically neutral. Everything has a
political meaning: it either fosters the interests of the people or
the interests of their class enemies—the bourgeoisie and the
imperialists. An act, for instance, that does not promote the
interests of the revolution is political in that it distracts people
from their priorities—it saps their energies by filling their minds
with alien concerns. This perspective applies to religion as to
everything else. Beliefs and religious practices which do not
promote the peoples' commitment to the revolution cannot but
be alienating elements damaging to the interests of the people
and the party. If necessary, the FSLN, the people's educator and
guide, should intervene to make sure that people do not suc-
cumb to harmful ideological influences. This was the rationale
for a campaign they launched to redefine religious symbols and
celebrations.

At the same time, the Frente realized that it had to proceed
with tact and caution in these matters—but act, nevertheless. It
could not afford to remain idle, neglecting the key task of reshaping people's consciousness. A secret document of the FSLN

regarding the celebration of Christmas, which accidentally fell into the hands of *La Prensa* in early 1980, reflects the tension between the Frente's call to revolutionize traditional religious practice and faith, and the need to do so carefully. The document was signed by Julio López, head of the Department of Propaganda and Political Education of the FSLN. It was addressed to the regional leaders of the party. Its subjects was how FSLN militants ought to approach the upcoming Christmas celebration (December 1979). Here are some excerpts:

> After the triumph of the People's Sandinista Revolution we are working to reorient the celebration of Christmas. We want to make it a special day for the children, one with a different content, fundamentally political. In essence, we want to rescue for the revolution a tradition that, although religious, is established among our people. It is thanks to our Sandinista revolution that now our children can celebrate their Christmas in freedom and grow up in a homeland that assures them their future and their happiness. This is the central thought of the celebration. . . .

> Only five months after the triumph of the revolution, it would be rather foolish to directly confront a tradition of more than 1979 years, because it would entail political conflicts and the inevitable loss of confidence of our people. . . .

> Sixty-two years of revolution in the Soviet Union have not been enough to completely eradicate this religious tradition. Therefore to pretend to uproot such a tradition from our people in such a short time could only constitute a petty bourgeois revolutionary attitude.

> At the same time, when interpreting the sense that the FSLN wants to give Christmas now, we ought to keep in mind that it is not propaganda campaigns that will erase a tradition of profound religious consciousness. It is the transformations of the material aspect of life that will definitely create the conditions that will allow effective development of a work of education and ideological formation of our people.

In this document, the FSLN states a clear intention to actively enter into the religious realm. It wishes to reorient the celebration of Christmas by giving it a fundamentally political content. With an awareness of the political costs of directly confronting religion, the Sandinista document recommends an indirect strategy for dealing with faith. It cautions the militants of the FSLN to be realistic, for even in the most advanced Socialist nation, the U.S.S.R., sixty-two years of revolution have not yet eradicated Christmas.

As early as fall 1979 the Sandinistas began taking a very active role in redesigning religious celebrations. The Ministry of Culture, in association with the Department of Propaganda and Political Education, printed thousands of posters to commemorate Christmas as the advent of the "new man," a Marxist term referring to the new unselfish man that will be born with socialism. The central message, as the secret memo of the Department of Propaganda had directed, was that the new man would now be possible in Nicaragua thanks to the Sandinista revolution.

I attended a meeting in November 1979 at which the Ministry of Culture asked for the collaboration of different sectors in distributing these Christmas posters. I asked why the FSLN had not consulted the Catholic bishops or other church leaders about the content of these materials. They answered that Fr. Edgar Parrales, a Sandinista priest who was then Vice-Minister of Social Welfare, was in agreement with the content. This amounted to saying that the government had bypassed legitimate church authorities. A couple of Nicaraguans who were in the meeting representing some artisans' shops from the town of Masaya shared with me after the meeting their alarm and disillusionment at the way the Sandinistas were handling religious issues. "They are just trying to divert more water to their mills," they told me, using an old proverb.

In their attempt to politicize religious meanings and events, many of the FSLN leaders also began joining in at Catholic religious festivities, appearing where possible side by side with church celebrants and often addressing the crowds. Conscious of the extraordinary ideological potential of religion, they wanted to harness it for their purposes.

One of the Sandinista comandantes most involved in this strategy was Tomás Borge, who, unlike other ideologists of the Frente such as Humberto Ortega, deliberately associated concepts of Sandinismo and Christianity. His goal was to promote a secularized Christianity by equating it with general goodwill devoid of any basis in the supernatural. Believing himself and his comrades to be men of great goodwill, Borge was by his definition a Christian.

> What it is to be a Christian? I am not an expert in theology . . . but if to be a Christian is to be good, if to be Christian is to be honest, if to

be Christian is to profoundly respect others, if to be a Christian is to fill the soul and the heart with love toward others, I am a Christian.[7]

The members of the national directorate of the FSLN, like most of the other members of the party's inner circle, were self-confessed atheists. They tried, however, to keep the lowest possible profile in this regard, at least for a time. Meanwhile they boasted of being more Christian than anyone else. A May Day 1984 speech by commander Jaime Wheelock illustrates their approach. Referring to the Beatitudes in the Gospel, Wheelock asked: "Who is the one who said, 'Blessed are the poor for they shall inherit the earth'?" The crowd answered: "Jesus Christ." Wheelock then asked: "And who are the ones here who are giving away land to the poor?" The people answered: "The revolution." Wheelock asked: "Who are, in a word, the ones who fulfill these Christian principles in the most direct way? The Sandinistas?" And the people answered, "The vanguard." Wheelock's closing comment was,

> Therefore, there is no contradiction [between Christianity and the revolution], and they [enemies of the FSLN] could even say that we are atheists. Well, let us admit it . . . that there are some inside the FSLN who, because of their ideas, their ideology, their studies, and their questions have begun to think that God does not exist; let us then admit it, but we shall not discuss this.[8]

The FSLN was aware that a strategy of trying to politicize religious meanings would be more effective than open rejection. The Sandinistas also saw it as important to emphasize the claim that the only true Christians were those who supported the revolution. Their strategy toward the churches, therefore, involved one of tolerance and even friendship toward those Christians or other believers willing to embrace the revolutionary process.

The Sandinistas found radical Christians within the churches who shared the FSLN's desire to politicize Christian beliefs and who, like the Sandinistas, classified their brethren on the basis of their stance toward the revolution. This strategy of cooperation with the revolutionary Christians had the powerful advantage of allowing the FSLN to continue the campaign of revolutionizing religious symbols with at least short-term impunity. The Frente could point to the revolutionary Christians as the source of the changes that they were trying to implement. At the same time, the FSLN could use its allies within the churches to minimize the political costs of confronting Christians unwilling to bend to all its policies. Cristophe Batasch, in *Le Monde Diplomatique,* commented on the sagacity of the Sandinistas "letting the leftist Christians take care of combatting the bishops."[9] The government simply provided its allies within the churches with access to the state-controlled media while restricting its availability to others. The government thus gave the appearance of allowing religious freedom, but with the qualification it had stated: only for religious leaders who defended the interest of the working class (the FSLN). Meanwhile, the FSLN would place greater and greater restrictions on the freedom of expression of Christians unwilling to recognize their hegemony over the church. In this regard, however, the Sandinistas were to confront a church with a history of withstanding government pressure.

THE CATHOLIC CHURCH IN NICARAGUA

The Nicaraguan Catholic Church of the late seventies was a vigorous body with a multitude of tendencies and outlooks. The Second Vatican Council (1963 to 1965) and the Latin American bishops' conference at Medellin, Colombia (1968) were having a profound influence on the Latin American Catholic Church, including the church in Nicaragua. These two landmark events decisively raised concern for social justice as a key issue for the church to grapple with. These assemblies of bishops also challenged some of the patterns of Catholic life that had developed over the centuries in Latin America and elsewhere, including a reduction of Christianity in practice to ritualism, passivity of lay people in relation to the clergy, and a privatization of religion that prevented it from transforming national life. By the late seventies, various Catholics were responding positively or negatively to the changes of direction which Vatican II and Medellin had mandated. In their approach to social and political issues, Catholic leaders fell into three general categories: the conservatives, the progressives, and the radicals or revolutionaries.

The Conservatives

The conservatives in Nicaragua, as elsewhere in Latin America, were Christians who either sympathized with the status quo or shied away from church involvement in politics and especially from open criticism of the sociopolitical system. In Nicaragua, these Christians included many members of the Catholic hierarchy who had taken office before the seventies. During the sixties some of the most renowned conservative Catholic personalities were in charge of educational institutions; for example, Fr. León Pallais, a Jesuit, who headed the Central American University. These men lost most of their influence during the early seventies, when the leadership of the Catholic Church in the country passed to progressive hands. (A similar process took place among Protestants in Nicaragua, but more slowly. Until the late seventies they tended to refrain from most forms of political involvement.)

The Progressives

The progressive Catholics took up the church's greater emphasis on social justice. They did this from the perspective of the Catholic Church's social teaching, with its rejection of both individualistic liberalism and collectivistic Marxism, and its insistance on the primacy of personal conversion to Christ.

In Nicaragua, the emerging progressives came to be led by Miguel Obando y Bravo, who was ordained archbishop of Managua in 1970. A man of Indian and mulatto family background, Archbishop Obando came to embody the Catholic Church's break with its conservative past. He organized the first Christian peasant unions in Nicaragua, and he refused Somoza's efforts to win him with gifts. He was the strongest voice in the Catholic Church denouncing Somoza's violations of human rights—a stand which led to threats and at least one attempt on his life and to a campaign of defamation in the Somocista press. Somoza's press called him "Commandante Miguel," meaning that he was just one more guerrilla leader. He was also accused of being Communist. The attacks against him drew many Catholics to close ranks in his defense and increased his popularity. The archbishop also served as an intermediary between the Sandinista guerrillas and the Nicaraguan government on the two occasions when the Frente kidnapped groups of Somocista officials.

Along with Archbishop Obando, the other Nicaraguan bishops, as well as many members of the clergy and the religious orders, began advocating a new social order. Their record in facing the Somoza dictatorship was so well established that later even the Sandinistas acknowledged it in their document on religion, published by the national directorate of the FSLN on October 7, 1980:

> The Catholic bishops on various occasions courageously denounced the crimes of the [Somoza] dictatorship, particularly Archbishop Obando y Bravo and Bishop Salazar y Espionoza, who, among others, suffered as a consequence the harassement of the Somocista thugs.[10]

The bishops' position during the seventies was delicate. On the one hand, they had to withstand the attacks of those on the far right who decried their involvement with political concerns and suspected them of being manipulated by the radical left. On the other hand, the bishops had to wrestle with those on the left who wanted to see the Catholic Church endorsing specific partisan agendas for social change. The bishops denounced rightist, authoritarian oppression and the dehumanizing features of a world driven solely by the profit motive, and also warned of the evil of totalitarian utopias that reduce men to the role of pawns of an absolute power.

In 1971, the bishops published a "Pastoral Letter on the Duty of Christian Witness and Action in the Political Realm." It expressed the middle road that they wished to take:

> A redistribution of resources is of the utmost urgency. . . .[12]
>
> To organize to defend oneself against forces inspired by greed and accumulation [of wealth] is a fundamental right of the citizen. . . .[13]
>
> [The goal of Christian teaching] is not to draw men to any system or political party in particular. . . .[14]
>
> Christian action . . . does not identify itself with institutions or organizations of a civic nature, nor is it a substitute for them.[15]
>
> Let us not repeat inappropriate clerical interventionism in matters which are the legitimate and free domain of the citizen. . . .[16]
>
> The continuity of power [the Somoza dynasty] is being questioned in our midst. Our young people and the general clamour of our nation point to new perspectives for life in the country.[17]

A pastoral letter the following year again reflected the bishop's effort to chart a course independent of both right- and left-wing pressures:[18]

There are abundant critics, from those who would like to isolate the church from these [socio-political] problems, and from those who would like to see her involved in every particular choice. . . .[19]

At times there have been insults and criticism of priests and even bishops who were fulfilling their duty of denouncing injustices and promoting peace, attacking their actions as undue interventionism in the political realm. . . .[20]

In their origins, the guerrillas are nothing but the irrepressible cry of a whole people that has become conscious of its situation and seeks a way to break the molds that imprison it.[21]

In their theological-political discourse, the bishops stressed the need for social justice, yet repeatedly stated that it was not their role to offer specific sociopolitical solutions.

We talk about changes and about the transformation of structures, but which are the solutions or ways proposed by the church? . . . The church does not offer solutions or practical proposals for concrete situations. . . . The mission of the pastors of the church is to offer the principles that derive from its faith, thus enlightening the human roads . . . and thus discerning the deviations that threaten such roads. Guided by that faith it is the task of the men who have in their hands the construction of their societies to explore the specific roads.[22]

Among the guidelines for achieving a just society, the bishops stressed the freedom to organize intermediate associations— trade unions, cooperatives, base communities, and so on; plurality of political choices; the duty of citizens to participate in the political process; the right to dissent; and the subordination of political parties to the rights of men.

In another pastoral letter, in August 1974, the bishops again defend their right to speak out on sociopolitical matters:

It is perverse and twisted to attempt to exclude [the church] from its participation in public life. . . . Action in behalf of justice and participation in the transformation of the world are clearly presented to us as one of the constitutive dimensions of preaching the gospel.[23]

The bishops criticized the attempt of any political party to monopolize power and deprive other political parties of their right to compete. This was a clear reference to Somoza, but also to the Leninist thesis of the Marxist party as the only vanguard of the people. The bishops also questioned elections without the necessary safeguards, which Somoza was trying to impose on Nicaragua as a way to legitimize himself:

> The vote . . . to be valid . . . requires the capacity to discern and freedom. Nobody can be forced to vote against his conscience. . . . If the vote must obey an order . . . it simply does not elect.[24]

The bishops further strained relations with the Somoza government after the 1974 elections, when Archbishop Obando refused to attend Somoza's inauguration ceremonies.

In 1977, as the Somoza regime launched an antiguerrilla campaign in the countryside, the bishops issued a communique that shook the regime.[25] Among its denunciations, it referred to the "state of terror that forces numerous peasants to desperately flee from their own homes and farms in the mountains of Zelaya, Matagalpa, and the Segovias."[26] The document also denounced government investigations "against citizens considered to be suspicious, using inhuman and humilating methods from torture to rape, and even resorting to summary executions."[27] Another issue the bishops addressed was the "accumulation of wealth and lands in the hands of a few."[28]

They also gave special attention to the many instances of harassment of religious personnel by government troops:

> In some places in the mountains of Zelaya and Matagalpa, army patrols have turned Catholic chapels into military barracks. Some Catholics, Delegates of the Word [lay leaders involved in evangelization], have been pressured into ceasing their collaboration with missioner priests. There are some cases in which Delegates of the Word have been captured by members of the army—some of them being tortured and some of them disappearing.[29]

(Church leaders were indeed being harassed and even physically attacked. For instance, in December 1977 a Jesuit priest, Fr. Pedro Miguel, was assaulted by a Somocista mob in his Managua parish. The archdiocese issued a statement, signed by spokesman Fr. Bismarck Carballo, excommunicating the aggressors.)

In addition to a concern for the overall political situation, the progressive leaders in the Catholic hierarchy worked to strengthen the spiritual life of church members. Archbishop Obando, in particular, was a strong pastoral leader, very much absorbed with ministering to his largely peasant flock. The vigorous lay conversion movements that existed in the country—the charismatic renewal, the Cursillo movement, the neocatechumenal movement, the Delegates of the Word, and so on—looked to Archbishop Obando as their spiritual leader. It was precisely because he was fundamentally a spiritual leader rather than a politician that the archbishop remained a force for peace in the country and was able to issue credible appeals for national reconciliation and dialogue, both to the Nicaraguan government and to the Sandinista guerrillas.

I joined Archbishop Obando in his effort when he organized a committee in 1978 called the Committee for Patriotic Reflection. He invited representatives from every political and civic sector to search for an end to the increasingly bloody civil war. On August 4, 1978, he issued a pastoral letter—in the drafting of which I participated—in which he publicly called on Somoza to consider resigning the presidency as a way to national peace. His call for dialogue between the government and the guerrillas was rejected by both.

On June 2, 1979, in the climax of the war, the Nicaraguan bishops conference, at the initiative of the bishop of Leon, Salazar y Espinoza, issued its last pastoral letter under the Somoza regime. It regretted the spiraling violence in which the country was caught up, but warned that "It cannot deny the moral . . . legitimacy [of revolutionary insurrections] in the case of evident and prolonged tyranny that gravely threatens the fundamental rights of the person and the common good of the country."[30]

The bishops welcomed the triumph of the revolution. They offered a celebration mass attended by the national directorate of the FSLN and one of the largest crowds ever assembled in the country's history.

The bishops' first postrevolution pastoral letter was issued on July 31, 1979. Its opening paragraph announced a new era: "We have the utmost duty of building it in a spirit of brotherhood and of reaffirming ourselves as a people characterized by faith and the spirit of freedom."[31] The pastoral letter included a statement thanking the "brother countries who have helped us in our liberation,"[32] and it expressed the bishops' confidence "in the high ideals that have encouraged our liberation movement."[33] But the letter also expressed the hierarchy's concern for safeguarding the church's independence: "As a church we must remain free . . . before any system, to opt always for man, for the oppressed, and for man's right to organize his own society."[34]

The bishops also stressed the need for God's help in the rebuilding process: "God is not only the source of life; he is also the source of a right and just social order. When this source is denied, a system of power takes its place and erects itself as an 'absolute.' " They quoted Psalm 127:1—"Unless the Lord builds the house, they labor in vain who build it."[35]

Two and a half months later, on November 17, 1979, the bishops issued their most comprehensive document on the position of Catholics in the new revolutionary period. They greeted the end of the civil war as an "exceptional opportunity for announcing and bearing witness to God's kingdom" and called on the Nicaraguan Catholic Church to face the future with confidence and determination:

> If through fear and mistrust, through the insecurity of some in the face of radical social change, or through the desire to defend personal interests, we neglect this crucial opportunity to commit ourselves to the poor . . . we would be in serious violation of the gospel's teaching.[36]

The document offered some guidelines which the bishops believed the revolution ought to follow.

> Our commitment to the revolutionary process cannot mean naiveté or blind enthusiasm, much less the creation of a new idol before which there is a duty to bow down unconditionally.
> We are asked what we think of socialism. . . . If it means, as it should, that the interests of the majority of Nicaraguans are paramount, and if it includes a model of an economic system planned with national interests in mind that is in solidarity with and provides for increased participation of the people . . . we deem it just. . . . If socialism implies that power is exercised from the viewpoint of the great majority and that it is increasingly shared by the people . . . again, it will find . . . only our encouragement and support.[37]

The bishops were thus favoring what could be called democratic socialism, a system geared to satisfying the needs of the people while respecting basic freedoms and a representative political process. The bishops rejected totalitarian socialism:

> For if . . . socialism gets adulterated, robbing . . . the people of their call to be free protagonists of history; if it attempts to blindly yoke

the people to the manipulation and dictates of those who would then arbitrarily exercise power, such false socialism we could not accept. [It would be] equally unacceptable to deny parents the right to educate their children according to their convictions. . . .[38]

The bishops ended the document's section on socialism with a statement that summarized their hopes regarding the new phase of history that Nicaragua was entering into:

> We also have confidence that the revolutionary process will be something original, creative, deeply national, and in no way imitative, because what we seek, together with the Nicaraguan majority, is a process that will result in a society completely and truly Nicaraguan, one that is neither capitalist, nor dependent, nor totalitarian.[39]

The Revolutionary Christians

The third trend among Christians in Nicaragua as they confronted the political situation was the approach of the radical, revolutionary Christians. As we have seen in the first section of this book, these Christians played an important role in the Sandinistas' coming to power and in the Sandinista government's consolidation of power and dealings with the churches.

The revolutionary Christians were an outgrowth of a student-based community founded by Fr. Uriel Molina in 1972, and were influenced by the early preaching of the Cardenal priest-brothers, Ernesto and Fernando. As stated before, throughout the period predating the revolutionary victory of 1979, the revolutionary Christians were a small, mainly middle- and upper-class elite, which was largely absorbed by the FSLN. Some revolutionary Christians also emerged from within the ranks of the Protestant churches, although, as one of their leaders has acknowledged, they remained a tiny faction for most of the seventies.[40]

The Nicaraguan revolutionary Christians claimed to be inspired by a Latin American theological movement known as liberation theology, particularly as that theology was taught by men such as Gustavo Gutiérrez, Jon Sobrino, Juan Luis Segundo, José Miguez Bonino, Leonardo Boff, and others. The views of these theologians and their Nicaraguan disciples differ in key regards from the views of the progressive Christians discussed above. First, the radical Christians place a much greater emphasis on the duty of political involvement. Whereas for the Catholic bishops involvement in the political process was *an* inescapable duty of the Christian citizen, for the revolutionary liberation theologians it was *the* Christian duty. "Liberation theology," according to Gustavo Gutiérrez, a seminal thinker in the development of liberation theology in Latin America, "involves a total immersion in the political process of revolution."[41]

This view is rooted in the belief that sin is embodied in specific social structures—usually identified as capitalism—and, therefore, liberation from sin demands a liberation of a political nature. On this issue, liberation theologians go beyond the progressive Christians and the mainstream of Catholic social thought. They insist that "doing theology" in the midst of a particular political situation ought to lead theologians to make specific choices for specific political forces. Which forces? The answer is forces representing the oppressed, the poor, the proletariat. The forces representing the poor are not abstractions, but concrete political parties and movements.

A Protestant liberation theologian, José Miguez Bonino, expresses this conviction in the following terms: "The theologian cannot remain any more above the realm of political options. . . . Latin American theology becomes therefore a militant theology—a partisan theology, perhaps."[42] Bonino thus praises liberation theologians such as Gutierrez, Assman, and Segundo for attacking the attempts "of such theologians as Kung, Metz, or Moltmann [European theologians] to remain at a nonpartisan level."[43]

In contrast, the Nicaraguan bishops had reiterated that the church itself was not to baptize partisan political options nor, least of all, to absolutize any particular option as the unique road to social liberation. Rather, they taught that the role of reflection and teaching by church leaders is to provide lay people with criteria which will equip them to make political choices in light of their faith.

Second, the liberation theology advocated by the revolutionary Christians in Nicaragua diverged from the views of the progressive Christians in regard to the use of Marxist social analysis. Whereas the progressives denied Marxism the status of a science and tended to be critical of its assumptions, most, if not all, the liberation theologians considered it to provide the key to understanding the Latin American situation.

Their acceptance of Marxist social analysis is implicit in their writings, and often even explicitly stated. An early advocate of liberation theology and lecturer in Nicaragua, the Italian Giulio Girardi, said that the incorporation of scientific Marxist analysis had been a "qualitative leap" for Christians. For Bonino, it has been "decisive for the theological task."[44] To understand the economic and political problems of Latin America, the liberation theologians adopted Marxist dependency theory, which attributes the continent's oppression and underdevelopment to a dependence on the capitalist nations. To understand social dynamics and conflicts, they adopted the Marxist theory of class struggle, which sees the world as the battleground of two irreconcilable forces that have been engaged in an agelong struggle: the oppressors and the oppressed. Final liberation will only come when the latter take power and abolish the root of all oppressions: the private ownership of the means of production.

Perhaps the clearest statements in support of this Marxist view of the world (even according to Bonino) are to be found in the writings of pioneer liberation theologian Gustavo Gutiérrez. The following are samples from a single essay:

> Only a class-based analysis will enable us to see what is really involved in the opposition between oppressed countries on the one hand and dominant peoples on the other. . . .
>
> [The] people must come to power if society is to be truly free and egalitarian. In such a society private ownership of the means of production will be eliminated because it enables a few to expropriate the fruits of labor . . . generates class divisions in society, and permits one class to be exploited by another. . . .
>
> Only by eliminating private ownership of the wealth created by human labor will we be able to lay the foundations for a more just society. That is why efforts to project a new society in Latin America are moving more and more toward socialism.[45]

As these statements by Gutiérrez suggest, these liberation theologians do not use Marxist social theory merely as a method, as they sometimes claim. Rather they adopt it as an ideology. Nowhere in their writings do they question its empirical validity.

The use of Marxist analysis characterized the work of the Nicaraguan revolutionary Christians from the start. "We had study sessions to analyze the Nicaraguan reality making use of the Marxist method," recalled Fr. Uriel Molina.[46] In the Solentiname community of Fr. Ernesto Cardenal, standard study texts in addition to the Bible were the speeches of Fidel Castro and the diary of Che Guevara.[47]

As a result of this analysis, the revolutionary Christians came to believe in revolutionary socialism as the one system capable of creating the conditions for the definitive end of oppression and injustice. In contrast with the bishops and the other progressive Christians, the revolutionary Christians usually looked to Cuba as an inspiring model of social change and did not reject the totalitarian features of Marxist governments. Evil, for them, was in capitalism; revolutionary socialism was the hope of the future. When questioned about the persecution of Christians in Communist countries, they contended that such an outcome was not inherent in Marxism; it was the result of Christian reactions.

As the political situation in Nicaragua deteriorated after the 1978 murder of Pedro J. Chamorro, and as the FSLN emerged as a powerful military force, a superficial unity was created between the revolutionary and progressive Christians. The mounting antagonism toward the Somoza regime fueled this convergence. Common opposition to Somoza drew many diverse elements together and tended to blur other fundamental issues. The Sandinistas, leaders of the opposition, came to be viewed by many as the bold heroes willing to fight corruption with their lives. The attacks of Somoza against communism, the guerrillas, and Cuba helped to make all of these look more benign.

Confusion was also spawned by a lack of clarity about Christian concepts that were being applied to the anti-Somoza effort. Terms such as the "option for the poor," widely used by both progressive and revolutionary Christians, were seldom defined with any precision. While the broad alliances against the dictatorship prevailed, the call to "opt for the poor" was often simply equated with joining the anti-Somoza struggle.

As we have seen, the FSLN meanwhile gained prestige by profiling itself as being in harmony with religion. They lauded the bishops' stands and avoided antagonizing the most influential religious groups. Although there was a struggle going on between the Catholic hierarchy and some of the most radicalized priests and theologians, who demanded that the bishops give all-out support to the FSLN and the armed insurrection, this dispute was not publicly aired before July 1979.

The alliance of anti-Somoza elements with fundamentally dissimilar views and the blurring of their mutual opposition changed once the revolution triumphed. The full radicality of the revolutionary Christians' beliefs began to emerge. Riding on the euphoria produced by the July 1979 victory, the most celebrated Latin American liberation theologians poured into Nicaragua to give conferences and seminars. Among them were Gustavo Gutiérrez, Enrique Dussell, Jon Sobrino, Hugo Assman, and Pablo Richard. Many other theologians of the same convictions moved permanently to the country. They came to staff and strengthen the Catholic, Protestant, and ecumenical centers which either sympathized with liberation theology or were beginning to do so. Among these centers was the Centro Antonio Valdivieso (CAV), officially "ecumenical," directed by Fr. Uriel Molina and by a newly-arrived Spanish theologian, Fr. Teófilo Cabestrero; the Instituto Histórico Centroamericano (IHCA), led by two Jesuit priests, Alvaro Arguello from Nicaragua, and Juan Hernández Pico, another newly-arrived theologian from Spain (IHCA also supervised the work of another Jesuit organization, the "Instituto Juan XXIII"); the Centro de Promoción Agraria (CEPA), Jesuit; and the Eje Ecuménico MEC-CELADEC (the "Ecumenical Axis"), linked with the World Council of Churches. A large evangelical Protestant organization, the Centro de Promoción y Desarrollo (CEPAD), also followed this path. CEPAD was an umbrella organization for the relief activities of several Protestant denominations and had been actively involved in development programs since the 1972 Managua earthquake. Although its leaders Gustavo Parajón, Benjamin Cortés, and Sixto Ulloa had no record of public opposition to the Somoza regime, after the revolution they suddenly became actively involved in the theological struggle, taking sides with the liberation theologians and the Sandinistas.

ABSOLUTE COMMITMENT TO THE REVOLUTION

Central to the teachings of these centers and of those Christians subscribing to their views was the contention that in order to be a good Christian, one had to be committed to the Sandinista revolution. Although the emphasis of this point varied among its proponents, it was constantly expressed in one way or another, sometimes very explicitly. The claim was rooted in Gutiérrez's— and other liberation theologians'—view that without concrete political commitment, love for the poor was abstract and "historically uneffective."

The revolutionary Christians active in Nicaragua translated this commitment to political action on behalf of the poor into a commitment to the Sandinista revolution and, after the victory of the revolution, commitment to the FSLN rather than to any of the other political parties.

The equation of Christian social concern and support of the FSLN was clearly expressed in a document of March 20, 1980, endorsed by a majority of the individual leaders and organizations of the revolutionary Christians.

> The only way to love God, whom we do not see, is by contributing to the advancement of this revolutionary process in the most sensible and radical way possible. Only then shall we be loving our brothers, whom we do see. Therefore, we say that to be a Christian is to be a revolutionary.[48]

A few lines later they add:

> Preference for and solidarity with the poor in Nicaragua today means to work under the guidance of the Sandinista Front.[49]

This equation perfectly coincided with the claim advanced by the Sandinistas themselves. It meant, in effect, that one's identity as a Christian depended on one's particular political commitments.

Many observers outside Nicaragua have been led to believe that the revolutionary Christians were only claiming that being a Christian ought not to be an obstacle to supporting the revolution; in other words, that the revolutionary Christians were claiming that cooperation with the FSLN should not be ruled out *a priori*. Sandinista slogans such as "There is no contradiction between Christianity and revolution" fostered this impression. But what many of the revolutionary Christians in Nicaragua were actually declaring was not only the possibility of Christians working with Marxist revolutionaries, but the *duty* of doing so. They have asserted that there is *no other way* to be a Christian in Nicaragua than by supporting the Sandinista revolution and party.

The revolutionary Christians explicitly rejected the idea of a plurality of political options:

> Christians should realize very clearly that they do not have more than two alternatives left: either they are with the revolutionary pro-

cess . . . or else they are unavoidably against such a process, regardless of how holy and humanitarian their intentions may be.[50]

Similar statements are found in Margaret Randall's interviews with some of the first Nicaraguan revolutionary Christians. For example:

> For me there is no Christian who is not a revolutionary. . . . If somebody tells me that some priest is a good Christian and that he does not love the revolution and does not understand it, for me he is not a Christian; he is the opposite.[51]

Amanecer, the magazine of Centro Antonio Valdivieso, edited by theologian Fr. Teófilo Cabestrero, editorialized on the church's duty toward the revolution in the following terms:

> In Nicaragua the revolutionary process asks the church to make its option for the poor concrete. Here one either choses for the poor people (supporting the radical changes of the revolution), or for the entrepreneurial class, supporting (either directly or indirectly) its political project.[52]

Gustavo Gutiérrez put it this way: "To opt for the poor is to opt for one social class over against another."[53]

For liberation theologians, as for the Sandinistas, the people are not the population as such but only those individuals, regardless of class affiliation, with revolutionary consciousness. For liberation theologian Hugo Assman, who has traveled to Nicaragua to speak, those who really represent the poor, and thereby understand the Word of God, are those "who fight for their liberation," "the ones who try to break their chains."[54] The Christians for Socialism movement, in which Fr. Uriel Molina had experienced his most decisive conversion to radical politics, had also expressed this view. People are "not only those who suffer acute exploitation directly or indirectly, but all others who place themselves at the service of their struggle."[55]

Thus the revolution and the poor—and by implication the FSLN—were treated as synonymous: "To defend the lives of the poor was to defend the revolution."[56] If the FSLN represented the revolution, to defend the revolution was to defend the FSLN. Individuals and churches could not remain neutral in regard to this duty:

The independence of the church is not neutrality. (If there were such a thing as neutrality, a neutral church would sin against God for abandoning the poor. . . .) Gospel freedom is the freedom to support the poor majorities.[57]

In another issue of *Amanecer,* Cabestrero clarified the church's duty in the revolutionary process. A church true to the gospel "would act in a way that would result in advancing the revolution, not denigrating it, affirming it in its popular values and not weakening it in its limitations; attracting in its behalf international solidarity and not suspicion, accusations, and aggression." This church, according to Cabestrero, "would not need to act outside or aside from the revolution."[58]

Cabestrero's remark echoes Tomás Borge's definition of freedom in Sandinista Nicaragua: "Pluralism within the revolution, but not outside or against it; freedom to further the revolutionary process, not to destabilize it."

Another editorial of *Amanecer* said that "Christian discernment is only prophetic and faithful to Jesus Christ if it is done from a sincere identification with the poor majorities. . . . In Nicaragua, the historical project of the poor majorities is the [Sandinista] people's revolution."[59] Participation in the revolution alongside the FSLN was thus a crucial responsibility no Christian could refuse.

This was the strongest and most consistently reiterated message of the revolutionary Christians in Nicaragua. From the Jesuit-run Instituto Histórico Centroamericano to the evangelical Protestant CEPAD, all shared this outlook. CEPAD's branch in Chontales (south-central Nicaragua) issued a communique in August 1982 informing Christians that "we have the duty to affiliate ourselves to the civil defense, to the revolutionary watch [espionage of the CDS's], to the productive cultural, social, and political tasks."[60] Benjamin Cortés, one of the leaders of CEPAD, said in late 1982 that "it is required that we as Christians understand that biblical faith is inseparable from [political] militancy."[61] CEPAD's international affairs director, Sixto Ulloa, took a practical step in this direction by affiliating himself to the FSLN and running on the Sandinista ticket in the 1984 elections.

If Christians were to support the FSLN, what kind of support should that be? Commitment to the FSLN must be absolute: "There is no other way for a Christian to show his faith in the kingdom than by committing himself absolutely to a contingent project," wrote Fr. Juan Hernández Pico, S.J., of the Instituto Histórico Centroamericano.[62]

This view was another outgrowth of the concept of the revolutionary party as the source of objectivity and truth. Christians must be absolutely committed to the truth; if the truth is embodied in a "contingent project"—the revolution as guided by the party—then Christians must be absolutely committed to it. In fact, this primary commitment to revolution ought to lead Christians to reassess the other aspects of their faith. According to Pablo Richard, a Chilean theologian and former Catholic priest who made Costa Rica and Nicaragua his base: "It is from a revolutionary commitment, which is assumed by itself, by its own rationality, that we want to rethink our faith."[63]

Everything was thus judged on the basis of whether it supported the revolution or not. A Catholic mass was good if it was a revolutionary mass. A priest or minister was a good priest or minister if he was revolutionary.

FOLLOWING REVOLUTIONARY PREMISES TO THEIR CONCLUSIONS

The setting up of the revolution as an absolute naturally affected every aspect of Christian life, including worship. Red and black banners (the FSLN colors) and posters of the FSLN began to appear in some Catholic churches, and new prayers were sung, using the words of the "Nicaraguan Peasant Mass," a collection of songs composed by FSLN militant Carlos Mejía Godoy. One of the prayers petitions Christ to stand in solidarity with the oppressed people, but not with the oppressing class. In another song, "Jesus Has Been Born in Palacagüina" (a peasant town of northern Nicaragua), we hear that Mary is thinking about her son's future as a carpenter, while the child Jesus is thinking that when he grows up he will be a guerrilla fighter. The process whereby the Christian meaning of religious symbols is replaced with political meanings is graphically illustrated by the cover of a book published by IHCA. Entitled *Christian Faith and Sandinista Revolution in Nicaragua*, the cover shows the image of Jesus Christ crucified superimposed on a larger image of a guerrilla fighter, his arms raised and brandishing a rifle: Jesus becomes incarnate in twentieth-century Latin America as a revolutionary. Some priests went even further and staged revolutionary baptismal ceremonies. Margaret Randall, in her book on Christians in the revolution, provides a glimpse of one of these involving Fr. Ernesto Cardenal:

> Some days later I happened to witness a baptism celebrated by one of the four priests [holding government office]. "Now we know," he said, "that original sin is the division of society into classes. . . . I command you, spirit of egoism, of capitalism, of Somocismo, to come out of this child." And while he poured the water on the forehead of the baby he ended with, "Now I give you your revolutionary membership."[64]

Not all cases, of course, were as extreme as this one. But the point is that the revolutionary Christians were putting into practice the FSLN's call to reinvest religious symbols and celebrations with new, revolutionary meanings. And they were doing so far more effectively than the Sandinistas could possibly have done themselves. In the liberation theology being preached in the country, the revolutionary Christians identified sin with capitalism; Satan with the bourgeoisie and U.S. imperialism; salvation, or deliverance from sin, with revolution; the Messiah—Jesus being a revolutionary zealot—with the vanguard, or revolutionary party; the kingdom of God with revolutionary socialism. All this was the Marxist-Leninist world view and eschatology; only the terms changed.

The theological centers promoting the new revolutionary theology were also explicit, especially during the first years after the revolution, in their effort to convince Christians of the virtues of Marxism-Leninism. IHCA, for instance, circulated pamphlets persuading Christians not to be afraid of communism and portraying Fidel Castro as a friend of Christianity.[65] A key contention was that Christians' traditional reluctance to accept communism was the product of decades of anti-communist, imperialist propaganda. Christians, in fact, had nothing to fear from communism, for both shared the same end: justice for the oppressed.

CEPAD, the evangelical Protestant center, in conjunction with two other revolutionary Christian organizations, published a popularly written book illustrated with cartoons in which Marx is praised and portrayed as a friend of Christians. It also presented the Cuban revolution as a model for Latin America.[66]

Ernesto Cardenal, as usual less restrained than his colleagues, openly claimed to be a Marxist Christian and stated:

Our only solution is Marxism. It is the only possible way to achieve freedom. I do not see any other course we can take, if the promises of history and of the gospel are going to be true. . . . For me the revolution and the kingdom of heaven, mentioned in the gospel, are the same thing. A Christian should embrace Marxism if he wants to be with God and all men.[67]

Fr. Miguel D'Escoto expressed the following in *Christianity and Crisis:*

About Marxism, I think of it as being one of the greatest blessings on the church. It has been the divine whip to bring it back. I know people with other experience from Western Europe or Poland or wherever; they speak from their perspective. Let me speak from my perspective, that leftist revolutions have never persecuted Christians for being faithful to the gospel, that it is the rightist governments, which sometimes are so pleasing to many of our distinguished bepurpled brothers, that are the ones who persecute the authentic church.[68]

The Baptist leader and head of the Ecumenical Axis (Eje Ecuménico MEC-CELADEC), José M. Torres, has expressed with gratitude how he came to learn about Marx's dialectical materialism in Cuba, where he was the student of Humberto Ortega.[69] Benjamín Cortés, of CEPAD, recalled how "It was then found that Marxism provided a scientific method to analyze the social, economic, and political problems."[70]

When the revolutionary Christians in Nicaragua realized that their frankness about Marxism made them vulnerable to charges of being Communist-infiltrated and Communist-inspired, they, like the FSLN earlier, adopted a more careful approach in their public statements. Marxism, and particularly its dogma of class struggle, however, continued to be the lens through which the revolutionary Christians saw reality. In fact, all of their insistence that Christians should side with the oppressed (the FSLN) and the accompanying secularizing of religious symbols and celebrations were rooted in a Marxist view of the world, legitimized with numerous Biblical quotations.

A seemingly inescapable conclusion of this view is that if justice and peace can only be achieved by the destruction of class division, and the destruction of class division is the result of the proletarian class rising against the bourgeoisie, then there is no need of religion; the work of Marxist revolutionaries is sufficient. Many statements, and later actions, of the revolutionary Christians showed that they did not flinch from following the logic of their position to its conclusion.

Predictably, they did not hold religious belief to be of key significance. What really mattered was commitment to revolutionary action. "Faith Without Revolution Is Dead," read a poster of the revolutionary Christians. In a statement to the press, in 1980, Fr. Miguel D'Escoto said:

> There are people who call themselves atheists. From the Christian perspective, in fact, this does not have great importance. The important thing is the behavior of people; it is the practice, not the theory.

Recalling his early participation with the revolutionary Christian movement, Commander Alvaro Baltodano, in charge of military education in the Sandinista army, said:

> Whether there was God or no God, was not the concern. Our concern was our current political practice. . . . For us to be Christians was to be with the poorest . . . and, at that time, it was to work with the Sandinista Front.[71]

This submission of belief to political action had been made explicitly in the literature of the founding fathers of liberation theology. They state clearly that orthopraxis, that is, right practice, is fundamentally more important than orthodoxy, or right belief (for example, Bonino and Gutiérrez). Faith, for liberation theologian Raul Vidales,

> entails a discovery of the world of the "other" in the light of the new scientific line of reasoning [Marxist social analysis] and also an option for their cause. . . . It means that the believer has made the basic option of entering into the conflict-ridden world of the exploited [political commitment to revolution].[72]

To say that faith, in this sense, leads to commitment to revolution, does not reflect the full meaning liberation theologians had in mind. What they implicitly were stating is that faith *was* commitment to revolution. A Christian who did not commit himself to revolution (variously expressed as the poor, the oppressed, the "other," etc.) was lacking something fundamental, while a Marxist revolutionary, an acknowledged atheist, was not. In some ways he could even be regarded as a "Christian incognito," an unconscious Christian.

As Marxist revolutionaries were, in this approach, regarded as unconscious Christians, nonrevolutionary Christians were regarded as unconscious atheists. The distinguishing factor was a person's relation to revolution. Those committed to it were believers, in deed if not in words; those who were not committed to it were atheists by their deeds. The atheism inherent in Marxism was of no concern. "The only atheism of which we should be afraid," stated Fr. Donald Mendoza in Nicaragua, "is the one which involves domination and injustice"[73]—which, in this view, only occur in capitalist countries.

The proponents of these views emphatically insisted that they were still Christians. When questioned, they would assert their belief in God, Christ, the resurrection, and so on. The problem, however, was how they understood these terms. And as they have redefined these realities in political terms, Christianity has gradually become almost superfluous to them. "Jesus Christ was not enough," claimed Fr. Juan H. Pico, S.J., of IHCA, because Christianity needs a revolutionary theory and praxis in order to carry out its mission in the world.[74] On the practical level, one revolutionary Christian drew out the implications of the secondary nature of Christianity: "I consider myself a Christian, but I am clear that if at some point in time I would have to choose between religion and the revolution, I am with the revolution."[75] Not all, of course, would speak so candidly, nor would all share this view. The majority would assert that there could not be contradiction between God and revolution, for one implies the other.

These views inevitably affected the way the revolutionary Christian centers practiced evangelization. As I pointed out in the first section, in their abundant literature the emphasis is never on the preaching of Jesus Christ or the incorporation of people into the body of Christ, the church. They do not preach to Marxists in order to attract them to Christ, but to Christians in order to draw them to Marx. The conversion of Christians to Marxism-Sandinismo is the main thrust of their evangelistic effort. Their recurrent appeal is: join the revolution! support the FSLN! and, at times, come to Marx! The paradox is that the ones who need conversion are the Christians. The revolutionaries, particularly the Sandinista commanders, do not.

It could even be said that the theological perspective adopted by the revolutionary Christians led them to an inferiority complex toward the Sandinista leaders. Since the Sandinistas were the most revolutionary, they were by definition the best Christians. Fr. Amando López, S.J., reflected this mentality when he told the commanders at a joint meeting of Christian leaders and Sandinista commanders:

> If I were to put it in concrete terms, what Christians would expect from the FSLN, I would say—and not as a literary expression—what Christians expect from the FSLN is that they make us Christians.[76]

This subservient mentality toward the FSLN and its leaders, rooted in the revolutionary Christians' theology, led them to relinquish any claims to offer leadership, or even an agenda of their own. They did not, as the progressive Christians had done through the Catholic bishops, provide a set of guidelines for structuring a more humane social and political order.

In this regard, they fell prey to one of the weaknesses of Latin American liberation theology: the absence of an agenda for the day after revolution. The revolutionary Christians' talk was often appealing, but almost always abstract: "solidarity with the oppressed," "the historical effectiveness of love," and so on. When it came to specific guidelines or policies for how to rescue the poor from oppression, however, all the revolutionary Christians did was to support the policies put forward by the FSLN. They did not proffer principles for just political action such as, for example, the rights and responsibilities of private property ownership, or the desirability of structuring society in ways that leave as much responsibility as possible with smaller units in society rather than centering all decision-making at the level of the national government—principles of Catholic social teaching promoted by the progressive Catholics. The radical Christians did not offer guidelines for how to structure a government that would truly be of the people and not just another dictatorship. Rather, they assumed, as Marxist theory suggests, that the overthrow of the bourgeoisie and the elimination of private ownership of the means of production would somehow usher in an end to oppression.

Consciously or unconsciously the revolutionary Christians looked to the FSLN as the vanguard of the poor and the gatekeepers of an earthly kingdom:

> [The revolution] was a project of the people, and we wanted to integrate ourselves into this process . . . but not with the pretense of

being the vanguard. It is the party which leads the proletariat and takes it to the conquest of power, and this is not the role of the church.[77]

The problem with this approach is not that the church does not spearhead social and political change; that is not her role. The problem is that the church then fails to fulfill its role of providing principles for a just ordering of society, drawn from the Christian revelation, which can be used to guide and evaluate efforts of social change.

NOTES

1. Ron Sider, mimeographed letter to Congress and religious leaders, 1983.

2. *Christianity Today,* April 8, 1983, p. 34.

3. Cardinal Karol Wojtyla, quoted in *L'Osservatore Romano,* English edition, November 9, 1978.

4. Ministry of Education, *El Amanecer del Pueblo,* Managua, 1980, Lesson 22.

5. Junta de Gobierno, "Mensaje de Año Nuevo," *Barricada,* January 1, 1981, p. 1.

6. FSLN National Directorate, *op. cit.,* "Documento de las 72 Horas," p. 21.

. 7. Tomás Borge, speech at a meeting of Central and South American religious organizations, in *Amanecer,* No. 7-8, March-April 1982, Managua, p. 9.

8. Jaime Wheelock, *FSLN es la Organizatión de los Trabajadores,* p. 13.

9. Batasch, *Le Monde Diplomatique,* October 22, 1981.

10. FSLN, "Comunicado de la Dirección Nacional del FSLN sobre la Religión," in *Nicarauac,* No. 5 [April-June 1981], p. 93.

11. Nicaraguan Bishops Conference, "Sobre el Deber del Testimonio y de la Acción Cristiana en la Orden Político," Managua: Episcopal Conference, 1971.

12. *Ibid.,* p. 4.

13. *Ibid.*

14. *Ibid.,* p. 7.

15. *Ibid.,* p. 10.

16. *Ibid.*, p. 21.

17. *Ibid.*, p. 20.

18. Nicaraguan Bishops Conference, "Sobre los Principios que Rigen la Actividad Política de Toda la Iglesia como Tal," Managua: Episcopal Conference, March 19, 1972.

19. *Ibid.*, p. 5.

20. *Ibid.*, p. 10.

21. *Ibid.*, pp. 11, 12.

22. *Ibid.*, p. 12.

23. Nicaraguan Bishops Conference, "El Hombre, La Iglesia, y La Sociedad, August 6, 1974, published in *La Prensa*, August 18, 1974, p. 7.

24. *Ibid.*

25. Nicaraguan Bishops Conference, "Renovando la Esperanza Cristiana al Iniciarse el Año de 1977," Managua: Episcopal Conference, January 8, 1977.

26. *Ibid.*, p. 1.

27. *Ibid.*, p. 2.

28. *Ibid.*

29. *Ibid.*, p. 3.

30. Nicaraguan Bishops Conference, "Mensaje al Pueblo Nicaragüense," Managua: Episcopal Conference, June 2, 1979, p. 2.

31. Nicaraguan Bishops Conference, "Mensaje de la Conferencia Episcopal al Pueblo Católico y a Todos los Nicaragüenses," Managua: Episcopal Conference, July 31, 1979, p. 1.

32. *Ibid.*, p. 2.

33. *Ibid.*, p. 3.

34. *Ibid.*

35. *Ibid.*, p. 2.

36. Nicaraguan Bishops Conference, "Compromiso Cristiano para una Nicaragua Nueva," Managua: Episcopal Conference, November 17, 1979, p. 12.

37. *Ibid.*, p. 7.

38. *Ibid.*, p. 8.

39. *Ibid.*, p. 9.

40. José Miguel Torres, "Cristianismo Protestante en la Revolución Sandinista," in *Nicarauac*, No. 5, April-June 1981, Managua, pp. 39-47.

41. Gustavo Gutiérrez, "Liberation Praxis and Christian Faith," in *Frontiers of Theology in Latin America,* Rosino Gibellini, ed. (Maryknoll, N.Y.: Orbis Books, 1979), p. 24.

42. Bonino, *Doing Theology in a Revolutionary Situation* (Philadelphia: Fortress Press, 1976), p. 80.

43. *Ibid.*

44. *Ibid.,* p. 71.

45. Gutiérrez, *op. cit.,* "Liberation Praxis and Christian Faith," pp. 17,1-2,18.

46. Molina in "El Sendero de una Experiencia," *Nicarauac,* No. 5, April-June 1981, Managua, p. 23.

47. Reported by Teresa Builes in *op. cit.,* Randall, p. 91.

48. *Los Cristianos Estan con la Revolución,* Costa Rica: Departamento Ecuménico de Investigaciones, 1980, p. 3.

49. *Ibid.*

50. Fr. Alvaro Arguello, S.J., *Fidel Castro y los Cristianos Revolucionarios,* Rutilio Grande Monographs, Managua: IHCA, undated, p. 5.

51. *Op. cit.,* Randall, p. 129.

52. Cabestrero, "Misión de la Iglesia en un Pueblo en Revolución," *Amanecer,* No. 1, May 1981, p. 13.

53. *Op. cit.,* Gutiérrez, "Liberation Praxis and Christian Faith," p. 9.

54. Quoted by Boaventura Kloppenburg, *Iglesia Popular* (Bogotá: Editorial Paulinas, 1977), p. 35.

55. *Ibid.,* p. 34.

56. Teófilo Cabestrero, "La Defensa la Paz y de la Vida," *Amanecer,* No. 4, December 1981, p. 12.

57. Teófilo Cabestrero, "Misión de la Iglesia en un Pueblo en Revolución," *Amanecer,* No. 1, May 1981, p. 13.

58. Teófilo Cabestrero, "Hacer Más Evangelica Esta Iglesia," *Amanecer,* No. 6, February 1982, p. 11.

59. Editorial, *Amanecer,* No. 5, January 1982, p. 2.

60. "Cristianos Evangélicos con la Revolución," *Barricada,* August 25, 1982, p. 5.

61. Cortés in *Reflexiones sobre Fe y Revolución* (Managua: CEPRI-CEPAD, October 1982), p. 22.

62. Pico in "Para Acercar el Reino: Compromiso Absoluto con un Proyecto Reletivo," *Cristianos Revolucionarios,* No. 3, Managua, 1980, p. 28.

63. Richard, "Volver a Repensar Nuestra Fe," *Cristianos Revolucionarios,* No. 4, Managua, 1980, p. 31.

64. *Op. cit.,* Randall, p. 47.

65. *Socialismo, Marxismo, Communismo! Les Tengo Miedo y Vós?,* Popular Pamphlets, "Gaspar García Laviana," No. 1, Managua: IHCA, undated; and *Fidel Castro y los Cristianos Revolucionarios,* Rutilio Grande Monographs No. 6, Managua: IHCA, undated.

66. *Capitalismo y Socialismo para Principiantes* (Managua: CEPAD/ CONFER/CEBIC, September 1980).

67. Ernesto Cardenal, "El Evangelio Me Hizo Marxista," interview, *Sábado Gráfico,* Madrid, October 1978.

68. Miguel D'Escoto, "Nicaragua and the World," interview, *Christianity and Crisis,* May 12, 1980, p. 144.

69. Torres in *op. cit.,* Randall, p. 189.

70. Cortes in *op. cit., Reflexiones sobre Fe y Revolución,* p. 19.

71. Alvaro Baltodano in *op. cit.,* Randall, p. 211.

72. Raul Vidales, "Methological Issues in Liberation Theology," in *Frontiers,* p. 45.

73. Mendoza, "Qué Reto Presenta a las Iglesias Cristianas el Proceso Revolucionario de Nicaragua?," *Fe Cristiana y Revolucion Sandinista* (Managua: IHCA, 1980), p. 136.

74. Pico in *Cristianos Revolucionarios,* No. 4, Managua, 1980, p. 9.

75. David Chavarria, a former member of Fr. Molina's Christian community, in *op. cit.,* Randall, p. 213.

76. López, *op. cit.,* in *Fe Cristiana y Revolución Sandinista,* p. 347.

77. Pablo Richard, *Cristianos Revolucionarios,* No. 4, Managua, 1980, p. 31.

CHRISTIANS AGAINST CHRISTIANS

The revolutionary Christians in Nicaragua fit the ideology and purpose of the FSLN. They echoed in theological terms the Sandinista contention that true Christians in Nicaragua would unfailingly support the revolutionary process. They provided a theological way to revolutionize the main contents of the Christian faith. They worked hard to dispel the deep-seated fear of communism that so many Nicaraguans felt and to present Marxism as mainly a neutral social science. But their most important service to the Frente was to provide the government with a rationale for bringing the Nicaraguan Christian churches into submission to the state. The government could profile itself as favorable toward religion by maintaining cordial relations with the revolutionary Christians; it would seem to oppose not religion itself, but only religion which was an expression or tool of bourgeois and imperialistic interests.

The revolutionary Christians themselves spearheaded the attacks on the Christians who did not unreservedly support the Sandinista government. The flip side of the revolutionary Christians' call to all Christians to throw their support entirely behind the FSLN was criticism of those unwilling to do so. Having defined the FSLN as the only vanguard of the oppressed, as we have seen, failure to support it fully appeared as the most serious failure to put the gospel into practice. The reluctance of the Nicaraguan bishops and other progressive Christians to follow this interpretation made them the target of increasingly bitter criticism from the revolutionary Christians.

The revolutionary Christians began by lamenting that the bishops were afraid of fulfilling their historical duty and that they were the victims of unreasonable fears of communism. Liberation theologian Jon Sobrino, for example, speaking in Nicaragua, said:

> In the present situation, I have the impression that the church states its problems from its fear of Marxism or the possibility of atheism. Then it calls on God to defend it from this danger. I think that deep down the church is afraid of God.[1]

Other revolutionary Christians charged that the bishops were incoherent, fearful, and indecisive[2] or were victims of an inadequate model of Christianity from which they were not fully liberated.[3] Although many of these theologians had praise for the November 1979 pastoral letter of the bishops welcoming the revolution, many others did not like the bishops' warnings about the danger of idolatry of the state and about totalitarian forms of socialism. They read in these cautions the imprint of "bourgeois, capitalist values."[4]

The revolutionary Christians' initial criticism of the bishops was not provoked by any anti-Sandinista stand of the bishops. It was based on the bishops' lack of an open and explicit acknowledgment of the FSLN as the vanguard of the Nicaraguan people and on the bishops' desire to keep the church above partisan politics. In the view of the revolutionary Christians, there could be no such a thing as a neutral church.

It was not until 1980 that some progressive Christians actually began to voice concerns about Sandinista activity. This took place as the broad alliance of forces that had fought against Somoza began to break apart and as the Sandinistas began to interfere in more direct ways in the life of the churches.

By the middle of 1980, the revolutionary Christians and the Sandinistas were on a collision course with the Christian churches. Their demands for complete submission to the Sandinista party met a Catholic Church which had developed habits of independence during a decade of opposition to the Somoza dictatorship. This church had welcomed the revolution and stated an openness to a socialism that truly was for the people. But it had no intention of relinquishing its freedom to criticize violations of human rights or policies that denied basic Christian principles about man and society. As Archbishop Obando y Bravo had emphasized in his 1980 New Year's message:

A Christian denounces the slaughter of men and women whatever their ethnic character, age, political creed, or condition. Christians denounce torture . . . they denounce all forms of oppression and exploitation of man by man, of man by the state.[5]

The revolutionary Christians and the Sandinistas were not ready to calmly accept a non-Sandinista, non-Marxist church. As was happening in the political realm, any show of independence or criticism of the government was greeted with ever-increasing hostility. "The present circumstances are ones that demand—from the reality of the [revolutionary] process—much more support than criticism," claimed theologian Juan Hernandez Pico, S.J.[6] The revolutionary Christians regarded criticism of the regime as a betrayal of the revolution and an implicit siding with the economic interests of the bourgeoisie.

Another foreign theologian, the Brazilian priest Frei Betto, claimed that

if we [Christians] have a criticism to make of the FSLN, that criticism should be made by our Christian militants inside the FSLN and not by ourselves, members of religious organizations, as if we had the historical privilege of ideological authority.[7]

Betto was advancing the strange proposition that only militants within the FSLN could criticize the FSLN and was expressing the revolutionary Christians' double standard. Under Somoza they had hailed the "prophetic denunciation" of government misdeeds as one of the greatest Christian duties. But now to criticize the regime from outside its own rank and file was an improper, almost sinful thing to do.

The revolutionary Christians refrained from criticizing the government and became apologists for nearly all of its policies, including many of the most controversial ones. The Centro Antonio Valdivieso, for instance, justified the mob attacks of dissidents in March 1981, after the MDN (Movimiento Democrático Nicaragüense) attempted to stage an authorized, indoor meeting. CAV described the attacks as an expression of the poor's anger in the face of provocations from its enemies.[8] A similar rationale was provided by Fr. Fernando Cardenal, S.J., coordinator of the Sandinista youth organization. In April 1981, after Sandinista mobs unleashed a night of terror against several dissidents and their families, an MDN leader who was a former friend of Fr. Cardenal wrote him an open letter in which he protested the horror that he and his family had suffered when mobs surrounded their home at midnight, throwing bombs inside and threatening to burn it down. In his public response, Fr. Cardenal addressed his former friend in these terms:

> Why did those people attack your house? To enable you to answer this question you have to bear in mind that you have identified yourself with the interest of a class—the class which kept these people in misery and exploitation for more than a century. The patience of the people is exhausted. Now it is known who are carrying out a project on behalf of the formerly forgotten and exploited majority and who are only defending their old privileges and interest as an exploiting class. I think it is very dangerous to live in the midst of the people while attacking the interest of that very same people.[9]

His statement reflected the dangerous totalitarian logic which sees in every opponent and dissident an enemy of a sacred cause and which blinds the observer to abuses committed by the power that he supports.

A further example of this attitude was provided by CEPAD, which praised the forceful relocations of the Miskito Indians in 1982, "as a plan to guarantee the right to life of the Miskito people" and did not have a word of criticism of the government's treatment of the Indians.[10]

The revolutionary Christians' uncritical attitude toward the FSLN contrasted with their propensity to openly criticize the Nicaraguan bishops and other independent Christians. They took a criticism-only-for-the-church approach. For example, the Spanish theologian of the Centro Antonio Valdivieso, Fr. Teófilo Cabestrero, after stating that the church ought not to denigrate the revolution but improve it, ought not to isolate the revolution but attract international solidarity in its behalf, turned his attention to church members, such as the bishops, whom he considers not to be taking this approach:

> This [policy of complete support of the FSLN] cannot be understood by any of those members of the church that keep only the name and words of the gospel, but not the spirit given to it by Jesus Christ, because it [the spirit of the gospel] was supplanted by the liberal-bourgeois, capitalist spirit. . . .
> They do not want nor do they believe in the gospel, for the same

reason that they do not want the revolution: they prefer their goods, privileges, and class advantages, which they defend and sanctify with a church which is not evangelical, with a gospel which is not evangelical.[11]

In this regard, the revolutionary Christians followed the FSLN-Marxist approach—critics were all motived by class-based economic interests, that is, by selfishness. Even when their criticisms were mild, critics were considered to be people who had been misled by the shrewd bourgeoisie. The Nicaraguan church, the revolutionary Christians argued, had a "preferential option for the rich;[12] it is impregnated by the values of capitalist, bourgeois society;[13] it is afraid of listening to the Word of God in the present history;[14] it is not willing to listen to God;[15] it has allowed itself to be determined by the criticism of the bourgeoisie.[16]

The Catholic hierarchy was not the only target of these attacks. Some Protestant denominations were also harshly attacked. The Centro Antonio Valdivieso began publishing pamphlets in 1980 that portrayed Protestant missionaries as Uncle Sam's wind-up dolls, sent to Nicaragua in order to destabilize the revolution. Favorite targets for attacks like this were the Seventh-Day Adventists, the Pentecostal churches, and some other smaller evangelical churches. (Another religious group which suffered verbal attacks by revolutionary Christians—and government harassment, such as the seizure of buildings—was the Jehovah's Witnesses.)

The charges against these groups were never substantiated with evidence. The attacks were rather the result of a decision to undermine the smaller and more vulnerable religious organizations, which, in the view of the revolutionary Christians and the Sandinistas, were engaged in a super-spiritualized form of religious life that was not attuned to the political demands of the times. The Sandinistas and the revolutionary Christians were angered, for example, by the Seventh-Day Adventist claim that Jesus would soon return in person. Such preaching was "diversionist"—it drew people's attention away from the revolution.

A RICH CHURCH AND A POOR CHURCH
The revolutionary Christians, with the Sandinistas, began claiming that the church in Nicaragua was divided along class lines.

There was a church of the poor, or "people's church," which represented the interests of the poor, and there was a "bourgeois church," or church of the rich, which represented the interests of the Nicaraguan bourgeoisie. As was the case with the Sandinista ideology, being bourgeious or poor or proletarian was not based on an objective condition, but on a subjective one: the adoption of a revolutionary consciousness. Thus the archbishop of Managua and the other Nicaraguan bishops, together with the bulk of the Nicaraguan-born clergy, who were of mostly humble origins, were considered to be bourgeois. But the Sandinista priests, above all the Cardenal brothers and Fr. Miguel D'Escoto, all from very wealthy backgrounds, were considered "of the poor."

The contrast between the rhetoric of the revolutionary Christians and the facts was further enhanced by the way the advocates of the people's church lived. Many, particularly Fr. D'Escoto and Fr. Ernesto Cardenal, live in luxurious homes (Fr. D'Escoto occupies the former residence of Roberto Incer, who was the president of the Nicaraguan Central Bank under Somoza; it is one of Managua's finest), drive Mercedes Benzs, and otherwise maintain a very expensive lifestyle.

The leaders of the so-called people's church claimed that it was an expression of the yearnings of the poor; that theirs was a church that was born from the Nicaraguan people. The reality is the opposite. The revolutionary Christians are an elite of mostly foreign, middle- and upper-class intellectuals and clergy. Mario Vargas Llosa, the Peruvian novelist, found:

> Its name notwithstanding, the "people's church" is largely composed of members of the religious elite—priests and laymen whose intellectual disquisitions and sociopolitical work lie beyond the scope of most of the Catholic poor.
> The efforts of the leaders of the "people's church" to combine politics and religion have only found a response in the intellectually militant members of the middle class, many of whom are already converts.[17]

The revolutionary Christians did not go to the people to listen to them, but to teach them and raise their consciousness. The matrix for their theology was not Nicaragua's slums or fields, but the classrooms of European and North American universities.

The revolutionary Christians tried to present themselves as

having a large social base in the "base communities"—grass-roots Bible-study and reflection groups, usually of eight to a dozen people each. But the number of Nicaraguan poor involved in base communities sympathetic to the views of the revolutionary Christians have never been more than a tiny percentage of the total Catholic population. In fact, many of the base communities in Nicaragua were formed by Fr. Benito LePlant and express a very different view of Christian faith and commitment—which is why Fr. LePlant was summarily expelled by the Sandinistas in 1984. (His expulsion on less than a day's notice was supposedly for taking part in a march organized by Archbishop Obando. He was not, however, present at the march.) A Jes priest, who was also expelled in 1984, told an interviewer t "the members of the famous 'base communities' [committed the Sandinistas] are very few—statistically speaking their num is negligible—they are usually managed and led by a partisan priest who is the one who imposes goals and strategies."[18]

The only significant numerical inroads that the advocates of the people's church were able to make was in the membership of some religious institutes of priests or nuns, particularly those with the foreign members—Jesuits, Dominicans, Franciscans, and the Ascension Sisters—and in some student circles. The problem with the students was that most if not a of the converts to revolutionary Christianity ended up doing what, as we have seen, the earlier members of the Movimiento Cristianos Revolucionarios (MCR) had done: they joined the FSLN and abandoned membership in the church.

This lack of popular support for the advocates of the people's church must have been a deep source of frustration for them, the more so because it contrasted so visibly with the massive support shown the archbishop of Managua and the rest of the Catholic hierarchy.

On October 19, 1981, the revolutionary Christians attempted to show their strength at a public mass in Managua following a demonstration in which they had protested the archbishop's removal of a Sandinista priest from a parish. According to estimates of the government press, no more than five hundred people attended. When seizing churches or holding sit-ins against the Catholic hierarchy, the revolutionary Christians usually have to mobilize people from distant locations and often fill out a crowd with Sandinista militants from the FSLN's mass organizations. I encountered an instance of this sort of thing at the chapel of a small university in Managua where I used to worship. After some three years of attending about three times a week, I knew practically all the parishioners. In September 1981, just as a service was ending, about eight revolutionary Christians entered the chapel to begin a one-week sit-in as a protest against Archbishop Obando. Neither I nor the other parishioners had ever seen any of these protesters before.

Archbishop Obando, on the other hand, draws crowds of mostly poor Nicaraguans wherever he goes. A survey conducted by the Centro de Estudios Religiosos—an independent lay organization to which I belonged—in August 1981, using a sample of nine hundred urban households, showed Archbishop Obando to be the most popular figure in the country. More recently, Stephen Kinzer of the *New York Times* spoke of the archbishop's popularity among the poor. "Archbishop Obando can draw an instant crowd anywhere in Nicaragua," wrote Kinzer after traveling with the prelate through some Nicaraguan towns in 1984. "Anyone who follows Obando on his trips in the countryside can see that he is venerated even more emotionally among the poor."[19] Visiting in 1985, Mario Vargas Llosa reported, "And I see it [evidence that Nicaraguan Catholics are loyal to the bishops] most of all in the excitement Monsignor Obando generates in his public appearances."[20]

There are many reasons for this phenomenon. One is the solid prestige that Archbishop Obando and other Catholic bishops gained during the dictatorship of Somoza. The people felt the bishops' stands were a reflection of moral convictions and not the result of political or social interests. Another reason is the bishops' clear Christian commitment. In the midst of political turmoil they have maintained their pastoral and evangelistic role. They have shepherded the Nicaraguan poor, responding to the religious and spiritual needs of their flock. They have remained enmeshed in the lives of the poor, whose racial and cultural background they share to a great extent.

The advocates of the people's church, by contrast, are generally white, upper-class, and foreign-born. Some, like Fr. Miguel D'Escoto and Fr. Ernesto Cardenal, are Nicaraguan and took a stand against Somoza, but in general have lived rather sheltered lives. Fr. D'Escoto lived outside Nicaragua for many years and did not return until after the Sandinistas triumphed. Cardenal spent most of the 1970s on the bucolic islands of Solentiname, in southern Nicaragua. He has been described by Geraldine Macias, former Maryknoll nun forced into exile with her husband Edgard in 1983, as an "upper class hippie," his only connection with the peasants since becoming Minister of Culture being that he often dresses like one. Fr. Fernando Cardenal and Fr. Uriel Molina had been secret collaborators of the FSLN before the revolution, and the latter led a very poor parish, but their revolutionary disciples were predominantly middle- and upper-class. The point is not that people from an affluent background cannot understand poorer people or win their support, but that the natural base of support of Nicaraguan peasants and workers is much stronger for the Nicaraguan bishops and the clergy loyal to them than for the leaders of the revolutionary Christians.

The Protestant leaders among the revolutionary Christians were people who did not get particularly involved in the anti-Somoza effort. Parajón, Cortés, and Ulloa, leaders of CEPAD, never took stands comparable to those of the bishops, nor did they ever face any kind of persecution or harassment under Somoza. José M. Torres, leader of the Ecumenical Axis, although a secret admirer of the Ortegas, also refrained from taking a public stand against Somoza.

Another factor in the revolutionary Christians' lack of broad popularity has been the fact that their theological discourse is much more political than religious. Their attention has seldom been on the spiritual needs of the mass of people, whom they consider to be too traditionalist. Rather, their liturgies and other celebrations of the sacraments tend to be couched in political terms (and their preaching at times is too intellectual for ordinary people). Their constant appeals in behalf of the revolution and the FSLN are little different than the propaganda available in the Sandinista press and on televison—which the people do not need to go to church to hear. For these and doubtless other reasons the poor in Nicaragua have balked at the new theologians and have maintained their commitment to their traditional spiritual leaders—to what the liberation theologians called the "church of the rich."

The revolutionary Christians' sources of power have been their theological centers, their access to the Sandinista-controlled media, and their international connections. They have received generous financial help from Christian organizations abroad, particularly the World Council of Churches. In April 1983, for example, the WCC gave the Centro Antonio Valdivieso $176,243 U.S.[21] American Protestants contribute to the funding of CEPAD. In 1981 the Church World Service of the National Council of Churches (U.S.A.) gave $375,329 to CEPAD (the NCC's Latin America department has refused to release financial information since 1981),[22] The United Methodist Committee on Relief gave $100,000, and the United Presbyterian Hunger Program gave $10,000.[23] (CEPAD was also the recipient of a $500,000 AID grant from the U.S. government in 1980.) Another center, the Instituto Nacional de Investigaciones y Estudios Sociales, a pro-Sandinista group, received $30,000 in 1982 from the Board of Global Ministries of the United Methodist Church.

With this sort of help, the centers advocating revolutionary Christian views in Nicaragua were able to set up well-funded offices where full-time theologians could devote themselves to the ideological battle on behalf of the FSLN—and against the non-Sandinista Christians. Some of these centers—CEPAD, for example—devote a large part of their resources to social programs. But they also use some of their money to print progovernment literature, to train Nicaraguan pastors in liberation theology, and to host groups of evangelical visitors who come to the country (mainly from the U.S.) to learn about the revolution. CEPAD has also helped to organize trips for Witness for Peace groups—groups of ten to fifteen people, mostly North Americans, who travel to northern Nicaragua to act as nonviolent interference to the contras—in an effort to increase solidarity with the Sandinistas. And even CEPAD-sponsored social programs have been used for the political purposes of the FSLN. For one thing, CEPAD channels at least some of its relief supplies through the Sandinista Defense Committees.[24] Also, according to the Jesuit priest Fr. Santiago Anitua, when aid arrives in some war-torn areas, Sandinista commanders are responsible for deciding who the recipients are going to be, and they add their customary political speeches at the time that the aid is being distributed.[25]

Organizations like the Centro Antonio Valdivieso, devote themselves exclusively to theological activities. They print numerous pamphlets and two international bulletins, *Informes CAV* and *Amanecer.* These periodicals, intended mostly for foreign consumption, are available in Spanish, English, and German.

This center publishes a daily column and other articles in the Sandinista-subsidized newspaper *El Nuevo Diario*. It also conducts seminars, panels, and roundtables with many of the most renowned Latin American liberation theologians.

The Central American Historical Institute (IHCA) publishes two sets of pamphlets: the *Cuadernos Rutilio Grande*, named after a priest murdered in El Salvador, and the *Cuadernos García Laviana*, named after a Spanish priest who died fighting as a Sandinista guerrilla in 1978. IHCA has established a branch at Georgetown University in Washington, D.C., and publishes from both offices a multilingual publication called *Envío*.

Centro De Promoción Agraria (CEPA) has devoted itself to printing pamphlets for peasants. The series *Cristo Campesino* and other catechetical materials are designed to raise peasants' political consciousness. The CEPA staff works in close collaboration with the Nicaraguan Ministry of Agrarian Reform.

The Instituto Nacional de Investigaciones y Estudios Sociales (INIES), directed by the Spanish Jesuit theologian Xavier Gorostiaga, uses a monthly magazine and a monograph series to explain to foreign audiences any advances of the Sandinista revolutionary process.

The full-time theologians and intellectual leaders of these centers tend to be foreigners who arrived after the triumph of the revolution. Such was the case with Fr. Gorostiaga of INIES, Fr. Pico of IHCA, Fr. Cabestrero of CAV, Fr. Plácido Herdozain, and others. José Arguello, lay theologian who joined CAV in 1981, and one of the few CAV staff members of Nicaraguan origin, spent most of his adult life in Germany.

In addition to their own published material, the revolutionary Christians make extensive use of media outlets provided to them by the FSLN. As mentioned earlier, a key part of the Sandinistas' strategy toward religion was to give the revolutionary Christians as much media space as possible, while gradually curtailing the freedom of expression of the other Christians. The revolutionary Christans have produced television and radio programs for the FSLN-owned media and publish columns in the FSLN's newspapers, particularly in the state-subsidized *El Nuevo Diario*. Their expensive international theological roundtables and conventions receive news coverage and are often attended by Sandinista commanders, who give speeches lauding the revolutionary Christians and lashing out at the "reactionary" ones.

With the passing of time, the non-Sandinista, non-Marxist

Christians have lost their access to the media. After a few years they became a silenced church. One step in this direction was the government's cancellation of Archbishop Obando's televised mass, which had been broadcast every Sunday for years on a formerly independent television station. The Sandinistas canned the program in July 1981, claiming that the archbishop had refused to share his space with more progressive priests. Even this pretext shows that the FSLN felt no qualms about interfering in the internal affairs of the church. Why should the government rather than the leaders of the church decide who is theologically progressive?

The more the government took control over radio programs and other of the remaining independent media, the narrower the freedom of expression for the independent churches became. The most serious blows came on March 15, 1982 when the government decreed the state of emergency which involved complete prior censorship of all media, and in August 1982 when the Catholic Church's radio station was forced to close for one month. When the station was allowed to reopen, it was placed under severe restrictions. For some time it could only broadcast music. After that it had to submit its programs to the state censors. By Easter 1983, the Sandinistas had decreed that homilies and sermons of church leaders had to be censored as a precondition for broadcasting.

Another policy of the Sandinistas to weaken the non-Sandinista churches was to decree that all foreign aid to private organizations had to be approved by the Nicaraguan government. When AID (a department of the U.S. government) tried to give the Catholic Church a grant for a social aid program in 1982—a grant one-third the size of the AID grant to CEPAD in 1980—the government would not allow the Catholic Church to accept it.

The irony was that what the revolutionary Christians called the "church of the rich" was in fact a poor church, and what they called the "church of the poor" lived and worked in luxury. The Catholic Church, the Protestant churches, and the other religious bodies that did not overtly support the Sandinistas lacked access to the mass media, had a fraction of the theological staff and resources that the centers of the revolutionary Christians had, and were limited in the ability to raise funds outside the country. Furthermore, the Nicaraguan government passed a law in the summer of 1981 making it illegal for any Nicaraguan to make declarations abroad that could be judged detrimental to the revolution. The law carried a punishment of three to ten years of imprisonment. Although some of the Catholic bishops have dared to defy this law on some of their visits to other countries, most non-Sandinista Nicaraguan Christians have clearly been inhibited from testifying against their government in international forums.

The revolutionary Christians, by contrast, keep a steady stream of spokesmen traveling abroad, giving Christians and others their views about the conflict in Nicaragua. A Maryknoll nun, Sr. Peggy Healy, for example, whom Tomás Borge has called an "angel," has traveled with companions to the U.S. to inform the Speaker of the House, Tip O'Neill, of the virtues of the Sandinista revolution. A Nicaraguan Christian with a different view who communicated his opinions abroad and wished to return to Nicaragua would do so only at great personal risk. This is the main reason why I left Nicaragua permanently in 1982. It was the only way to freely testify about events in my country.

NOTES

1. Jon Sobrino, "Dios y los Procesos Revolucionarios," in *Apuntes para una Teología Nicaragüense*, CAV-IHCA, ed. (San José, Costa Rica: Departamento Ecuménico de Investigaciones, 1981), pp. 107, 108.

2. Juan Pico S.J., "Marxismo y Cristianismo Hoy," in *ibid., Apuntes para una Teología Nicaragüense*, pp. 146, 147.

3. Juan Pico S.J., "Los Cristianos y el Poder en Nicaragua Hoy," in *ibid., Apuntes para una Teología Nicaragüense*, pp. 134, 135.

4. Elsa Tamez, "Cómo Abordar el Problema de la Mujer en un Proceso Revolucionario?" in *ibid., Apuntes para una Teología Nicaragüense*, p. 184.

5. Archbishop Obando y Bravo, "Mensaje de Año Nuevo, 1980," in *Revista del Pensamiento Centroamericano*, July-December 1980, Managua, Nicaragua.

6. Juan Pico S.J., "El Proceso Global en la Nicaragua Revolucionaria y los Retos que Propone a la Fe Cristiana Social," in *op. cit., Apuntes para una Teología Nicaragüense*, p. 26.

7. Frei Betto, "La Iglesia que Surge del Pueblo," in *ibid., Apuntes para una Teología Nicaragüense*, p. 90.

8. CAV, *La Media Docena de Desafíos Revolucionarios,* La Trocha Collection, No. 1 Managua, 1981, p. 16.

9. *La Prensa,* May 1981.

10. CEPAD, "Pastoral Letter to the U.S. Christian Churches," *El Nuevo Diario,* March 16, 1982, p. 5.

11. Teófilo Cabestrero, "Hacer más Evangélica Esta Iglesia," in *Amanecer,* No. 6, February 1982, p. 11.

12. Pablo Richard, "Identidad Eclesial en el Proceso," in *op. cit., Apuntes para una Teología Nicaragüense,* p. 96.

13. *Op. cit.,* Elsa Tamaz, "Cómo Abordar el Problema?," p. 184.

14. *Op. cit.,* Jon Sobrino, "Dios y los Procesos Revolucionarios," p. 118.

15. *Op. cit.,* Elsa Tamaz, "Cómo Abordar el Problema?," p. 184.

16. See Boaventura Kloppenburg, "Síntesis," in *Centro América en Llamas* (Bogotá, Colombia: CONFE, 1982), p. 203.

17. Mario Vargas Llosa, "In Nicaragua," p. 46.

18. Fr. Santiago Anitua, S.J., "The People's Church in Nicaragua," *Latino,* Los Angeles, CA, undated, p. 18.

19. Stephen Kinzer, "Nicaragua's Combative Archbishop," *The New York Times Magazine,* November 18, 1984, pp. 90, 93.

20. *Op. cit.,* Mario Vargas Llosa, "In Nicaragua," p. 76.

21. Source: Institute on Religion and Democracy, "Church Support for Pro-Sandinista Network," report, Washington, D.C.: IRD, 1984, p. 14.

22. *Ibid.,* p. 10.

23. *Ibid.*

24. CEPAD, "Informe Anual 1981," Managua: CEPAD, 1982, p. 9.

25. Fr. Anitua, "The People's Church," pp. 17, 18.

THIRTEEN

THE SANDINISTAS VS. THE CHURCH

Less than one year after the end of the war with Somoza, the Sandinista government and the Christians independent of the FSLN were moving toward a crisis. The Sandinistas' political messianism and the theology of their Christian supporters clashed sharply with the views of the Nicaraguan bishops and with those of numerous Protestant bodies. The issue was one of independence.

Obscuring the nature of the growing conflict was the fact that the Sandinistas and their allies within the churches interpreted all opposition or lack of compliance by Christians in exclusively political terms. The conflict between revolutionary and other Christians was merely the historical class struggle between the haves and the have-nots working itself out in the ecclesiastical sphere. Christians who claimed to be concerned for the integrity of their faith were using this as a pretext to mask their more basic, economic interests.

There is no doubt that the defense of political, social, and economic interests drew segments of the Nicaraguan middle and upper classes to side with the bishops and the non-Sandinista churches. But what about the poor? Why did they massively back their traditional religious leaders? And why were the bishops, who had shown no propensity under Somoza to side with power or with elites, suddenly driven by crass class interest? The same might be asked for the independent Protestant churches, whose membership was overwhelmingly made up of poor Nicaraguans. In fact, from the point of view of self-interest, joining in with the Sandinistas was the wisest path to follow.

Although by April 1980 the broad alliance of forces that fought against Somoza had broken up and widespread misgivings were being voiced in regard to Sandinista policies, the Catholic Church had refrained from any public criticism of the regime. The first recorded expressions of discontent from the church came after the revolution was a year old. In August 1980 the Catholic bishop of Juigalpa, a rural province in southern Nicaragua, issued an open letter to church leaders in the area, denouncing the following actions of the Sandinistas:

> 1. . . . There have been repeated instances of political organizers and leaders trying to dissuade people from attending the meetings of our church community. They have sown divisions in the midst of the community, openly proclaiming that religion is no longer necessary, and that instead it is an obstacle to the development of revolution. They say that what is going to count from now on is the science [of Marxism] and the force of the people's organizations.
> 2. It has frequently been the case that political activists stage their meetings on the same day and at the same time as our church community meetings. You have denounced [to me] the arbitrary occupation of local chapels [by the FSLN] to celebrate political meetings, including the painting of the walls with slogans of the Sandinista Front. Another type of interference has been to try to persuade church leaders to fully commit themselves to partisan political activism, making the people believe that religion and Marxism-Leninism are the same thing.[1]

Other Christians, including myself, also began voicing their concerns. After much hesitation, in September 1980 we at *La Prensa* finally published the FSLN's private memo about Christmas. We had withheld the document from publication since it came into our hands in December 1979, because it was our policy to avoid antagonizing the Sandinistas. But by September of 1980 we felt we could wait no longer. The Sandinistas' campaign to politicize religion was growing stronger, as was their drive to compel Christians to join the FSLN.

On October 7, 1980, the FSLN issued a statement of their official policy on religious matters. It began by asserting that reactionary forces were trying to sell the idea that the FSLN was using religion as part of a longer-term plan to eradicate it altogether.[2]

The Nicaraguan bishops' conference immediately answered the FSLN with a document of its own, in which for the first time the Catholic hierarchy clearly expressed its reservations about the Sandinistas' intentions. It is worth quoting from both documents at length, because they reveal much about the religious and political views of both sets of authors.[3]

The FSLN:

> No one can be discriminated against in the new Nicaragua for publicly professing or spreading his religious beliefs. This right also pertains to those who do not profess any religious faith.
>
> Within the partisan framework of the FSLN there is no room for religious proselytism, since such activity would destroy the specific character of our vanguard and would introduce elements of division, since the Sandinista Front gathers comrades with different or no religious beliefs.

The bishops:

> This implies, logically, that there cannot be privileges for those who do not profess any faith. . . . Therefore neither the government nor the FSLN should boast of atheism or allow ideological proselytism opposed to religious belief to be promoted under the protections of its structures. . . .
>
> How [do we] reconcile this declaration [no discrimination or privileges on the grounds of religious belief] with what at the official and public level is being done against the faith and against religion through the official organs of the state? . . . There is [ideological] indoctrination and there are pressures, by various and known means, against religious beliefs and sentiments. . . . To be an atheist as an individual right is a different thing from promoting atheist proselytism through the state institutions.

This last remark was a reference to the fact that soldiers in the army and members of the FSLN were being intensively trained in Marxist-Leninist ideology using the resources of the state.

The FSLN:

> For the revolutionary state, religion is a private matter. . . . The revolution and the state have an origin, goals, and a realm of action completely different from those of religion.

The bishops:

> It would be a great mistake . . . to continue speaking of religious life and socioeconomic life as though they ran parallel, without interpenetration and claims upon one another.

In fact, it was curious that while praising the Christians' and the churches' involvement in the overthrow of Somoza, the FSLN now wanted them confined to the private sphere, thus replicating one of the arguments that Somoza had used against the church's involvement in politics.

It was not that the bishops were rejecting the notion of the separation of church and state. They insisted on this separation, but they claimed for the church the right to have a say in the shaping of the new society. To deny the church such a right, restricting its influence to a purely private sphere, was characteristic of totalitarian rather than democratic societies:

> Totalitarian systems, by virtue of their materialistic philosophy, deny the church all qualitative participation in public affairs. . . . They seek to use the church as a tool. . . . They accept for strategic reasons, the desirability of gaining the church's participation, but only as an instrument to consecrate and bless the movement toward a monolithic and absolutist system. . . . Under these conditions the church does not serve the interest of man but the totalitarian power of the state.

One concrete issue in this discussion was the situation of four Catholic priests, who, despite the wishes of the hierarchy, held positions in the Sandinista government. Was not this an instance of the kind of participation that the church sought? In defending the priest's participation in the state the FSLN stated:

> It is the right of all Nicaraguan citizens to participate in the managing of the political affairs of the nation.

To this the bishops responded:

> It is one thing to call a priest to exercise his ministry [within the political arena] and another very different thing to insert himself into a system in order to justify it or give it religious legitimacy. Religion cannot be at the service of partisan interests.

Thus, for example, a Catholic priest might serve as a chaplain of a government body or take part in consultations on political and economic matters in government councils, as these would be ways of bringing Christian faith and social principles into the arena of government. But a priest should not take a political post, because he is by definition an ordained, official leader of the Catholic Church, and his exercising a political role would be interpreted as a sign of Catholic Church approval of the nature and policies of the government. In Catholic teaching, there is a distinction of spheres of responsibility between clergy and laity. Political roles should be filled by lay men and women, guided by Christian principles taught by the clergy. Priests and bishops, in order to teach these principles fairly and credibly, should not be identified with particular parties and governments. In taking this position, the Nicaraguan bishops were consistent with the teaching of Vatican Council II and contemporary popes and with the practice of bishops elsewhere. In recent years U.S. and Canadian bishops have asked priests to resign seats in Congress and parliament for these reasons.

The bishops then quoted from the documents of the Third General Conference of the Latin American Catholic Bishops held at Puebla, Mexico, in 1979:

> The shepherds, by contrast [with the laity], since they should be concerned for unity, will put aside all partisan political ideologies that may condition their attitudes and judgments. They will thus have the freedom to evangelize the political realm as Christ, from a gospel without partisanship.

The bishops closed their remarks on this subject with the following statement:

> The church is at the service of the people, but not at the service of power.

This was just the sort of statement that infuriated the Sandinistas, for they believed that they and "the people" were synonymous. To imply that there was FSLN power distinct from the people was to challenge one of the basic dogmas of Marxist-Leninist and Sandinista ideology: the claim that the revolutionary vanguard was the embodiment of the people.

The FSLN:

> The FSLN has a profound respect for all the celebrations and religious traditions of our people and it makes an effort to rescue their true meanings. . . . We find that this respect should express itself not only in guaranteeing the conditions for their free expression, but also in preventing their utilization for political or commercial purposes. It is obvious that if some political parties or individuals try to turn these religious celebrations into acts which are contrary to the revolution

(as has happened in the past), the FSLN declares its right to defend the people and to defend the revolution. No Sandinista militant as such should give opinions about interpretations of religious issues which exclusively pertain to the different churches.

To this intention to rescue the "true meaning" of religious celebrations, the bishops responded:

The principle according to which the interpretation of religious issues is the exclusive jurisdiction of the churches is annulled if the FSLN arrogates to itself the right to interpret which religious festivities or activities do or do not oppose its revolution. . . . There are also objective facts that already confirm the tendency to intervene in religious celebrations and interpret them as something political and partisan. . . . We all know the plans for the celebration of Christmas. And those used for the festivity of the Virgin Mary and in the celebrations of patron saints. . . . For a social or political group to truly respect religion . . . it is not enough that it recognizes their existence. It is necessary that it does not . . . try to strategically undermine them.

The bishops ended their document by addressing charges which had been made in the FSLN-controlled media that the Catholic Church was opposed to social change and to the revolution:

Could there be anyone so nonsensical that they could accuse the church or the Christian people of opposing the revolution because it might offer culture, medicine, and a system of labor and production more attuned to human dignity and to social development?

We Christians want—and have been demanding—serious and profound transformations. We are radicals, but not extremists. We demand these revolutionary changes, but we must always ask ourselves: What kind of revolution are we to make and how are we to make it?; what are our values and what is our basis?

It is not the church or the Christians who are against the Nicaraguan revolution, but those who, driven by their ideology, turn it against the religious feelings of our people.

The bishops' document restated their position vis-á-vis the revolution and their objections to the FSLN. They continued to stand for deep and serious social changes in behalf of the poor. They were for revolution. What they objected to was the FSLN attempt to make religion a tool of partisan politics, the Sandinistas' efforts to interfere in religious matters and redefine religious truths, and their manifestations of disregard for basic human rights and freedoms.

The revolutionary Christians reacted in anger to the bishops' document. They refused to discuss the bishops' analysis of the role of religion and claimed that the statement was being used against the people. The revolutionary Christians did not address the problem of the division in the church. Instead, they accused the bishops of the "grave evil" of dividing the revolution.[4]

Speaking on the state-owned Radio Sandino, the revolutionary Christians voiced the Sandinistas' anger at the bishops' reference to a distinction between the people and the FSLN.

> We are disquieted by the bishops' judgment of the FSLN, which attempts to separate and even put the poor people at odds with their legitimate and recognized vanguard.[5]

After this, the campaign of criticism against the bishops and other non-Sandinista Christians became more systematic and bitter. Yet the Catholic hierarchy still spoke in moderate tones in reference to the Sandinistas. And their references were not always negative. Archbishop Obando still characterized the regime in early 1981 as pluralistic and on a trip to Venezuela told the press, "The church is carrying out its task in Nicaragua without government intervention, a situation contrary to that experienced during the previous regime, when our gospel was persecuted by official proclamation."[6]

Just a few days after these remarks, the bishops faced new tension with the FSLN. Its origin was in the Catholic hierarchy's opposition to priests holding positions in the Sandinista government. The Nicaraguan bishop's conference held a series of meetings with the priests involved from January 17, 1981, through the middle of the year, trying to persuade the priests that their political role was incompatible with their priestly ministry. The meetings yielded no results, and on June 4, the bishops issued a statement demanding that all priests occupying government office return to their pastoral callings.

The Sandinistas and the revolutionary Christians responded with an agitation and propaganda campaign against the bishops. Among the first acts in this campaign, the priests involved issued a document defying the bishops. It ended with these words:

Finally we declare our unbreakable commitment to the people's San-dinista revolution, in loyalty to our people, which is the same as saying, in loyalty to the will of God.[7]

This remarkable statement by the revolutionary priests elicited this commentary from the Colombian writer Carlos Corsi:

Fidelity was given not to the church, but to the people, and since the people were led to liberation by the FSLN, itself led by the com-manders, then fidelity to God was fidelity to the commanders who became absolute interpreters of God's will on earth.[8]

Knowing the significance of the debate, the revolutionary Christians launched the base communities that they controlled on a series of rallies, sit-ins, and other protests against the bish-ops. The Sandinista media gave these actions and the Christians responsible for them constant coverage. The FSLN was aware of the asset these priests represented in their strategy of portraying their regime as one in which Christians and secular revolutionar-ies worked side by side. Radio Sandino described the protests of the base communities as a "decision to support the revolution."[9] The base community in the barrio Larreynaga charged that "our bishops' attitude obviously shows that the Catholic Church has never considered or worried about the well-being of the poorer classes."[10]

Sandinista leaders also joined in the attacks, becoming more directly involved in the conflict than they had before. Junta member Sergio Ramírez referred to the existence of two churches: a revolutionary church and a nonrevolutionary church. As for the revolutionary church, Ramirez argued that it was a

church of change. This church became the people's ally. . . . [It] committed itself to this revolution . . . and is incorporating the patriotic and revolutionary priests, of whom we are very proud, into the government.[11]

In an ominous reference to the "other" church, Ramirez warned that "there have been revolutions against the church and revolutions without the church because it remained outside." Speaking before a rally of the Sandinista Children's Associ-ation, Tomás Borge reminded his young listeners of how the church, under the Inquisition, used to persecute people. Borge announced that the FSLN ought to protect Christians from being persecuted by the hierarchy.

> We must struggle to keep them from being persecuted. We must strive to save Christians from persecution. For the first time in a revolution, Christians are being persecuted by a sector of the high-ranking church hierarchy.[12]

Very few Christians outside Nicaragua spoke out in defense of the bishops. Confidence in the Sandinista revolution was still too strong. Interpretations of the growing conflict by Christians abroad were usually made with little understanding of the background of the Catholic bishops or of their detractors and almost always favored the Sandinistas.

The centers operated by the revolutionary Christians contributed to the confusion of many non-Nicaraguan Christians. These centers began hosting many short-term visitors and, with their resources and international connections, they were able to spread versions of the conflict that outside audiences were in no position to contradict. Christians in Western Europe and North America especially found it credible that the Nicaraguan Catholic hierarchy was a body of authoritarian reactionaries whose prejudices put them at odds with the revolution for political rather than theological reasons. CEPAD, which many U.S. Protestants mistakenly took as the voice of Nicaraguan evangelicals, contributed substantially to the confusion over the nature of the conflict.

The hierarchy-is-reactionary version of the conflict between the bishops and the Sandinistas was especially persuasive when it came from Catholic priests themselves. The Central American Historical Institute later wrote, for instance, that:

> In Nicaragua there certainly is religious persecution, only in contrast to what happens in El Salvador, Guatemala, or Honduras, it is not the government which carries it out, but the very sold-out church.[13]

FROM VIOLENT WORDS TO VIOLENT ACTIONS

Through the middle of 1981, most of the attacks made against Catholics were vocal only. Aside from the harassment and interferences reported in August 1980 by Bishop Vega, the Sandinista government engaged in few direct actions against Catholic leaders or other Catholics. The government's treatment of Protestants in the populous Pacific coast region, where most Nicaraguans live, also followed the same pattern through mid-1981: verbal attacks in the government media but no direct repression, with one exception.

In mid-1980 the evangelical preacher Morris Cerullo, on a tour of Latin America, was expelled by the Sandinistas as soon as he landed at the Managua airport. The government justified this action by accusing Cerullo of being sent by the CIA. At the time, his expulsion seemed to many Nicaraguan Christians an isolated event. Furthermore, Cerullo did not have an organized church in Nicaragua which could protest his treatment. And since ecumenical solidarity is not a strong feature of the Nicaraguan churches—a fact consistently exploited by the FSLN—his expulsion passed with little protest. We did editorialize about it in *La Prensa,* but that was about all the coverage it received. The FSLN claimed that even this little show of concern was a cover-up for our counterrevolutionary political intentions.

The small Jewish community in Nicaragua was also a target of early harassment by the Sandinistas. In 1978 the Sandinistas, chanting anti-Semitic and PLO slogans, attacked Nicaragua's only synagogue. Once in power, they confiscated it. They also confiscated the property of many Jewish families on the grounds that they had been Somocistas—some had, some had not. Abraham Gorn, the informal leader of the Jewish community, was arrested in 1979. Other Jews received threatening phone calls advising them to leave the country. Most fled.

The Cerullo incident and the experience of the Jews proved that it was easier for the Sandinistas to manhandle the more isolated, numerically weaker religious groups than it was to confront the larger and more well-established churches.

The first Christians to experience direct government repression were Moravian missionaries based in the isolated Atlantic Coast region where the Miskitos and other Indian minorities live. As mentioned earlier, the Sandinistas began soon after the triumph of the revolution to replace the leadership and influence of the Moravian missionaries with that of Sandinista militants, many of them Cubans. In the wake of the unrest that these actions stirred among the Miskitos, the Sandinistas jailed several missionaries and killed some of them, alleging that they were inciting the Miskitos to rebel against the authorities and were CIA agents.

During the summer of 1981, the hostility of the government and of the revolutionary Christians to Christians who did not fully agree with the FSLN became more intense. On July 7, 1981, the government suspended the televised mass that the archbishop of Managua had celebrated for many years. Meanwhile, public presentations by the revolutionary Christians bitterly criticizing the hierarchy multiplied. Simultaneously, many religious billboards put up around the capital by groups of Catholics (for example, those of Sister Ana Zavala which exhorted people to love their enemies) were destroyed or defaced. Reporting this fact cost *La Prensa* its first temporary closing (the government claimed that we had lied about the billboards).

More significant than the destruction of billboards were physical attacks on Catholic bishops and priests. The first took place toward the end of 1981 when a Sandinista mob threw stones at the bishop of Juigalpa, Pablo A. Vega, while he was leaving a church. Some weeks later another mob in Managua destroyed the windows and tires of Archbishop Obando's jeep.

On January 13, 1982, five North American Catholics (three nuns and two priests) were expelled from the country. The government attributed the expulsion to a bureaucrat's mistake. It announced that the five could return, although not to their original parishes. Two of them returned. The bishop of the Atlantic coast, Salvador Schlaefer, experienced similar treatment (by 1985 he had been expelled from his diocese four times).

In March 1982, the government gave clear indications that it was preparing for a more generalized campaign against the non-Sandinista religious groups, both Catholic and Protestant. The government started this campaign by loudly repeating the charges against the Protestant denominations that the Centro Antonio Valdivieso had been making. On March 3, 1982, *Barricada,* the official voice of the FSLN, published the first of a series of reports on the Protestant denominations, disparagingly referred to in the articles as "sects." They were ridiculed as superstitious and fanatical and invariably linked to North American imperialism. The charges were nonspecific and mostly speculative. Although many of the bodies being attacked had U.S. origins, many other North American religious groups were active in Nicaragua with the blessing of the FSLN, such as the Mary-knoll nuns, some U.S. Franciscans, and some of the evangelicals. The main reason for the open attack on the Protestants singled out by the government seems to be that the Sandinistas had no hope of converting them to the revolution or to Marxist liberation theology. In the eyes of the FSLN, they were too concerned with spiritual and supernatural matters and hence kept their people distracted from the all-important task of supporting the revolution. Their leaders—unlike the leaders of CEPAD—had failed to express their explicit adherence to Sandinismo.

A group that particularly annoyed the Sandinistas was the Seventh-Day Adventists, who preached the imminent return of Christ. The reason was expressed by *Barricada* journalist Margaret Randall:

> It is common to see on the walls in any neighborhood in Managua, "Christ Shall Come"—a sentence that is threatening and lying. The "Christ Shall Come" of the counterrevolution is in direct opposition to the Christ that has already arrived in Nicaragua with his liberating preaching through the revolutionary triumph. . . . Christ already came to Palacaguina and to Nicaragua, dressed as a triumphal people. . . . The Christ that is present in the daily labor of our people does not need to be advertised as something remote or in the future.[14]

The propaganda campaign against these groups staged by *Barricada* and the ecumenical Centro Antonio Valdivieso was followed by violence. On March 15, 1982, a state of emergency was decreed, originally for one month, but subsequently extended at each expiration. This signaled the end of the remaining margin of free expression in the country; for example, it meant complete prior press censorship. Assured of the silence of their critics, the Sandinistas stepped up their attacks on independent churches. After May, over twenty churches of the Moravians, Adventists, and some other evangelical denominations were confiscated by the authorities. Roughly a dozen buildings belonging to the Mormons and the Jehovah's Witnesses were also seized. All these groups were accused of working with the CIA. As in other instances, the charges were not supported with proof of any sort, nor were the victims allowed to defend themselves in court.

In a public address, Tomás Borge accused Protestants, in addition to having CIA alliances, of being allied with the Somocistas. The mob of FSLN militants listening to him began to chant "que se vayan"—"get them out." They proceeded to attack and occupy Protestant churches and religious buildings. On Monday, August 9, 1982, the FSLN mobs took over twenty such buildings.

According to the Sandinista press, these mob attacks were "acts in defense of the revolution."[15] If this official defense of mob terror was a disturbing symptom of the state of civil liberties, the response of the revolutionary Christians was even more unsettling as a repudiation of Christian solidarity and a rejection of the spiritual dimension of the gospel. In words that faithfully echoed those of the FSLN, the Centro Antonio Valdivieso stated:

> It has become evident in recent years that there has been an alarming growth of sects and fanatical elements that influence people into not joining the militias, not preparing the defense, boycotting the people's health [FSLN] campaigns, and breaking with the revolution because that would be the will of God. The people defends itself from this destabilizing fanaticism by taking over the churches. In the last weeks the people's organizations have taken over more than 30 churches of religious sects. . . . The people [now] devote these places to be centers for the education and the culture of the people.
>
> The theological formation of these sects and of some of the evangelical denominations that are part of them are part of a pro-American ideological scheme—a theology only interested in the spiritual, with a strong emphasis on the next life, forgetting the here and now. Theirs was therefore a theology without any social perspective capable of making the believer meditate on the commitment of his faith. . . . All this was reinforced with anti-Communist, anti-Marxist materials.[16]

It is noteworthy that the revolutionary Christians of the ecumenical Centro Antonio Valdivieso sided with the FSLN completely in a conflict involving Protestant denominations—a conflict which had involved not just harsh words but violence and illegal seizure of church buildings. It is also worth noticing that the concern of the CAV is ultimately political rather than theological. Despite the theological critique of the evangelicals—that is, that they concentrate on the spiritual side of Christianity and do not involve themselves in political efforts for social justice—the specific accusations of the CAV are political and partisan: the problem with the evangelicals is that they are not supporting the

FSLN. They do not join the militias; they do not prepare the defense; they do not commit themselves to the Sandinista revolution.

The CAV's defense of the takeover of churches of these Christians for whom Sandinista Nicaragua had no place ended with a paragraph so similar in style to the FSLN's secret Christmas memo of 1979 that it could have well been written by the same author. It reads:

> It has become necessary to create a pedagogy that will enable us to uproot profound ideological roots, a task which is not possible to achieve overnight.[17]

TRUE BELIEVERS

The FSLN has been unyielding in its attempt to uproot every ideological and religious belief different than its own. Yet it has recognized that this task requires time and strategy. But it would be erroneous to think that everything the FSLN did in this regard was the result of calculated planning. When the Sandinistas printed prayers to the Virgin Mary in which she is asked to intercede for the vanguard, they clearly did so as part of a premeditated plan of action. But when they proclaim slogans like, "Sandino Yesterday, Sandino Today, Sandino Forever," or print on billboards, "The FSLN Is Immortal," they are not necessarily copying from the Scriptures (Hebrews 13:8—"Jesus Christ is the same yesterday, today, and forever") or consciously trying to twist the Christian belief in the eternal nature of God. These slogans may in fact be authentic expressions of the religious nature of the Sandinista ideology, for in many important respects the revolution and its ideology have the flavor of a religious faith.

For example, in 1983 Sandinista television broadcast a series of five or six programs about the "revolutionary saints." Every evening, programs would show the photographs of different Sandinista guerrillas who had died in the war. "These are the saints," a solemn voice explained. "These are the saints who died killing and who have been resurrected in our midst." A song in honor of Carlos Fonseca, the founding father of the FSLN, claimed that he had defeated death. He is alive, together with Sandino. He is present in the defense and in the work. He will be watching us, protecting us. His sacrifice has redeemed the Nicaraguan people.

Some revolutionary priests, such as Fr. Uriel Molina, contributed to this hero-worship by placing posters of Fonseca, Sandino, Che Guevara, Farabundo Martí (founder of El Salvador's Communist party), and others inside their churches. It was the by-product of both a theology and an ideology which apotheosized revolution.

The Sandinistas' and the revolutionary Christians' religious reverence for revolution led them all the more emphatically to deny Christian virtue in others. Daniel Ortega stated in 1982 that the Catholic bishops had Christian habits, but that they were not Christians. Tomás Borge has called them "false prophets" and even prostitutes.

By contrast, the Sandinistas attempted to profile a pro-Sandinista priest, Fr. Arias Caldera, as the true shepherd of the Nicaraguan Catholics. The FSLN newspaper *Barricada* dubbed him the "archbishop of the poor." The aim of both the revolutionary Christians and the Sandinistas was the same: to bypass the authority of the church's appointed leaders, replacing them with their own true believers.

THE GOVERNMENT MANUFACTURES AN INCIDENT

The Sandinistas' growing resolve to break the bishops' hold on Catholics' loyalties, aided by their complete control of the media, led to an escalation of hostilities. On July 20, 1982, the Catholic bishops sent *La Prensa* a courteous, open letter, asking the government to clarify the situation of Bishop Schlaefer of the Atlantic Coast, who had been ousted for the third time from his diocese, and to cease the antireligious campaign. *La Prensa* was prohibited by the government censor from publishing the letter. The next day Sandinista mobs attempted to take over several Catholic churches in protest of the decision of the archbishop of Managua to move Fr. Arias Caldera to another parish in Managua. The mobs, encouraged by the state-controlled mass media and enjoying the logistic support of government vehicles, attacked several priests. In one incident, the auxiliary bishop of Managua, Bosco Vivas, was beaten. The Nicaraguan Priests Council protested the attack, but the government's censor also prevented the publication of their letter.

Another serious governmental intervention occurred on July 31, 1982, when the Sandinista regime banned the publication of a letter from Pope John Paul II to the Nicaraguan bishops in which he expressed his concern for the unity of the Nicaraguan church. Only after three closings of *La Prensa* and vigorous protests was the ban lifted, fully one month after the Pope's letter had arrived.

The following month brought a further and particularly painful attack. On August 11, the government publicly announced that Fr. Bismark Carballo, spokesman for the Catholic archbishop's office, had been caught in a tryst. The following night Sandinista television presented a documentary. In it, Fr. Carballo was seen being removed naked and bleeding by police from a house in the quiet residential neighborhood of Las Colinas. A crowd mocked him from outside. The priest, who was visiting a female parishioner who had insistently requested him to come, reported that when he entered the house, a man armed with a pistol had appeared and demanded that he undress. As soon as he did so, police arrived and dragged him out to the street, where a crowd of about seventy people, including reporters from the Sandinista newspapers and a crew from the Sandinista television, was gathered. According to the government, they were there by sheer coincidence. It was also a coincidence that the front door of the house happened to be open so that the photographer from *Barricada* could get a shot of the struggle while it was taking place inside the house.

In their first report the Sandinista media did not give the name of the alleged offended husband, although a picture was published. When the government began the trial, however, the alleged husband turned out not to be the man whose picture had been published at first. When *La Prensa* sought to publish this incongruity, the government censor prohibited it.

The censorship of this discrepancy, and the government's prohibition of any discussion of the incident by those friendly to Fr. Carballo (letters of protest by the Managua Priests Council, peasant base communities, and others were denied publication in *La Prensa* by government censors), clearly indicated the government's intention to defame him. The woman involved was interviewed by *El Nuevo Diario* and *Barricada,* to whom she confessed, apparently without qualms or fear of her aggressive "husband," that she was having a love affair with the priest. She also happened to be a former mistress of Carlos Mejía Godoy, a Sandinista singer, and composer of the "Nicaraguan Peasant

Mass," and a woman with many connections high in the Sandinista government.

Later, in the face of domestic and international outrage, the government took the position that it had erred in *publicizing* the incident. However, the manner in which the government consistently suppressed evidence favorable to Fr. Carballo demonstrates that the government not only made a tactical error by playing up the incident in the media, but that the government had manufactured the incident in the first place as a way of undermining the Catholic Church and the archbishop of Managua by destroying the reputation of one of the church's leading spokesmen.

Evidence regarding how the Sandinistas set up the whole plan to defame Fr. Carballo was later provided by Miguel Bolanos, an agent in the Nicaraguan Intellegence Service who defected in May 1983. Among other things, Bolanos reported that Interior Minister Tomás Borge and Managua Chief of Police Lenín Cerna watched the whole Carballo episode from a van with tinted windows parked near the house where the event took place.

When the Sandinista regime broadcast the pictures of the naked and bleeding Fr. Carballo and accused him of immoral behavior, the reaction of many Nicaraguans was violent. In an explosion such as had not been seen before under the Sandinistas, thousands of Catholic students went on strike and occupied their school buildings. Significantly, the Monimboseno Indians, living in the Indian district which had been the first to rise against Somoza, rioted, improvising barricades and attacking police stations—the toll being three dead and several wounded.

In reprisal, the Sandinista government expelled from the country two priests belonging to the Salesian order on the pretext that they had incited violence against the government (a Salesian school was among those occupied by striking students in protest against the treatment of Fr. Carballo). This spurred a further outcry of protest both in Nicaragua and abroad.

The Salesians sent a vigorous protest in which many of the government's false accusations and arbitrary measures in regard to their schools and the congregation were exposed. Outside Nicaragua, Vatican Radio, the Catholic bishops of Venezuela and Costa Rica, and the president of the U.S. Catholic bishops conference, Archbishop John R. Roach of Minneapolis-St. Paul, released statements protesting the Sandinistas' actions. The revolutionary Christians, however, remained silent.

TWO STEPS FORWARD, ONE STEP BACK

This show of support for Nicaraguan Christians caused the Sandinistas to back off in embarrassment. Although they did not allow Fr. Moratalla to return to Nicaragua, they did return to the Salesian congregation the school they had confiscated.

Also sensing that they had gone too far in regard to the Protestants, the Sandinistas backed off a bit. Although CEPAD took a consistently apologetic and supportive position toward the government, the massive takeover of Protestant churches had stirred a lot of controversy and tension within CEPAD's affiliated denominations—many of them being affected directly. A massive loss of membership was at stake if CEPAD remained passive. Its leaders thus petitioned the FSLN to reconsider some of its most recent actions. The Sandinistas agreed to return some of the occupied churches.

But the return policy was selective. Only those pastors and churches willing to express support for the Sandinistas would receive their confiscated property back. Some Protestant leaders thus found that the only way to buy more time was by expressing sympathy toward the government, especially to foreign visitors who would often later quote their remarks. To do otherwise was to risk losing everything they had in Nicaragua.

An uneasy truce followed these developments. In hindsight, they could well be interpreted as an instance of Lenin's famous tactic of "two steps forward, one step backward": move suddenly and forcefully against your adversary and take from him as much as you can get away with; when he reacts, negotiate with him and give back part of what you took. If the government negotiates skillfully enough, it may end up convincing bystanders—and sometimes even the victim himself—of how reasonable and yielding it is. With the assault on the Protestant churches, the Catholic media, and Fr. Carballo, the Sandinistas took several steps on the churches. When the outcry got too loud, the Sandinistas made concessions. Some Protestant churches were returned to their congregations; the Salesian school of Masaya was returned to the Salesians; the Sandinistas criticized themselves for the media coverage of Fr. Carballo's "sexual" affair. But in the end there were fewer Protestant churches than before, one less Salesian priest, and Fr. Carballo had been humiliated and his reputation damaged.

The Sandinistas took one step backward, however, only in the Pacific region. In the Atlantic region, the geographical isolation and the silence created by the Sandinistas' cut-off of information made the situation worse for Christians. According to Edgard Macías, former Vice-Minister of Labor in the Sandinista government, by mid-1982 the government militia had destroyed at least fifty-five churches in that part of the country—a tragedy of immense proportions, according to Macías, for these churches had been the sole organized source of social services for many of the Miskitos.[18]

In January 1982 two Moravian church leaders, the Rev. Fernando Colomes and Norman Bent, were forced to leave the Atlantic region and go to Managua. In May 1982 Sandinista authorities announced the closing of the Committee of Social Action of the Moravian Church, which was in charge of providing social and relief services to the Miskitos. They also arrested the Rev. Santos Clevban, who was held incommunicado from July 11 to 25.

An authoritative witness, Berkeley professor Bernard Nietschmann, who was well-acquainted with the Miskitos from several periods when he had lived among them before the revolution, spent two and a half months in Miskito territory in 1983. He gave the following testimony in regard to religious persecution on the Atlantic Coast:

> Only in those villages now under the protection of Miskito warriors [anti-Sandinista rebels] are religious services being held. For some villages I visited, that protection had only recently been secured. And even in this large zone many villages cannot hold church services because their religious leaders are in jail or are in exile in Honduras or Costa Rica.
>
> During the Sandinista military occupations of villages, churches have commonly been used as jails, to detain men and women accused or suspected of counterrevolutionary activities. Churches have also been used to house the Sandinista soldiers. Bibles and hymn books have been destroyed. Villagers accuse the Sandinista soldiers of defecating and urinating in the churches. . . .
>
> The Miskitos are a very religious people, and they have suffered greatly from the denial of their freedom of religion. In almost all of my discussions with hundreds of Miskito men and women, this was a principal grievance they reported to me.[19]

As the events that took place on the Atlantic Coast show, the Sandinistas' policy toward the Christian churches did not follow the same pattern in all parts of the country. The Sandinistas might be acting with relative restraint and tolerance in some regions, while in others they were engaging in open persecution. As a rule, the more remote and isolated the setting, the harsher the Sandinistas were. But harshness was inconsistent. There were periods of almost complete calm—weeks, and even months, would pass when pastors and Christians in general would go unmolested and the Sandinistas would speak of dialogue. But then suddenly there would come an outburst of inflammatory accusations, mob attacks, and other physical and psychological harassment. Sometimes the abrupt change appeared to come in response to some specific event—the Sandinistas would say, "provocations." But at other times they seemed to come out of nowhere.

While I was still in Nicaragua, the Sandinistas' unpredictability surprised me. Their repression, for instance, did not seem to follow a clear pattern. Some people who were very outspoken in their criticism of the regime would come and go undisturbed. Others, for only the mildest criticism, might suddenly be jailed, mobbed, or beaten. Sometimes criticism by *La Prensa* that might be expected to ignite the fury of the Sandinistas would get a green light from the censors. But at other times even a casual remark about the taste of the supermarket's onions would be censored.

As time went by, we became convinced that this unpredictability was not so much the outcome of immaturity or incompetence or disagreements among the Sandinista leaders as it was the application of a deliberate strategy. We began to observe the political payoff this approach had for the Sandinistas. It confounded their adversaries, who were often caught off-guard. It confused visitors, who, being skillfully hosted by the Sandinistas and the revolutionary Christians, would perhaps witness an outspoken priest give an anti-Sandinista sermon with impunity, or talk with a real political opponent who usually got visas and permits from the government when he needed them. The fate of any particular opponent could change overnight, but the inconsistency meant that there were always plenty of exceptions around. For most Nicaraguans, this strategy introduced a subtle uncertainty and diffuse fear. Since there was no apparent pattern or clear-cut rules, no one could be sure of what would happen next.

In the last months of 1982 the Nicaraguan government, taking a new tack, began to court some Catholic bishops while stepping up its attempts to portray Archbishop Obando as the source of all tensions between the church and the state (a claim that was picked up by some North American visitors and publicized in the religious press; for example, by Fr. Vincent Giese in *Our Sunday Visitor*).

SANDINISTA EDUCATION AND THE CHURCH

But a new round of attacks against all bishops began in December 1982. The reason was the growing concern of the bishops and many other Christians about the increasingly Marxist and atheistic nature of materials being used in the Nicaraguan public schools. The Ministry of Education made it mandatory for all high school students to study Marx's theory of dialectical materialism, regarded, in the official pamphlets distributed to teachers, as the "basis of all scientific endeavor."

In general, the Sandinistas were stepping up their drive to politicize education and cultural and artistic endeavors. The determination to bring these areas under their hegemony, already outlined in the 1969 and subsequent programs of the FSLN, had been reiterated by several Sandinista leaders after the triumph of the revolution. Commander Bayardo Arce, for example, had said: "We are convinced that cultural activity should be seen as it is: as an ideological activity."[20] Government junta member Sergio Ramírez had said:

> The culture is also a political function, and it should exist as a political function, that is, as a revolutionary function of transformation. . . . We could never accept the existence of a culture isolated from the revolutionary process.[21]

The revolutionary Christians shared this view of culture. Fr. Ernesto Cardenal, for instance, in his role as Minister of Culture, said:

> To those of us who have had a Christian education, it was taught that everything should be subordinated to God. But true Christianity teaches that God is love to men; we thus have to say that everything should be subordinated to the love of men. So there is no room for

art for the sake of art itself; art has to be subordinated to the love of men, that is, to the revolution—as does everything else.[22]

In a document of the Nicaraguan Ministry of Education, released in September 1982, entitled "Ends and Goals of the New Education," the Sandinista government stated that one of the major objectives of the new education was "to form new generations in the values and principles of the Sandinista people's revolution," and to "form the new man in the thoughts and example of the heroes and martyrs [of the revolution]." The document stated that one of the general objectives of the new education would be to provide a humanistic, scientific, techno-logical, political, ideological, and moral formation compatible with the principles and programs of the revolution. Likewise, the "new man" to be formed would be patriotic and revolutionary, anti-imperialist, internationalist, for peace and against every form of exploitation. He was to be self-critical, with a "scientific view of the world and society." Moreover, he was to understand "that the interests of the individual must harmonize with the social and national interests." The document also promised that the right of parents to choose schools different from those of the government would be respected. But, in fact, it deprived parents, as well as the private schools themselves, of the right to choose the type of education they wished to provide.

Speaking sometime later, in 1984, Deputy Education Minister Hernan Sotelo said that education had to be comprehended as a process of integrating the populace into the revolution, as a political means to an end. Those who objected to this, he added, "belong to the classes which have been shunted aside by the power process." The basic goal of education was "political and ideological transformation" for the maintenance of the "people's power."[23]

To provide Nicaragua with teachers and technicians trained in a Marxist class-conflict mentality, the Sandinistas began in 1979 to send a yearly average of five hundred elite secondary school pupils and five hundred top university students to Cuba and East European countries. On April 19, 1985, *Barricada* pub-lished a full list of the students selected to pursue higher educa-tion abroad. There were two hundred for the USSR, twenty-five for Czechoslovakia, thirty for Bulgaria, thirty-seven for East Ger-many, and four for Hungary. Many others would be assigned to

Cuba. The Ministry of Education also chose two thousand Nicaraguan teachers to fly to Cuba in March 1985 for a four-month intensive course in "pedagogy." (In 1984 Nicaragua had sent fifteen hundred teachers to Cuba.)

Sotelo also explained that the state has the right to influence the personnel policies of private educational institutions. In fact, since about 1982 private school teaching positions have increasingly been filled with Sandinista teachers.[24] The same phenomenon was reported by Chris Hedges in the U.S.-based *National Catholic Reporter:*

> The Sandinista government has been forcing Catholic schools not only to hire teachers whose ideology has been approved by the state, but also to use a curriculum that is little less than a primer for Sandinista ideology. In many state-run schools, religion itself has become a forbidden topic.[25]

An examination of the textbooks used in Nicaraguan schools supports the veracity of these assertions. For instance, topic one of the grammar book for children in their third year of elementary school begins with a conversation between Commander Carlos Fonseca and a Moscow boy. Adapted from Fonseca's book *A Nicaraguan in Moscow,* the conversation opens with the child, Vladimiro, asking Fonseca whether it is true that in Latin America most children cannot attend school. After Fonseca answers that such is the case, Vladimiro explains that in the Soviet Union all children can go to school, although before the revolution the situation was the same as it is in Latin America. Vladimiro then describes how peace-loving the Soviets are, and so on. The grammar lesson asks the young readers: Who was talking in the story? How do the Soviet children live?, etc.[26] Topic four teaches that Latin America is awakening. A poem in the lesson begins:

> If Nicaragua sparked the flame,
> El Salvador shall continue.
> Then all America will follow
> Becoming a closed fist.

Questions of the reader are: What is the reading about? (answer: Latin America awakens); what are the children of Latin America to do? (answer: to fight); what will a united Latin America be? (answer: a fortress against the exploiters).[27]

Hedges, in the article mentioned above, picked out another feature of Nicaraguan education that has also been addressed by the Catholic bishops: the lack of a critical, open, or searching spirit. Schoolchildren are instructed to sing the Sandinista anthem and then shout: "The nine [the FSLN national directorate] command me!" Television interviews with students, noticed another observer, "generally produce an outpouring of deadly earnest slogans without individual variation. Among such organized youth there is little sign of the often evoked 'tenderness of the revolution.' "28

University curricula have also been reshaped with Marxist-Leninist propaganda. A description of the situation at the National University (UNAN) was given in 1985 by the former Sandinista director of planning of the Nicaraguan International Reconstruction Fund, the economist and former UNAN professor, Jorge Alaníz. Referring to the Department of Economic Sciences, changed after the revolution to the Department of Political Economy, Alaníz mentions with irony how, in a single stroke,

> the teaching of "bourgeois economics," the false science of capitalism, was suppressed and replaced by the science of all sciences, Marxism-Leninism, as understood and revised by Professor Stalin. The former texts have been replaced by the *Manual of Political Economy* of the Academy of Sciences of the USSR and by another manual, *The Principles of Dialectical Materialism.* Lenin's *Imperialism: The Higher State of Capitalism* and *State and Revolution,* in addition to some Cuban publications and pamphlets containing economic propaganda of the FSLN, complete all the basic readings for the whole degree—from the first year to the last.29

Not surprisingly these developments in education brought a strong reaction from the Christian community. If the state was nonconfessional and committed to granting privileges neither to believers nor nonbelievers (FSLN Official Communique on Religion, October 1980), how could it now be imposing the specific ideology of a political party on the educational system? The bishops had stated in their first postrevolution pastoral letter (November 1979) that they would not recognize as valid a socialism that would deny parents the right to educate their children according to their convictions and beliefs. But now in Sandinista Nicaragua the state was imposing a Sandinista education on the whole educational system, regardless of whether the schools were public or private.

The first Nicaraguan Christians to protest this educational policy were a couple of organizations of Christian parents: the Unión Nicaraguense de Asociaciones de Padres de Familia de Colegios Cristianos (UNAPAFACC) and the Unión de Padres de Familia por la Educación Cristiana (UPAFEC):

It is not our intention to antagonize the government with Christianity. But we cannot avoid rejecting the aforementioned document ["Ends and Goals of the New Education"], for it is contrary to our Christianity. There is the pretense that the orientation for education in Nicaragua comes from the directorate of the FSLN as if God would have changed his plan and no longer entrusted the family, but a partisan political institution, with the basic task of education.[30]

The Nicaraguan bishops conference issued a carefully worded pastoral letter on December 8, 1982. In it the bishops acknowledged advances made in education by the Sandinista regime, particularly the literacy campaign and the increase in overall student enrollment. But they deplored

the tendency to treat some aspects of the formation of youth from a purely materialist perspective . . . a gradual loss of criticalness [reasoned analysis] in the education . . . the promotion of class struggle . . . the fostering and fueling of hatred between brothers . . . the propaganda in behalf of a literature which is alien to our people and which is in disagreement with its values and Christian beliefs [an oblique reference to Marxism-Leninism].[31]

Finally, the bishops conference condemned the instances in which officers of the Ministry of Education had obstructed the work of religious centers, "going so far at times as to interfere with the church's right to establish and freely run schools. . . ."[32]

In reaction the government launched a renewed campaign of attacks on the bishops conference. Both the Sandinistas and the revolutionary Christians scornfully rebuked the bishops. Junta member Sergio Ramírez announced that in Nicaragua, "There would be no parallel education, never"—meaning that there would be no education in any way different from the official education mandated by the state.[33] The revolutionary Christians, also writing in El Nuevo Diario, commented:

It would be sad [for the church] to cry because education might be in danger of not being Christian, when education is being provided for a people who have never had it.[34]

In January 1984 another conflict erupted between the Sandinistas and the Catholic Church when the Ministry of Education did not allow the Catholic La Salle High School to rehire seven teachers who had been fired by a former director of the school, the pro-Sandinista Christian Brother Edwin Maradiaga. The dispute led to protests from the Nicaraguan bishops conference—their statement was banned from publication by the state censor—and from the Nicaraguan Federation for Catholic Education and to a strike by the high school's teachers. The government did not yield. It announced that it would review the case in a year's time.

In May 1985, criticism of the partisan political nature of Nicaraguan education by UNAPAFACC (Unión de Padres de Familia de Colegios Cristianos) led to the detention and torture by State Security of its president, Sofonías Cisneros. As an example of how the Sandinistas had rewritten textbooks for elementary level students with the party's propaganda, Cisneros had quoted in a UNAPAFACC statement a passage—among many others—from a lesson in introductory French. It read: "Sergio Ramírez [Nicaragua's vice president] est grand, Napoleon Bonaparte est formidable, Humberto Ortega [commander in chief of the Sandinista army] est formidable."[35]

NOTES

1. Bishop Pablo Vega, "Circular Letter to All Leaders of the Community and to the Collaborators in Evangelization," Juigalpa, Nicaragua, August 27, 1980.

2. FSLN, "Comunicado de la Dirección Nacional del FSLN sobre la Religión," *Nicarauac*, No. 5, April-June 1981, p. 95.

3. All excerpts are from *Centro América en Llamas*, pp. 62-75.

4. Kerry Ptacek, *Nicaragua: A Revolution Against the Church?* (Washington, D.C.: The Institute on Religion and Democracy, 1981), p. 8.

5. Radio Sandino, October 22, 1980, quoted in *ibid.*, Ptacek, p. 9.

6. Agence France Presse, January 13, 1981, quoted in *ibid.*, Ptacek, p. 10.

7. Departamento Ecuménico de Investigaciones, *Sacerdotes en el Gobierno Nicaragüense: Poder o Servicio?* (San Jose, Costa Rica: DEI, 1981), p. 12.

8. Francis Francou, Carlos Corsi, and Cristina Corsi, *La Iglesia en Nicaragua* (Bogotá: CONFE, 1982), p. 51.

9. Radio Sandino, June 6 and 8, 1981, quoted in *op. cit.,* Ptacek, p. 12.

10. Radio Sandino, June 10, 1981, quoted in *ibid.,* Ptacek, p. 12.

11. Radio Sandino, June 10, 1981, quoted in *ibid.,* Ptacek, p. 13.

12. Radio Sandino, June 20, 1981.

13. IHCA, "Nicaragua en la Encrucijada," *Encuentro* (magazine of the Central American University), No. 19, Managua, July 1983, p. 56.

14. *Op. cit.,* Randall, p. 53.

15. *Barricada,* August 11, 1982, p. 1.

16. "Conflicto con las Sectas," *Amanecer,* No. 12, September 1982, Managua, p. 5.

17. *Ibid.*

18. Edgard Macías Gómez, *Revolución Sandinista y Religión* (San José, Costa Rica: n.p., 1982), p. 5.

19. Nietschmann, "Statement Before the OAS," p. 12.

20. Bayardo Arce, speech at the First National Encounter of Cultural Workers, in *Nicarauac,* No. 1, 1980.

21. Ramírez, speech, in *ibid.*

22. Cardenal, speech, in *ibid.*

23. Beat Ammann, "Nicaragua: 'One Great School,' " *Swiss Review of World Affairs,* January 1985, p. 7.

24. *Ibid.,* p. 6.

25. Chris Hedges, "Nicaragua: Strife within Church 'Really War of Western Socialist Mores,' " *National Catholic Reporter,* September, 1984, pp. 1, 25.

26. Ministerio de Educación, *Los Carlitos 3: Libro de Texto de Español para Tercer Grado,* Managua, 1985, pp. 9-10.

27. *Ibid.,* p. 201.

28. *Op. cit.,* Ammann, "Nicaragua: 'One Great School,' " p. 7.

29. Jorge Alaníz P., *Nicaragua: Una Revolución Reaccionaria* (Panama: Editorial Kosmos, 1985), p. 102.

30. UNAPAFACC-UPAFEC, "Commentarios Preliminares Sobre el Documento de Trabajo del Ministerio de Educatión, 'Fines y Metas de la Nueva Educación,' " Managua: UNAPAFACC-UPAFEC, 1982, p. 4.

31. Nicaraguan Bishops Conference, "Carta Pastoral del Episcopado Nicaragüense sobre la Educación Católica," Managua: Episcopal Conference, December 9, 1982, p. 8.

32. *Ibid.*

33. *El Nuevo Diario,* December 16, 1982, p. 10.

34. *Ibid.,* p. 2.

35. "Interroga Seguridad del Estado al Presidente de la Unión de Padres de Familia de Colegios Católicos," *Diario Las Américas,* Miami, May 22, 1985, p. 6.

FOURTEEN

THE VISIT OF
THE POPE AND AFTER

In March 1983 Pope John Paul II visited Nicaragua as part of a pastoral tour of Central America and the Caribbean. The visit drew a great deal of international attention because of the well-known tension between the Sandinista government and the Catholic hierarchy. By the time the Pope left, some were accusing him of sowing discord, while others were claiming that he had never been treated so disrespectfully. An examination of the Pope's brief time in Nicaragua provides important insights into the Sandinistas' mentality and their approach to religion in the new Nicaragua.

Leaving aside the points on which a consensus does not exist among the journalists present, the following description would be supported by relatively impartial observers. It is drawn from reports in the *Washington Post,* the *New York Times,* the major U.S. television networks, and the Vatican newspaper, *L'Osservatore Romano.* Many of the particulars can also be seen on the videotape made by Sandinista television.

1. The Catholic Church and the government agreed that the Pope's appearances in Managua and Leon were to be wholly religious and apolitical. The Catholic authorities warned parishioners against politicking and exhorted them not to carry partisan symbols or placards. Sandinista political supporters, however, carried political banners and posters and chanted slogans through megaphones.

2. The Sandinistas did not allow Nicaraguans the freedom to assemble to greet the Pope. Traffic was halted throughout most of the country, and only the Sandinista Defense Committees were entitled to transport people to the meeting places.

3. The Sandinistas prevented people from gathering ahead of time at the sites where the Pope was scheduled to appear. In Managua, police fired automatic weapons over the heads of people who attempted to get early places. Sandinista partisans were thus enabled to pack the front rows in the plaza.

4. An ABC-TV crew from the United States was detained and roughed up and their videotapes confiscated by police.

5. John Paul II was interrupted during his sermon in Managua, and then for the remainder of the mass, by heckling and the chanting of slogans. The police who were assigned to control the crowds frequently led the chants. Members of the Pope's entourage later stated that they had never before seen such behavior on a papal tour.

6. Government technicians connected microphones to the main loudspeaker system and the television sound system, to amplify the cry of agitators and the chants of "people's power."

7. During the celebration of the mass, all nine members of the Sandinista national directorate—including Tomás Borge and Daniel Ortega—joined the crowd in waving their left fists and shouting "people's power." They ended the mass by singing the FSLN anthem.

The Sandinistas and their supporters insist that far from trying to interfere with the public gathering to see the pope, the Nicaraguan government provided transportation and expensive logistic support. Heckling and interruptions during the mass in Managua took place, they acknowledge, but they assert that these were the result of spontaneous outbursts of people who were simply asking the Pope to pray for the "martyrs of the revolution" and for peace. When he did not, they became annoyed. The Sandinistas have been adamant in their refusal to apologize for the incidents during the Pope's time in Nicaragua and in their insistence that the people were justified in venting their indignation.

But, in fact, the FSLN deliberately intervened in every aspect of the visit, even to the extent of selecting beforehand the hundred persons to receive communion from the Pope.[1] As for the "spontaneity" of the hecklers at the Pope's mass, the videotape made by Sandinista television shows the police escorting groups of agitators armed with megaphones to a special location in the plaza where they were separated from the rest of the huge crowd by a line of FSLN militiamen in military uniform. Sandinista intelligence defector Miguel Bolanos later revealed that the

FSLN prepared most of these actions, including the chanting of slogans, well before the Pope's arrival.[2] The fact that the voices of agitators were connected to the main loudspeaker and television sound systems, so as to drown out, at times, the voice of the Pope, betrayed efforts which could not have been spontaneous.

The interruptions came, in fact, from a small minority of people. The great majority of Nicaraguans assembled to greet the Pope gave him and Archbishop Obando great ovations. Even the reports of the revolutionary Christians acknowledge this point. A book written by some pro-Sandinista foreign professors, including IHCA theologian Fr. Juan H. Pico, S.J., *The Pope in Nicaragua,* admitted that the people in the plaza with "clear political consciousness and with a liberating religious consciousness . . . were a minority," whereas people "religiously and politically confused" were a "great majority."[3]

The government's explanations, false or misleading as they are, nevertheless indicate the Sandinistas' general approach and mentality. While the government provided transportation to the Pope's events, their transportation, entrusted to the Sandinista Defense Committees, was the only transportation allowed; individual Christians or churches were prohibited from providing their own. Behind the government's alleged wish to help, there was a determination to channel and control events which they could not prevent so that they would be as much as possible a political gain. The FSLN could not stop the Pope from visiting Nicaragua without paying a great political cost. Yet, on the other hand, they were determined not to allow the visit to develop independently of their purposes.

Their attempt to control and politicize the event was acknowledged by the revolutionary Christians as the natural thing for the Sandinistas to do. The book mentioned above states that "The Front accepted the visit of the Pope . . . but it worked to use it as a clear support for its search for peace and as a clear denunciation of imperialist aggressions."[4]

Finally, it is important to note that the typical objections of the Sandinistas and their sympathizers to the way the Pope conducted himself were not that he said things critical of the revolution (he made no criticism of the Sandinista government), but that he did not *endorse* it. "I think the message of the Pope in Nicaragua was full of great omissions. The problem is not so much what he said but what he failed to say."[5]

According to the Sandinistas, their anger at the Pope was a

result of his failure to pray for the "martyrs of the revolution." In Leon, however, a town closer to the actual battlefront during the civil war, the Pope greeted the victims of violence. From the outset of his trip to Central America, the Pope insisted that the visit was undertaken as a pastoral, as opposed to an official or diplomatic, mission. This was something that the Sandinistas were unwilling to grant. Indeed, the pastoral rather than political nature of the Pope's visit was precisely what the Sandinistas objected to. His pastoral goals did not support their political agenda and, as in his sermon in Managua on the unity of the church, implicitly ran counter to Sandinista goals.

The government's resentment at John Paul II's failure to endorse the Sandinista revolution was vividly illustrated at the Pope's mass in Managua. On the Sandinista television broadcast of the event, the loud cry of a female Sandinista agitator was heard while the Pope distributed communion. Her remark reflects the Sandinista mentality: "Holy Father, if you are truly the representative of Christ on earth, we demand ["te exigimos"] that you side with us."[6] The revolutionary Christians also explicitly criticized the Pope for not supporting the FSLN. The back cover of The Pope in Nicaragua contains the following quote:

> The Pope did not tell us anything. . . . The Holy Father did not assume a stand of commitment in the Christian struggle for peace.[7]

It is significant that on this occasion the Sandinistas acted in full view of the international media. People who are prepared to engage in such disdainful treatment of a revered world religious leader can hardly be expected to act with respect for religious rights when dealing with less well-known believers outside the glare of international publicity.

Nicaraguan revolutionary Christians reacted bitterly toward the Pope. Fr. Ernesto Cardenal, speaking in Freiburg, Switzerland, on June 4, 1983, commented:

> It has been said that the Pope is very thankful to the CIA for the work it has done in Poland and the Pope has come to repay them in Central America.[8]

Less expected was the reaction of some well-known theologians from other parts of the world. In May of 1983 an international group of theologians published an open letter to John Paul

II in which they gave their support to the Nicaraguan revolutionary Christians and criticized him, but did not express so much as
a word of concern for the way the Sandinistas handled his Nicaragua visit. Signed by theologians Johannes Baptist Metz (Germany), Leonardo Boff (Brazil), Enrique Dussel (Mexico), Virgilio
Elizondo (director of the Mexican American Cultural Center in
the United States), Hans Kung (Germany), and others, their letter
stated that:

> In spite of all the difficulties and lack of understanding, we recognize
> in the church of the poor the true faith of the apostles. . . . We regret
> that the people did not feel confirmed in their faith when they
> received the visit of the Pope, who thus frustrated the petition of the
> people for peace and for the honorable remembrance of their fallen
> ones.[9]

For whatever reasons, these foreign theologians have given the
embrace of solidarity and support to an elite group of Christians
in Nicaragua who have allied themselves with the party in power. But the support that this self-defined "church of the poor"
has been unable to secure is that of the Nicaraguan poor—and
even less so after the Pope's visit. The whole incident hurt the
Sandinistas and the revolutionary Christians, alienating them
even further from most ordinary Catholics in the country. The
decline of the advocates of the "people's church" became more
evident later in the year when the Confederation of Religious of
Nicaragua, an association of members of Catholic religious orders and institutes, formerly a stronghold of the revolutionary
Christians, elected a new board of directors, all of whom were
faithful to the hierarchy.
    In the aftermath of the Pope's visit, the advocates of the
people's church shifted the focus of their proselytizing efforts
from Nicaraguans to foreign Christians. The revolutionary Christian became more concerned with convincing foreign Christians
of the virtues of the Sandinista revolution than with convincing
Nicaraguan Christians that they should support the FSLN. Their
theologians and theological centers shifted their concentration to
multilingual periodicals and pamphlets, to hosting foreign visitors, to organizing tours to Nicaragua, and to traveling abroad
to visit foreign churches and campuses.
    Along with this shift of focus, the revolutionary Christians
dropped their open advocacy of Marxism and adopted a more

detached tone when giving their analysis of the Nicaraguan situation. As mentioned, open espousal of Marxism was proving to be counterproductive. The revolutionary Christians needed to protect their credibility within the churches if they were to affect Christians, and critics were using their Marxist references against them in the polemical battles going on outside of Nicaragua. The revolutionary Christians therefore adopted their own version of the Tercerista strategy, out of a need to make their advocacy of the Sandinista revolution more effective. IHCA now claimed that some statements of the revolutionary Christians, uttered during the first phase of the revolution, had expressed some immaturity.

One of the major tactics of this revised game plan was to try to convince the international audience that the FSLN was not really committed to Marxism-Leninism. Another thrust was to provide foreign visitors with justifications for the policies of the Sandinista government in regard to the independent churches in Nicaragua. Finally, they set themselves to continue undermining the reputation of the Catholic bishops and other politically independent Christians, typecasting them as bourgeois reactionaries. Fr. Juan H. Pico, S.J., for example, IHCA's main theologian, expressed the following in June 1983:

> The Nicaraguan Church hierarchy is clearly identified with the interests of the bourgeoisie, and, at the same time, it is made a tool by it, being taken as its massive (political-religious) symbol and as its voice. It is foreseeable that this hierarchy will become increasingly identified with the "contra" itself. For this reason, and given its [the "contra"] support within its own organizations, it will almost turn into a political party of counterrevolutionary opposition.[10]

The gravity of this accusation in the Nicaraguan political context can scarcely be grasped outside Nicaragua. It amounted to saying that the Catholic bishops were guilty of treason, and it was therefore almost an invitation to the Sandinistas to escalate their attacks against the Catholic Church.

By the middle of 1983 the Sandinistas were, in fact, toughening their stand vis-á-vis the independent Christian churches. The first hints were provided by Tomás Borge, when, in the spring of that year, he announced that the Ministry of the Interior was keeping track of "counterrevolutionary priests" who were preaching dissent in the churches.

CONTINUING ATTACKS ON THE CHURCH

In May 1983, Fr. Timoteo Merino, a priest who for many years had been serving the peasants in the remote and extremely poor province of Rio San Juan, was expelled from Nicaragua on charges that he was "an ideological agent of the counterrevolutionary groups."[11] Knowing beforehand what the Sandinistas were preparing against him, Fr. Merino had offered to respond to any specific accusations before the appropriate authorities. The Sandinistas, however, offered him no opportunity to make a defense. Nine priests of Fr. Merino's diocese, as well as his bishop, protested the action against him. The priests included a reference to cases of harassment and threats against other priests "that have not been made public."[12] In a final letter to his parishioners, Fr. Merino explained why the Sandinistas were after him: "The true reason is that they have been unable to bend me to the demands of those who want the church to become an instrument . . . to serve a Marxist-Leninist political project, instead of the integral gospel."[13]

On August 29, 1983, the Nicaraguan bishops conference issued a pastoral letter criticizing a military draft law enacted by the government. The bishops expressed a concern shared by many Nicaraguan parents and youth: the Sandinista army was a partisan organization—an official branch of the FSLN—and not a truly national army. To force all Nicaraguan youth to serve in such an army was therefore a violation of the human right of freedom of association (no one should be forced to join a partisan organization) and was also objectionable on grounds of conscience (no one should be forced to serve a party with an ideology opposed at many points to one's religious convictions).

The Sandinistas responded by speaking of treason by the bishops. In an attempt to divide the bishops and isolate the archbishop of Managua, they portrayed the document, which in reality came from the whole episcopate, as "the Obando document."

Universal conscription into the Sandinista party army went into effect on September 30. One month later, on Sunday, October 30, in a wave of coordinated simultaneous attacks, Sandinista mobs, some of them armed with shotguns, stormed twenty-six Catholic churches in various towns—eight in Managua—interrupting mass, smashing doors and windows, and savagely beating several parishioners. According to a report issued by the archdiocese of Managua, "Many parishioners suffered a brutal beating inside the sacred precincts." Participants in a procession in honor of the Virgin Mary were also beaten, as was the auxiliary bishop of Managua, Bosco Vivas, who in addition received death threats.[14] The attacks resumed during the evening, when the doors of some other churches were ripped off.

On Tuesday, November 1, two Salesian priests, Fr. Luis Corral Prieto and Fr. José María Pacheco, were deported. According to a government communique, the two priests had urged people to ignore the military service law and supported the counterrevolutionaries by demanding a dialogue between the government and the rebels.[15] Fr. Pacheco, who had been expelled by Somoza on September 8, 1978, on the charge of interfering in political issues, said that many Nicaraguan youth were refusing to join the army, arguing that although they are ready to die for their country they are not ready to give up their lives for a political party.[16]

The Vatican newspaper, *L'Osservatore Romano,* condemned the attacks on the churches and the expulsion of the two priests as a new episode of "provocation and religious intolerance," adding: "It is difficult to accept the rationale of the government to the effect that the security services had discovered a plan to launch a campaign against military service."[17]

Even more serious were reports of worsening repression in the countryside. They came from two Catholic bishops: Bishop Pedro Vilchez, from northern Jinotega, and an area where the Sandinistas were engaging the so-called contras in battle, and Bishop Pablo Vega, from the south-central rural province of Chontales, who was elected president of the Nicaraguan bishops conference in late 1983. Bishop Vilchez sent a letter to the civilian and ecclesiastical authorities of the country in which he reported events such as the following:

> The people of this place flee when they learn that the "compas" [members of the Sandinista army] are coming, for they are afraid of the tortures, violations, and killings that come with charges of what constitute today the greatest crime in the mountains: threatening state security. They often jail members of the diocesan pastoral teams and of Catholic Action [a Catholic lay organization active throughout most of Latin America]. . . . The Sandinistas have an espionage network made up of members of State Security; they keep detailed records on all priests, nuns, and members of religious orders, as well as on all Christian lay movements, their members, their pastoral activities, what they say in their meetings, what they do, their politi-

cal participation. . . . There is a very well-planned infiltration [of Christian movements] to hinder all pastoral activity. Their program is wholly oriented to establishing a Marxist system. They have removed all crucifixes from the classrooms, they have prohibited prayer before classes.[18]

Bishop Vilchez also refers in his letter to several instances of actions like those reported by Professor Bernard Nietschmann and Bishop Vega: the military occupation and desecration, as well as the outright burning, of several country chapels—the chapels of Del Tigre, Aguascalientes, Kaisiguás, and Aguasás are specifically mentioned. Bishop Vilchez reports that the Sandinista authorities demand from religious leaders lists of all those who attend religious services in their areas.

Bishop Vega, in Chontales, documented even graver crimes. In a report released on November 2, 1983, he denounced the murder of lay Christian leaders of his diocese, as well as instances of harassment, threats, and other aggression against many church leaders.[19] The following is the brief story of the murder of Alfonso Galeano, lay activist of Las Pavas county:

> On some occasions he had been threatened with death because of his Christian activities. One day a group of men, who appeared to be thieves, assaulted his home while he and some other people were there. They did not steal anything and only [Galeano] was killed. It later came to light that the apparent robbers were members of the Sandinista militias. They were arrested but later seen moving about freely.

Another case was that of Daniel Sierra Ocon:

> He was arrested, accused of counterrevolutionary activities—a charge which was never substantiated. After he had been declared innocent of the charges and [the Sandinistas] had promised to release him, his wife was told that [he] had committed suicide in the officers' barracks.

Another case: Yamilet Sequeira de Lorio, a woman in charge of evangelization in San Miguel:

> She had been pressured to join State Security on several occasions. She was arrested along with her husband and another person by the local State Security chief. Their bodies were discovered some days later in an uninhabited area in the vicinity of San Miguel, showing signs of violence and grotesque tortures.

According to later remarks by Bishop Vega, "These cases are not frequent, but they constitute a way of intimidating and silencing everyone responsible for the evangelization programs. The greatest tragedy is that those families who have suffered these aggressions do not dare to make their complaints public because they are afraid of the reprisals."[20] The cases being reported, in other words, were only those which happened to break the barrier of silence and intimidation.

Sometimes they did so through fortuitous circumstances. An example is that of a Pentecostal pastor named Prudencio Baltodano. According to Baltodano, a group of Sandinista soldiers who were engaging some "contras" in combat captured him, apparently believing that he and his family were helping the rebels. When they found out that he was an evangelical pastor, they decided to torture him. Baltodano said that they declared themselves to be Communists and challenged him to pray to his God to see if He would save him. He was beaten and tied to a tree, and then his ears were cut off. One of the soldiers stabbed him in the neck with his bayonet, and they left him to bleed to death. The knife, however, missed the jugular. After hours of attempts, Baltodano was finally able to free himself. He wandered through the jungle for two days before coming upon a friendly family, who took care of him and later helped him to reach the Costa Rican border. He was later able to testify about his ordeal and the cold-blooded murder of four members of his community, El Tendido. I met Baltodano in the U.S. where I heard his testimony. He showed me his mutilated ears and the big scar on his neck. Baltodano's narrow escape had allowed the curtain of silence to be briefly lifted.

The stories reported by Bishops Vilchez and Vega and by Baltodano are examples of intense, government-promoted hostility toward Christians unwilling to get behind the FSLN. The omnipresent and incessant hammering of the Sandinista media, as well as the political education campaign within the army, portray these Christians as counterrevolutionaries, assassins, vipers, pharisees, and traitors. No wonder that this demonizing of a specific group of people takes its toll in violence.

NOTES

1. SEDAC, Episcopal Secretariat of Central America, *Juan Pablo II en América Central* (Costa Rica, 1984), p. 142.

2. *The Washington Post,* July 19, 1983.

3. *El Papa en Nicaragua* (Madrid: Editorial IEPALA, 1983), p. 221.

4. *Ibid.,* p. 222.

5. Tomás Borge, quoted by Agence France Presse, March 2, 1983 in *Diario las Américas,* Miami, March 4, 1983, p. 6.

6. The Papal Mass in Managua, Nicaragua, Friday, March 4, 1983, excerpts taped from the official Sandinista Television broadcast, distributed by the Nicaraguan Information Center, St. Charles, Mo.

7. *Op. cit., El Papa en Nicaragua,* back cover.

8. *Op. cit., Juan Pablo II en América Central,* p. 144.

9. "Carta de Apoyo a la Iglesia de los Pobres que esta en Nicaragua," in *op. cit., El Papa en Nicaragua,* p. 281.

10. *Ibid.,* p. 219.

11. *Barricada,* May 3, 1983, p. 7.

12. Statement by the priests council of Juigalpa, May 5, 1983.

13. Fr. Timoteo Merino, "Last Will to the Brothers and Sisters of the Communities of San Carlos, La Azucena, Sábalos, El Castillo, and Morrillo," undated letter.

14. *The Miami Herald,* November 4, 1983, p. 3.

15. *The New York Times,* November 2, 1983.

16. *La Prensa Libre,* Extraordinary Edition, San José, Costa Rica, November 2, 1983.

17. Spanish Language Edition, November 2, 1983, p. 1.

18. Bishop Pedro Vilchez, "Open Letter," Prelature of Jinotega, November 9, 1983.

19. Bishop Pablo Vega, "Cases that We Consider Aggressions Against the Church," Prelature of Juigalpa, November 2, 1983.

20. Bishop Vega, lecture at the Galveston-Houston Chancery, published in *La Voz,* Houston, Texas, July 10, 1984, p. 4.

FIFTEEN

THE BISHOPS' CALL FOR RECONCILIATION

The crisis between the Sandinista government and the independent Christian churches deepened throughout most of 1984. A focal point of tension was the "Pastoral Letter on Reconciliation" that the Nicaraguan bishops conference issued at Easter. The letter deplored the civil war taking place in the country and called attention to the fact that sin was at the root of the difficulties facing the Nicaraguan people. Young men are dying on the battlefield, children are subject to atheistic ideological indoctrination, families are divided by political differences, some of the mass media incites hatred, and so on. In response to this turmoil, the bishops pleaded for conversion, reconciliation, and a dialogue encompassing all sectors of Nicaraguan society.

> It is dishonest to constantly blame internal aggression and violence on foreign aggression. It is useless to blame the evil past for everything, without recognizing the problems of the present. All Nicaraguans inside and outside the country must participate in this dialogue, regardless of ideology, class, or partisan belief. Furthermore, we think that Nicaraguans who have taken up arms against the government must also participate in this dialogue. If not, there will be no possibility of a settlement, and our people, especially the poorest among them, will continue to suffer and die.[1]

The bishops' letter drew severe criticism from the Sandinistas. Interior Minister Tomás Borge called it "criminal." Daniel Ortega suggested that the letter had been written at the American embassy and that it would not be at all surprising if the bishops were working under instructions from the CIA. He later called the bishops "anti-Christians," "dishonest," and "immoral." *Barricada* accused the Nicaraguan hierarchy of being corrupt, Somocista, and made up of "sanctified hypocrites."[2] Sandinista Comandante Dora Téllez said the letter had been written by "wolves dressed in sheep's clothing."[3] These statements were part of a furious campaign of invective against the bishops unleashed by the Sandinista media, and focused particularly on Archbishop Obando. Despite the fact that the letter had been issued by the entire bishops conference, the Sandinistas insisted on calling it Obando's letter.

As usual, the revolutionary Christians echoed these accusations and gave them a theological rationale. The Ecumenical Axis (MEC-CELADEC) expressed

> indignation at the participation of Msgr. Obando y Bravo in activities against the peace and life of our people. . . . It really fills us with sorrow to see the low level to which he has descended, thus contradicting his much acclaimed moral quality in a complete negation of the image and righteousness that he hypocritically tries to sell. . . . It is outrageous, besides, to discover the intentions, which are not at all Christian or humanitarian, of Msgr. Obando y Bravo.[4]

José Arguello, a Centro Antonio Valdivieso theologian, characterized the bishops' letter as biased in behalf of the imperialist political policies of the Reagan Administration. He asked how dialogue could ever take place with the "assassins" of the Nicaraguan people (the "contras").

A director of one province of the Jesuits, the Spanish-born Fr. Inaki Zubizarreta, published an open letter criticizing the bishops and defending the position of the government. His letter, presented to the Sandinistas as an official letter from the Society of Jesus, was repudiated by many local Jesuits, who restated their support for the bishops. The Superior General of the Jesuits intervened in the dispute and criticized the provincial's action:

> I cannot but formally disapprove of the statement criticizing the pastoral letter issued by the Nicaraguan bishops last Easter, because [Fr. Zubizarreta's statement] was formulated without following the norms of dialogue with the ecclesiastical hierarchy and within the Society of Jesus itself.[5]

Outside Nicaragua, the harsh reaction of the Sandinistas and their allies prompted condemnations from liberals and conservatives alike. In the U.S., Senator Ted Kennedy in a speech before Congress termed the Sandinistas' response to the bishops "unacceptable." He continued,

> This is not the language of tolerance or religious freedom. These are not the words of people who are genuinely pledged to pluralism. This is not the rhetoric of a leadership determined to bring peace and reconciliation to all of the people of Nicaragua.[6]

The Vatican and several conferences of Catholic bishops in other nations also expressed their concern over the verbal campaign against the Nicaraguan episcopate.

The reason for the Sandinistas' aggressive reaction to the bishops' letter was probably the fact that the bishops did not accept the view that the war in Nicaragua was a war between Nicaragua and U.S. imperialism. Rather, the bishops regarded the conflict as a civil war. The Sandinistas do not recognize the "contras" as Nicaraguans with valid political interests. As mentioned earlier, they are ordinarily referred to in the Sandinista media as beasts, dogs, Somocistas, mercenaries, or assassins. No dialogue is possible with them.

This Sandinista stance toward the contras is not only a necessary consequence of their black-and-white view of the world; it is also tactically useful. The portrayal of the conflict as fundamentally international (between the U.S. and Nicaragua) rather than fundamentally internal (between Nicaraguans committed to diametrically opposed visions for the nation) helps the Sandinistas to legitimize the repression of their opponents, who are seen as traitors rather than political opponents. The Sandinista view also gives them a rationale for their policy of enforced conscription. It also wins them sympathy in the international forum, where they present themselves as the victims of foreign aggression, forced to defend their hard-won revolution. The bishops' statement enraged the Sandinistas by its refusal to endorse the Sandinista view of things and its recognition of the war as a civil one which ought to be resolved by dialogue rather than the total elimination of the Sandinistas' opponents.

In fact, the bishops' view is more realistic than the government's. Whatever one thinks of the contras' willingness to take up arms and of the degree to which they deserve foreign support, they are no less Nicaraguan than the Sandinistas. In terms of foreign technical, logistical, and financial support, there is little difference between the Sandinistas and the contras. The contras have been financed in part by the U.S. government through the CIA; the Sandinistas, on the other hand, have received over $4 billion from abroad since coming to power, a third of which has been destined for defense. The contras have been trained and advised by the CIA, the Sandinistas by thousands of Cuban and East European military advisors.

In terms of those who are actually doing the fighting, both armies are overwhelmingly Nicaraguan. The charge that the contras are mainly Somocista former National Guardsmen does not stand up to scrutiny. Somoza's armed forces never had more than eight thousand to ten thousand members, and many of these were unfit for combat, being essentially parasites who made their livelihood through bribes and corruption. One tenth of the military died during the war. Most of the remainder were captured in Managua in July 1979. At most, two thousand escaped from the country. Even assuming that all of them joined the contras, which would be highly unlikely, they could constitute only a fraction of the roughly fifteen thousand contra forces. In fact, perhaps as many as four thousand of the rebels are Miskito Indians. As many as four thousand are defectors from the Sandinista militias. Former Sandinista militia compose the bulk of the southern army led by former Sandinista commander Edén Pastora. Most of the remaining contras are peasants.

The bishops believed that if there was no dialogue between the rebels and the Sandinistas, the war would continue to drag on. The Sandinistas, however, flatly turned down any consideration of dialogue. "We shall only dialogue through the barrel of a gun," said junta member Sergio Ramírez.

SANDINISTA REPRISALS: THE FATHER PEÑA AFFAIR

A new phase in the struggle between the Sandinistas and the Catholic Church opened in June 1984. On Sunday, June 17, a mass concelebrated by the nine Nicaraguan bishops in the town of El Sauce and attended by nearly three thousand Catholics was attacked by a Sandinista mob of about three hundred trained cadres. The next day Tomás Borge announced a press conference to disclose how the government had dismantled a conspiracy against the revolution. At the conference, held two days later, Commander Lenín Cerna, chief of State Security, presented a man named Pedro Espinoza (captured on Monday, June 18, the same day that the press conference was originally announced), who claimed to head an organization called the Counterrevolutionary Internal Front. In his declarations he indicted several reputable Nicaraguan dissidents, but most noteworthy, he included Fr. Amado Peña, a Catholic priest responsible for one of the largest working-class parishes in Managua and a firm supporter of the Nicaraguan bishops.

Commander Cerna then showed a black-and-white film in which Espinoza appears with Fr. Peña in a small living room with some other people. There is conversation about subversive activities. The scene shifts to another room, where the dialogue between Fr. Peña and Espinoza is now about arms and the way to handle them. Whereas Espinoza's face is seen and his words are clearly audible, all that is seen of Fr. Peña is his back, and all that is heard from him are softly spoken words, not nearly as audible as in the first scene. For the Nicaraguan government, this was "irrefutable" evidence of the priest's involvement in the counterrevolution and of the Catholic Church's hypocrisy in preaching peace and dialogue.

The same day, a few hours before the press conference, another incident involving Fr. Peña had taken place. A man, whom Fr. Peña later affirmed he knew by sight, gave the priest a ride. Before reaching his destination, the man stopped the car and asked Fr. Peña to deliver a piece of luggage he was carrying to another man waiting in a nearby car. Fr. Peña was doing this favor when the police arrived with a Sandinista TV crew. They asked the priest to open the case; it was filled with explosives.

Filmed twice while conspiring against the government, there was no escape for Fr. Peña. Tomás Borge called the archbishop of Managua and told him that if the church wanted to avoid the arrest of the counterrevolutionary priest, they had better ask him to seek asylum at the Vatican delegation to Nicaragua.

After consultation with Fr. Peña, Archbishop Obando rejected Borge's suggestion. Fr. Peña stated that he remembered the first living room where he had been shown in the film, saying that it was in a house where he had been invited to give his blessing and stay for a party. But, he added, he did not remember the second room, nor could he figure out why in the film there were so few people, whereas at the party there had been many more. He signed a statement describing details of what he characterized as a trap to discredit him and the Catholic Church.

Catholic officials were soon convinced that the whole affair was a government setup. "With films you can do many things: people can even fly in them," remarked one official. From a technical point of view, indeed, there was no problem in splicing together genuine and staged scenes and impersonating Fr. Peña's voice, especially when he was not facing the camera.

In support of Fr. Peña, the Nicaraguan bishops conference reminded Nicaraguan Catholics of the Carballo incident and other occasions when the Sandinista government had lied in matters concerning church officials. They had publicly announced that Bishop Salvador Schlaefer had been murdered by the contras when, in fact, he was accompanying some Miskito Indians in a massive escape from a government relocation camp; that Archbishop Obando was visting President Reagan when he was visiting the Pope; and that Bishop Pablo Vega had smuggled arms for the contras although he had not.

Unbending to the request of Borge, Fr. Peña, with the support of his superiors, decided to go back to his parish and continue his pastoral ministry. The next day, June 21, while he was celebrating mass, a Sandinista mob surrounded the church and burned several tires on the sidewalk. Other militants got on top of the building and began to tear the roof off. When the suffocating parishioners tried to escape, they were beaten by the mob. Fr. Peña took refuge at a seminary, where he remained under house arrest until being "pardoned" almost a year later.

THE EXPELLING OF TEN CATHOLIC PRIESTS

In response to this incident, the Catholic bishops organized a silent march in support of Fr. Peña. Government reaction was swift. Next day, in retaliation it expelled ten foreign-born priests without advance notice or legal procedure.

Two reasons for the expulsions were given by the Sandinista regime. The first was that the priests had been involved in a subversive political action by participating in an antigovernment demonstration. In fact only five of the ten priests had taken part in the march, which could, in any case, be considered subversive only by a government which held all forms of dissent as subversive.

The government's second charge was that the priests were using their pastoral ministries to preach against the Nicaraguan revolution and promote opposition. The government did not supply evidence, in spite of requests by Catholic Church authorities and the Spanish ambassador (some of the expelled priests were Spanish). According to one of the expelled priests, Fr. Santiago Anitua, S.J., "We were not priests doing politics from the pulpit. But we did have some things in common. One is that we were all working in areas that the government regards as particularly key and sensitive areas."[7]

What were these areas? An analysis by Fr. Anitua provides further indications of the FSLN's strategy toward the churches. Fr. Anitua was a Jesuit priest who moved to Nicaragua in 1953. He had extensive experience with lay Christian movements and was himself a leader of the charismatic renewal movement in Nicaragua. At the time of his expulsion, he was professor and spiritual director at the Nicaraguan Catholic Seminary. The following is Fr. Anitua's brief description of the other expelled priests:

> Fr. Mario Madriz, a Panamanian, was the director of the large Don Bosco High School, which educates thousands of poor young people in the Indian neighborhood of Monimbó, in Masaya. Another priest, Fr. Montero, from Costa Rica, was the director of the even larger Don Bosco Youth Center of Managua. Fr. Mario Fiandri, from Italy, was in charge of youth sports, and on Sundays he rallied some 10,000 young people to play sports at the Catholic Youth Center in Managua.
>
> If we turn to the peasants, we see that the government expelled Fr. Benito LePlant, from Canada. He was immersed in the lives of the peasants. He had founded 352 peasant communities and several cooperatives and was a leader of the Delegates of the Word, a network of peasant evangelizers which spread through the Nicaraguan countryside.
>
> If we turn to the urban poor, we find something very striking: the government acted against four priests whose parishes were adjacent and which together comprised what is called the "barrios orientales" or eastern barrios, a collection of very poor neighborhoods which played a strategic role in the insurrection against Somoza when they took up arms in 1979. These four priests were Fr. Benito Pitito, parish priest of Sabana Grande; Fr. Vincente Gaudelli, priest of the Barrio Oriental; Fr. Amado Peña, who is now confined to the seminary, but who was in charge of Bello Horizonte and the western marketplace area; and myself, priest of Villa Venezuela, Villa Libertad, and Los Laureles. All of our parishes were close to each other, all were poor. . . .
>
> The government also expelled the parish priest of the Indian Monimbó barrio in Mayasa, Fr. Huerta, from Costa Rica. He was the second priest of Monimbó to be expelled by the Sandinistas.
>
> If we continue down the list of priests who were expelled, we find another set of coincidences. Fr. Francisco San Martin, from Spain,

was the shepherd of the Cursillo movement [a Catholic evangelistic movement] and other influential lay organizations. . . . As for myself . . . I was the spiritual director of the seminarians and, as such, I was influential in the formation of the next generation of priests. I was also a leader of the charismatic renewal movement.

In a nutshell, you see that the Sandinistas targeted a group of the foreign priests who had the greatest influence in the most sensitive areas, in order to weaken the influence of the Catholic Church.[8]

In a single blow the government removed strong, independent Catholic leaders from among the poorer youth, from the rural and urban poor, especially in areas which had played a key role in the insurrection against the previous government, from popular religious movements, and from the training of new priests.

A revolutionary Christian leader had already argued for the importance of removing such independent Catholic leadership in an article in 1983 entitled, "Local, Traditional, and Reactionary Church." In the article Fr. Juan H. Pico, S.J., expressed great concern over the "particularly grave reactionary stand of the younger priests and of the seminarians"—with whom Fr. Anitua was working. He accused the charismatic renewal, "The City of God" lay movement, and the Catechumenal movement of being reactionary influences. Among their sins, Fr. Pico mentioned their providing emotional support, manpower, and financial aid to the hierarchy; their striving to strengthen the image of the Pope; and their attempts to "depoliticize Christians and to spread the fear of . . . atheist Marxism."[9] Three of the expelled priests—Fr. Anitua, Fr. San Martin, and Fr. Castells—were the respective spiritual counselors or leaders of the three "reactionary lay movements" criticized by Fr. Pico.

On July 30, 1984, the bishops conference issued a brief, public statement recapitulating recent events and thanking Christian organizations around the world that had expressed their solidarity with the Nicaraguan bishops. The bishops explained that following the expulsion of the ten priests they asked the government to present evidence, according to the law, that would justify their action. "Up to now," the bishops said, "we have not received any reply."

We have also received many messages from bishops' conferences in different parts of the world which express to us their surprise, their consternation, and their protest about what is happening to the church in Nicaragua, and their solidarity with us. We are grateful for such demonstrations of Christian solidarity.[10]

The revolutionary Christians, on the other hand, demonstrated their solidarity with the Sandinistas. Sixto Ulloa, a leader of CEPAD, when asked what he thought of the expulsion of the ten Catholic priests, answered: "You can't go around saying what these priests have been saying and not expect the government to react."[11]

In the wake of the controversy between the Sandinistas and the church, new interpretations of Nicaragua's recent past began to appear. The Sandinista leaders now tried to portray the bishops as Somocistas. Tomás Borge was interviewed by *El Nuevo Diario* and asked about Archbishop Obando's mediations on behalf of the guerrillas back in 1974 and 1978, and about some other stands taken by the archbishop and already praised by the FSLN in their October 1980 Communique on Religion. Borge denied that the archbishop had faced any danger; he said that his stand against Somoza had been "pusillanimous" (the 1980 FSLN document had called it "courageous"). He also said that what the archbishop had done as an intermediary between the Sandinista guerrillas and the Somoza government, he had done in order to gain celebrity, publicity, and prestige.[12]

TRICKS, SURVEILLANCE, AND SUBTERFUGE
In August 1984, an FSLN plot against a Venezuelan Catholic bishop who was visiting Nicaragua, and who was very supportive of his Nicaraguan colleagues in the episcopate, failed. The bishop was Baltazar Porras Cardozo. On his first attempt to enter Nicaragua he was denied entry at Managua's international airport and so flew to Panama. The Nicaraguan ambassador in Venezuela was contacted, and he explained that there had been a mistake and that the bishop was now able to enter the country. He did so, and later told the following story of an experience he had in Nicaragua:

> On August 6, I went with three priests to Lake Jiloa to do some swimming. While we were there, suddenly, three well-dressed women, all in black, appeared before us and completely undressed in obvious provocation. One of the priests understood that this was another "strange coincidence," and we all left at once. Just then, a police patrol arrived at the site.[13]

A Nicaraguan prelate whom I met on one of my trips overseas, and who asked me not to divulge any names, told me the story of a Nicaraguan priest who worked for the bishops conference, whom the Sandinistas tried to disgrace by a similar setup. An official of the Ministry of the Interior asked a male friend of the priest to invite him to a certain beach on a specific day. Once at the beach the friend was simply to embrace the priest in a sexually affectionate way. Photographers from the secret police with telescopic lenses would do the rest. When the friend refused to take part in this plot to slander the priest as a homosexual, he was threatened with death. He sought refuge in a neighboring country.

Christians who try to remain independent of the Sandinista government are now subject to a wide variety of attacks on their reputation, interference in their activities, and surveillance. For the most part this pervasive government pressure goes unnoticed outside the country. A typical story of interference, which is designed as much to erode morale as it is to impede religious activities, was the obstruction of delivery of some repair parts ordered by Catholic Radio. The parts arrived in Nicaragua at the end of 1984, but were not released by Nicaraguan customs officials for months. Each time employees of the station asked for the parts, the authorities asked them to return to fill out new and different forms from those of the day before. Reports of this delay were repeatedly censored.

The government has interfered with the importation of Bibles—something it did not do during the first years after the revolution. While it still allows Bibles to be brought into the country by pro-Sandinista Christian groups, others now encounter difficulties. In one incident, Nicaraguan customs officials repeatedly denied that Bibles which had been ordered had arrived, but then suddenly announced that the Bibles had had to be returned to the sending country because nobody came to pick them up—when in fact the priest who placed the order had been paying a daily visit to the customs office for several weeks.

As mentioned before, a considerable intelligence effort is directed at Christian leaders. In September 1984, while government media censorship was relaxed slightly prior to the November elections, *La Prensa* published a copy of a questionnaire being used by the Sandinista Defense Committees entitled, "Outline of the Religious Characteristics of a Region."[14] The questionnaire is designed to gather detailed information on every priest or minister in the various regions of the country. The information to be collected includes where they live, where they travel to, which vehicles they use, who visits them, what the characteristics are of those they minister to, and so on. One of the questions asks for a profile of the religious leader according to whether hs is: (a) a smoker; (b) a drug addict; (c) a drinker; (d) a gambler; (e) a chaser of women; (f) a homosexual; (g) someone with a pro-Somocista background; (h) someone without a pro-Somocista background. Another question asks for a classification of the leader according to his attitudes toward the government: revolutionary, progressive, vacillating, reactionary, or counterrevolutionary.

Specific information is even requested for those identified as Sandinista Christians. The questionnaire asks whether they are members of the July 19 Sandinista Youth, base communities, or a Sandinista Defense Committee, specifying the exact zone and block number of the committee.

Other instances of spying on the activities of Nicaraguan Christians have been reported by Protestant ministers. In a statement to two North American visitors in 1984, Moravian Bishop John Wilson, then of the Atlantic Coast, acknowledged that in fact the Sandinistas were taking "security measures" in regard to the church. "Our provisional synod was held in Bluefields in 1983. . . . There were security officers in plain clothes present at all the sessions."[15]

Another enlightening example of the kind of tactics the Sandinistas are using on Christians in Nicaragua is the way the government interfered with an evangelistic crusade by Argentine evangelist Alberto Mottessi in January 1984. At a news conference held to publicize the event, a reporter from El Nuevo Diario demanded that Mottessi make a statement in favor of the Sandinista revolution and against "U.S. imperialism." Mottessi refused, saying, "You have no right to put words in my mouth. I am not here to make a judgment for or against any political system. My mission is one of peace and reconciliation."[16]

Hours before the crusade's scheduled opening in Managua, the government canceled the permit to use a large arena, and the crusade was forced into a much smaller stadium, without lights or sound equipment and with seating for only eight thousand, while attendance numbered from thirteen to eighty thousand (most people had to stand on the playing field).

The crusade's surprising success was followed by a government crackdown on the sponsoring organization, the National Council of Evangelical Pastors (NCEP). NCEP leaders were questioned by the authorities and forbidden to hold further events.[17] (The NCEP, not CEPAD, is the organization that represents evangelical pastors in Nicaragua. While CEPAD is often described as fulfilling this function, CEPAD was founded as a social service agency for evangelicals after the earthquake of 1972. Unlike CEPAD, NCEP does not promote Christian alignment with the FSLN. While it has not officially adopted a critical stance, NCEP officials have independently expressed misgivings about the government's policies regarding religion—a fact which has brought them under government pressure, amplified at times by leaders of CEPAD.)

Campus Crusade for Christ, another evangelical organization which has been the victim of Sandinista harassment, including office break-ins and beatings of its leaders, has reported that when it submitted the film *Jesus* to the Ministry of the Interior for the required prior censorship, the film was returned so badly damaged as to be barely usable. The Sandinista censor allowed Campus Crusade to show the film, but required that all notices for the movie must include a disclaimer saying the film was not recommended for minors.[18]

RENEWAL AMIDST CONTINUED STRUGGLE
Despite evidence of religious persecution, many visitors to Nicaragua had been confused about the situation of religion by signs of intense religious renewal and growth in church membership over the past few years. Many wonder whether this does not contradict the charges that the Sandinistas are engaged in crippling independent religious life. In fact, there has been impressive religious renewal and growth. Several Protestant denominations have multiplied their membership, attendance at religious celebrations has increased, the circulation of Bibles has reached unexpected levels. Yet, as Protestant observer Kate Rafferty has suggested, this is a "reflection of the bold spirit of freedom that Christ gives in the midst of any situation and a willingness to die for what one believes," not a product of the Sandinistas' willingness to see religion flourish.[19]

Rafferty provides another example of this dynamic—the Month of the Bible, a campaign that local evangelicals organized in Nicaragua in September 1984. According to her, it was the result of the "growing strength of Nicaraguan evangelicals, not the goodwill of the Sandinistas." The Sandinistas, in fact, tried to stop it, and when they could not do that, to control it; for example, asking evangelicals to hold their meetings indoors. But people outside Nicaragua who heard about the campaign did not generally learn about the government's restrictions, and probably credited the Sandinistas with practicing religious tolerance.

I witnessed a strong religious revival also taking place in the Catholic Church—a response, in part, to persecution. The atmosphere at religious ceremonies which were in danger of attack by Sandinista mobs was very intense—with apprehension, but also with renewed meaning. The prayers, the ritual, the reading of the Psalms, all had a special reality that often seemed lacking in calmer times. During this time I saw many friends who had been only nominally Christian growing closer to the church and discovering the values of their faith, perhaps for the first time. But these were unintended consequences of Sandinismo, very much like what has happened in Poland, where the confrontation with the Communist regime has had a bracing effect on the church.

The elections in late 1984 and the debate about aid for the contras taking place in the United States in early 1985 gave the Nicaraguan government reasons for avoiding blatantly repressive measures against religious groups, thus allowing independent Christians a respite. But events during this time highlighted the instability of any truce.

The president of the Nicaraguan bishops conference, Bishop Vega, criticized the elections in terms very much akin to the ones used by the Catholic bishops in regard to the elections staged by Somoza in 1974. Bishop Vega claimed that the elections did not meet the minimum requirements for a free electoral process. The Centro Antonio Valdivieso, on the other hand, defended them. When Commander Daniel Ortega was to be installed as president, it published a prayer for him adapted from a Hebrew psalm which is a prayer for the king, normally interpreted by Christians as applying to Christ, the Messiah-King. The prayer was interspersed with the Centro Antonio Valdivieso's comments:

O Lord, grant your wisdom and your justice to him that is a son of kings. . . .

We thus ask God that he grant President Ortega the precious gift of wisdom. . . . A gift that the Spirit of God grants to those who participate in the mission that brought the Messiah: restore justice in the world. . . . Ortega will measure up to his commitment, for he is a son of kings.

Elected President of Nicaragua: the Lord entrusts us to your mind and to your heart. . . . May you return to Nicaragua the honor and joy that it deserves, that in the future its inhabitants may call you blessed.[20]

Yet, despite the bishops' view of the elections, just weeks before the inauguration of Daniel Ortega as president of Nicaragua, the government called for a dialogue between church and state. Suspecting that the FSLN primarily wanted to have them attend the inauguration, the bishops asked that the dialogue be held after inauguration day. The Sandinistas lost interest.

Direct actions against the Catholic Church resumed shortly afterwards. In April 1985 another Catholic priest was expelled, Fr. Gregorio Raya, of the diocese of Chontales. The government accused him of helping several youngsters to evade the draft. In his farewell letter Fr. Raya told his parishioners:

My beloved people: this system that calls itself "popular" is afraid of the people; it is afraid of you and of the fruits of your Catholic faith. . . . In Nicaragua there has never been a revolution, but a treason imposed by those who have turned our dreams for a free country into a military, Communist dictatorship.[21]

There is no cause for thinking that more priests will not be expelled or more Christians will not be physically and verbally attacked, especially those with leadership responsibilities.

A ray of hope came in April 1985 when Pope John Paul II named Archbishop Obando a cardinal of the Catholic Church. Implicit in his appointment was the Pope's awareness of the difficult role that the prelate has been playing in Nicaragua since he was first made a bishop in 1970. Indeed Archbishop Obando's experience symbolizes the tension that Christians are called to face in a continent polarized between right- and left-wing extremes.

The national and international circumstances of the Sandinista revolution will no doubt continue to determine the speed at which the Sandinistas move toward achieving their goals in the religious sphere. The way in which local Christians decide to act and the solidarity they receive from fellow Christians abroad will also have an important bearing. None of these factors, however, will change the FSLN's goals themselves.

A remark of Commander Joaquín Cuadra, Chief of Staff of the Sandinista Army, candidly made to his comrade Margaret Randall, provides an unambiguous clue to what to expect. Speaking of the FSLN's relations with the churches, Cuadra said:

> I think that before anything else, the Sandinista government should maintain in this regard an intelligent policy. It could be counterproductive . . . to promote a confrontation now which would end up . . . in the church splitting, perhaps into two churches, thus forcing the Nicaraguan government to say, well, this one is the church that we recognize; the others must go. This would undoubtedly be a matter with great international repercussions. It is not convenient for us, not in these times of so much danger. . . . But historically it seems to me that this has to happen some day. We should be sure that this happens at the most opportune moment and with the least consequences.[22]

NOTES

1. Nicaraguan Bishops' Pastoral Letter on Reconciliation, *Catholicism in Crisis*, June 1984, pp. 45, 46.

2. Editorial, *Barricada*, April 30, 1984, p. 3.

3. *El Nuevo Diario*, April 26, 1984.

4. Eje Ecuménico, communique, in *El Nuevo Diario*, May 19, 1984.

5. Fr. Kolvenbach, "Communique, July 16, 1984," quoted in "Jesuit Superior General Gives Ultimatum to Cardenal," *National Catholic Register*, July 29, 1984, p. 3.

6. Senator Ted Kennedy, *The Congressional Record-Senate*, p. S 6247.

7. Fr. Anitua, "The Expelling of Ten Catholic Priests from Nicaragua," The Puebla Institute, *Occasional Bulletins*, No. 4, October 1984, p. 3.

8. *Ibid.*, pp. 4, 5.

9. Juan H. Pico, S.J., in *op. cit.*, *El Papa en Nicaragua*, p. 220.

10. "The Bishops of Nicaragua Ask for Dialogue and National Reconciliation," *L'Osservatore Romano*, English Language Edition, September 3, 1984, p. 6.

11. Sixto Ulloa, interview by Ken and Rhoda Mahler, "Nicaragua: Tracking Down the Persecuted Church," *Panama Update*, Panama, August 1984.

12. *El Nuevo Diario*, June 4, 1984, pp. 1, 8.

13. Quoted in Osvaldo Cuadra M., *Persecucion en Nicaragua* (Buenos Aires, Argentina: Anunciando el Evangelio Publishers, 1984), p. 54.

14. Although *La Prensa* was able to publish the questionnaire in September, it was not able to publish a letter to the government from the archdiocese of Managua protesting the state's denial of reentry visas to two Catholic priests: Fr. Bellanger, a Canadian, who for several years had led the Christian Family Movement in Nicaragua, and Fr. Vicente Cerezo, a Spaniard stationed for several years at "Las Palmas," a Managua parish. Denial of visas has been a regular feature of the program to gradually eliminate non-Sandinista priests and ministers.

15. *Op. cit.*, "Nicaragua: Tracking Down the Persecuted Church," p. 2.

16. "Nicaragua," *Open Doors*, Orange, California, May-June 1984, p. 23.

17. Alberto Mottessi Evangelistic Association press release, February 21, 1984; *Latin America Evangelist*, July-Sept. 1984, p. 11.

18. Kate Rafferty, Interview, "Who Speaks for Nicaragua's Evangelicals?," Institute on Religion and Democracy Briefing Paper, No. 5, January 1985, p. 4.

19. *Ibid.*

20. Quoted in Otto Fonseca, "La Apoteosis de Ortega," *La Nación*, San José, Costa Rica, 1985, p. 14A.

21. Fr. Raya, quoted in "Noticiero Nicaraguense," *Diario las Américas*, Miami, April 21, 1985, p. 6.

22. Joaquín Cuadra in *op. cit.*, Randall, p. 219.

SIXTEEN

A TIME FOR
DISCERNMENT AND SOLIDARITY

A review of the history of the Sandinista National Liberation
Front shows a guerrilla movement born in the early sixties
among radical middle-class students, and heavily influenced by
the Cuban revolution, growing to be a political and military force
capable of bending the circumstances of the Nicaraguan revolution to its purposes and achieving complete control of the government only eighteen years later. Shaped by the ideas of Carlos
Fonseca, the Frente was from its inception a Marxist-Leninist
movement that looked to Cuba and the Soviet Union as models
and developed close ties with Castro and Third-World guerrilla
movements. From the beginning, the Frente saw itself as the
vanguard of a new world order, the redeemers of Nicaragua, and
the force that would unite Central America. Although they took
their name from Sandino, the legendary nationalist, the Sandinistas' world view was always internationalist; their goal to bring
Nicaragua first, and then the rest of Central America, to revolutionary socialism and into the orbit of the most progressive
Socialist nations—Cuba and the Soviet Union.

The FSLN was originally made up of only a revolutionary elite.
But developments in the late sixties and early seventies led them
into strategic alliances with leftist Christians and later with
democratically oriented individuals and institutions seeking the
overthrow of Nicaragua's dictator, Anastasio Somoza. These alliances brought about a restructuring of the Frente to allow its
banner to fly over a wider circle. The inner core was directed by
the revolutionary elite, which placed great emphasis on ideological formation and unity and retained tight control of the organ-

ization as a whole. The second circle was made up of leftist Christians, radical social democrats, and others who only partly shared the ideology of the movement. In the outer circle was a congeries of individuals and groups who often shared with the Frente little more than a common commitment to oust Somoza. Through this restructuring, or adding of nonideological layers, the FSLN was able to change its public profile in the late seventies and position itself as an umbrella organization committed to pluralism, democracy, and religious freedom.

Ignorance of the FSLN's basic ideological commitments, its strategic shrewdness, and its layered structure underlay the hopes that so many democrats and Christians harbored toward the Sandinistas during the initial stages of their rule. It has continued to be the major source of confusion in the debate over why the Sandinistas broke their promises of political pluralism and turned toward the Soviets. A review of the Sandinistas' literature readily shows that their break in 1980 with the non-Marxist forces who had fought against Somoza had been fully anticipated by the FSLN leadership. The same can be said of what has seemed to some to be their drift toward totalitarianism and into the Soviet orbit. The Frente's documents show that they never regarded their alliance with what they called bourgeois political sectors as more than temporary and that their fundamental intention was to travel the road to revolutionary socialism laid down by the Cubans and the Soviets. Far from being pushed in a totalitarian direction, the Sandinistas have simply been following out the consequences of their own fundamental choices. The expectation that the Sandinistas can evolve toward a more democratic form of socialism if left unmolested or treated as friends fails to take account of their stated goals. It also fails to recognize the fact that the Sandinistas began taking decisive steps toward internal social control and toward the Soviet sphere when all domestic and international forces, including the U.S., were on good terms with them.

The Sandinistas' stated goals and strategy provide the key to making sense of their seemingly conflicting actions both before and after the war with Somoza—alliance with non-Marxist groups and individuals followed by conflict with the labor unions, relocation of the Miskito Indians, press censorship, confrontation with the churches, repression of independent political parties and other groups, and so on. By no stretch of the imagination were the Sandinistas facing in the majority of these cases stubborn resistance from right-wing Nicaraguans striving to defend selfish economic interests. Rather, in general, the Sandinistas were confronting progressive forces, which had fought for the end of the Somoza dictatorship and which yearned for the kind of revolution that the FSLN promised in 1979 to bring about.

The Sandinistas came to power calling for a radical restructuring of society that would put the needs of the majority ahead of the privileges of the few. But while they have increased certain social programs aimed at helping the poor, their fundamental goal has been political control and they have denied people, particularly the poor, the status of persons entitled to freedom, respect, and genuine participation in shaping society. Nowhere has this contradiction been clearer than in the case of the Miskito Indians. The Miskitos, the poorest of the Nicaraguan poor, rebelled not against the deprivation of social services, but against the deprivation of their human dignity and the destruction of their existing mechanisms for exercising social responsibility— their structure of leadership, communal land use, religious institutions, and the rest.

The significance of this painful episode is to challenge the widespread presupposition that the Third-World poor are beings eager only to be fed and willing to allow government to take total control of their lives in order to provide for them. This presupposition arises from a caricature of the poor in the minds of people who remain at a distance from their feelings and priorities. Freedom and personal dignity are not bourgeois aspirations; they are demands of the human heart. Man does not live by bread alone. All people, including the poor, have spiritual as well as material requirements, which they will not happily suffer to be violated by social engineers and armed revolutionaries.

The Sandinistas' commitment to a state-controlled model of development, which has proved to be so ruinous in so many underdeveloped countries, has been a major cause of the economic disaster that has befallen Nicaragua. The Sandinistas have followed this course for ideological reasons and out of power considerations. They have not acted in the interest of the needs of the poor majority, but have clung to failed economic dogmas whose main merit for the government is the increase in state control that they bring about.

The conflict with the Christian churches has likewise been an inevitable result of the Sandinistas' drive to assert their political and ideological hegemony over all sectors of Nicaraguan society. As documents of the FSLN reveal, the Sandinistas anticipated conflict with the churches and designed a campaign to bring religious beliefs and ceremonies into conformity with their ideology.

The Sandinista ideology precludes the existence of institutions which claim for themselves a jurisdiction and a loyalty independent of the state. Although the Sandinistas portray their conflict with the church as a clash between benevolent social reformers (the true Christians, the people's church) against an elite of reactionaries fearful of losing their privileges (the bishops and others), the reality is something quite different. The issue dividing the churches in Nicaragua today concerns not an "option for the poor," but an option for the Sandinistas: "Everything inside the revolution, nothing outside the revolution." An independent church is a contradiction to the Marxist vision; coexistence with Christians is only possible to the degree that Christians yield their essential beliefs and identity.

To carry out their objectives regarding religion, the Sandinistas have used the willing collaboration of Christians drawn to their revolution by the tenets of a radical liberation theology. Contrary to the expectations of many people, the participation of revolutionary Christians has not helped to Christianize or moderate the Sandinistas. It has not promoted within the revolution a "third way," a new, humanitarian socialism. Rather, the participation of revolutionary Christians has advanced the totalitarian march of the revolution by providing it with a theological rationale to justify its policies and its attacks on opponents. As Castro and others have explicitly acknowledged, the "strategic alliance" with Christians is nothing more than a Marxist tool wielded where convenient for their purposes.

Working from the tenets of radical liberation theology, revolutionary Christians have "Christianized" the revolution by accepting the Marxist revolutionaries as the agents of the Christian mission. In essence, they are emptying their faith of its contents and replacing them with Marxist-Leninist concepts. No reciprocal movement is occurring. The Sandinista leaders do not preach to their cadres the riches of Christian faith. They do not claim that in order to be a good revolutionary one must discover Jesus Christ. The preaching is in one direction only—toward the Sandinista revolution, its Marxist ideology, and its drive toward total social control.

The role these revolutionary Christians have played in Nicaragua is fourfold:

—They have provided a theological rationale for the messianism of the Sandinistas by making revolution a near synonym of salvation, with the party its only agent.

—They have lent credibility to the Sandinistas' contention that their regime is not Marxist-Leninist, but one in which Christianity and revolution can walk together.

—They have served as a visible front to attack the Christian churches and to undermine their authority and teachings, thus reducing for the Sandinistas the political cost of a more direct confrontation.

—They have been instruments of a subtle ideological campaign to substitute the Marxist creed for the Christian gospel, and loyalty to a totally secular political organization for the unconditional loyalty due to Christ and His teachings.

Contrary to their claims, the pro-Marxist Christians' liberation theology is not rooted in the actual experience of the poor. Making a political ideology out of Christianity could hardly be more alien to the Nicaraguan poor. The revolutionary Christians' theology is largely a foreign intrusion, one promoted and financed by foreigners and having very little grass-roots support.

It is ironic that by equating the "option for the poor" with unquestioning loyalty to the Sandinistas, the advocates of this theology turn a deaf ear to the poor, such as the Miskito Indians, the independent workers, the youth drafted into an ideological army, and the small merchants, who have known the pain of the government's policies.

A conclusion to be drawn from this is that Christians who share a legitimate concern for the poor in Latin America and elsewhere in the Third World need to be more aware of the complexity of social movements for change, and need to be more effectively equipped with approaches to social change that are constructed on clearly articulated Christian principles.

Christians must learn that there are many liberation theologies which are not liberating at all. In Nicaragua, a testing ground for liberation theology, it can be seen that radical liberation theologies have led Christians from opposition to right-wing dictatorship to support for left-wing totalitarianism. These theologies have identified themselves with a political force which seeks to repress and divide the churches and which will improve neither the spiritual or material lot of the poor they claim to represent.

Christians in the West need to be more discerning of movements and revolutions whose lofty rhetoric often disguises an ideology and goals deeply at odds with Christian faith and life. A romanticized view of Third-World revolutionaries bravely leading the charge against shocking injustices and inequalities needs to be tempered by a sober understanding of the nature and causes of injustices and inequalities, and hence how most effectively to change them. Enthusiasm for revolutions must also be moderated by the very pragmatic but all-important realization that despite their professed ideals, Marxist-inspired revolutions often contain the seeds of even more cruel oppressions than the ones they are striving to dethrone.

In a 1984 document on liberation theology the Vatican warned that

> [a] major fact of our time ought to evoke the reflection of all those who would sincerely work for the true liberation of their brothers: millions of our own contemporaries legitimately yearn to recover those basic freedoms of which they are deprived by totalitarian and atheistic regimes which came to power by violent and revolutionary means, precisely in the name of the liberation of the people. This shame of our time cannot be ignored: while claiming to bring them freedom, these regimes keep whole nations in conditions of servitude which are unworthy of mankind. Those who, perhaps inadvertently, make themselves accomplices of similar enslavements betray the very poor they mean to help.[1]

The experience of the Nicaraguan revolution clearly suggests that what have been regarded in some circles as the most advanced forms of liberation theology (the ideas of theologians such as Gutiérrez, Boff, Sobrino, Bonino, Segundo, and others) have in practice been little more than justifications for Marxist-Leninist revolution clothed in a religious garment. Terms that in academic discussions have sounded appealing and expressive of Christian values—"option for the poor," "siding with the oppressed," "struggling against the institutionalized forces of death"—have been translated into positions that "sacralize politics and betray the religion of the people in favor of the projects of the revolution."[2]

What we have broadly characterized as progressive Christians, on the other hand, particularly the Catholic bishops, have exhibited a far more consistent position on behalf of the poor. They raised their voice against the injustices of Somocismo. After the revolution, despite concerns based on their knowledge of the Frente's ideology, they did not refrain from calling for and participating in the work of building a new society. But as the progressive Christians did not give theological protection to the privileged and powerful under Somoza (as more conservative Christians did), so they have not given religious legitimization to the Frente's claim to be the sole interpreter and transformer of the social order (as the revolutionary Christians have done).

It might be argued that if anything has slowed the pace of the Sandinistas, it has been the courageous stand of the independent churches. In the opinion of Peruvian novelist Mario Vargas Llosa, "It is . . . the church's frontal attack against Marxism, perhaps more than the economic crisis or external pressures, that has been a moderating influence on the regime."[3]

Indeed, the Sandinistas are not completely impervious to change. But they will only give ground if they are confronted with resolute resistance, and then only so long as their hold on power is not seriously threatened. Sandinista Nicaragua is not yet the kind of entirely closed police state that Cuba is. But what remains of private ownership, pluralism, and tolerance of dissent are largely the products of strong domestic and external resistance. Using the past as a basis for predicting the future, it must be said that every concession that the Sandinistas might conceivably make to democracy or human rights or the freedom of religion is but the product of pressures which endanger their hold on power during the transition phase. If after more than six years of Marxist revolution Nicaragua is less totalitarian than Cuba was after the same period of time, it is only because the Sandinistas have found in Nicaragua more formidable barriers for moving in that direction.

Might it be expected that they will end up learning the "bourgeois art of compromise" and settle for something more democratic than the revolutionary socialism that they have so persistently sought? The historical record of Marxist revolutions and the Sandinista revolution in particular does not point in this direction. Both the democrats and the Christians who have supported the Sandinistas with the hope of moderating them have underestimated the profound incompatibility between their ideals and those of the FSLN. The social control that the Frente is building leaves only two options to independent subgroupings in Nicaragua: resistance or assimilation. It appears that the best that can be expected is that the Sandinistas will pace their advance toward revolutionary socialism according to pragmatic political considerations of what they deem necessary for their survival. Where they feel secure, or detect weakness or lack of resolve in their historical class enemies, they will take as many steps forward as they can. Compromises can be expected to be unstable and probably short-lived.

As I said in the introduction, my aim in communicating about Nicaragua has not been to influence the foreign policy of any country. My purpose has been to help Christians outside Nicaragua understand the religious dimension of recent events there. They are important events, which touch on issues that affect how Christians will perceive their mission in the world in the years ahead. But I hope this book provides more than intellectual enlightment to Christians outside Nicaragua. To develop a realistic understanding of the situation of Christians in Nicaragua is a first step. To act in solidarity with them is the second.

I think that if enough Christians outside Nicaragua were to express their concern and solidarity with their brethren there, it would have a powerful effect on the way the Sandinistas relate to the church. If every time a Nicaraguan Catholic priest, Protestant pastor, or other Christian leader were expelled, beaten, or abused by the government, Christian churches around the world were to voice their concern or protest, the Sandinistas could be moderated in their repression at least long enough for Nicaraguan Christians to consolidate their position and equip themselves to relate to government pressure.

The Sandinistas, as the Soviets, are sensitive to public opinion in the West. That is why it is so important for those who suffer persecution under oppressive regimes to get the support of their brothers and sisters from abroad. Silence and indifference only make matters worse.

Whether Christians and other concerned citizens outside Nicaragua favor the actions of the Sandinista regime or not, all can help the persecuted Christians inside by demanding from that government that it respect the freedom and the dignity of all Nicaraguan churches. Frequently, however, Christians have adopted a critical and demanding attitude toward those who resist the Sandinista government, while granting the Sandinistas their unqualified support.

Nowhere is this more clearly apparent than in the countless articles written by foreign visitors, often invited and hosted by CEPAD, IHCA, "Witness for Peace," and other organizations who sympathize with the Sandinistas. In their one- or two-week visits they fail to discern the true nature of the Nicaraguan situation. Many of the visitors are channeled through model prisons, model state farms, model revolutionary parishes, with the techniques of hospitality that Marxists have used skillfully in other countries. Visitors' unwitting vulnerability to such techniques is often exacerbated by the common tendency to ignore the background of the country, its political and religious life and history, the revolution, and the intricacies of Nicaraguan culture. Sometimes, in addition, there is a subtle North American paternalism at work, which assumes that "less sophisticated" Central Americans do not mind if they are subjected to exercises of government force which North American journalists, religious figures, union leaders, and so on would vehemently resist.

Such visitors are often also betraying ideological prejudices. Foreigners who apply to Nicaragua double standards regarding elections, freedom of the press, the contras, human rights, the vilification of religious leaders, and so on often share with the Sandinistas and their pro-Sandinista hosts a totalitarian frame of reference. They will sometimes acknowledge that the government does do some indefensible things. "But these are always, at worst, merely 'mistakes.' They are never moral wrongs, and never are they crimes. Only opponents of the regime can commit such deeds. . . . Under this concept, Sandinismo embodies the ultimate truth. Those who serve it are above any judgment."[4]

The use of double standards and Western Christians' naivete about Third-World Marxist revolutions and about some forms of liberation theology have conspired to deprive Nicaraguan Christians of support in an hour of trial. No statements of support for the independent Nicaraguan Christians have been forthcoming from the majority of churches and religious groups in the United States and Europe, nor are prayers for them a feature in the worshiping life of most Christian churches. In fact, in general, the pleas of support of many North American and European Christians have not been for the Nicaraguan Christians who suffer under state repression, but for the Sandinistas who are struggling for existence in a hostile world.

Armando Valladares, a Cuban Christian and poet released in 1982 after twenty-two years' imprisonment in Cuba, expresses what this means for those who suffer:

> During those years, with the purpose of forcing us to abandon our religious beliefs and to demoralize us, the Cuban Communist indoctrinators repeatedly used the statements of support for Castro's revolution made by some representatives of American Christian churches. Every time that a pamphlet was published in the U.S., every time a clergyman would write an article in support of Fidel Castro's dictatorship, a translation would reach us, and that was worse for the Christian political prisoners than the beatings or the hunger. Incomprehensibly to us, while we waited for the embrace of solidarity from our brothers in Christ, those who were embraced were our tormentors.

This same process is taking place in Nicaragua. It is not too late to stop it. It is not too late to step out in Christian solidarity with those who suffer for their faith.

NOTES

1. Congregation for the Doctrine of the Faith, "Instruction on Certain Aspects of the 'Theology of Liberation,' " Vatican City, 1984, p. 32.

2. *Ibid.*, p. 34.

3. Mario Vargas Llosa, *op cit.*, "In Nicaragua," p. 77.

4. Sister Camilla Mullay, O.P. and Father Robert Barry, O.P., *The Barren Fig Tree: A Christian Reappraisal of the Sandinista Revolution* (Washington, D.C.: Institute on Religion and Democracy, 1984), p. 42.

CHRONOLOGY
OF EVENTS

1909   U.S. Marines land in Nicaragua to back a Conservative party revolt against Liberal party President José S. Zelaya.

1928   Liberal party wins in U.S. supervised elections.

1933   U.S. Marines leave Nicaragua. After a short-lived truce, troops of nationalist General Augusto César Sandino engage the newly created Nicaraguan National Guard (GN) in battle.

1934   Sandino assassinated by officers of the National Guard.

1936   General Anastasio Somoza Garcia, head of the GN, ousts President Juan B. Sacasa in a coup.

1944   Creation of the pro-Soviet Nicaraguan Socialist Party (PSN).

1951   Beginning of the Nicaraguan cotton boom. The country modernizes and Somoza further consolidates power.

1956   General Somoza assassinated by a young Liberal Party dissident. Somoza's son Luis succeeds him in the presidency, initiating a period of significant political liberalization and tolerance.

1957   Carlos Fonseca Amador, future founder of the FSLN, travels to Moscow as the PSN's delegate to the Sixth World Student Festival.

1959   Jan. 1: Revolution led by Fidel Castro triumphs in Cuba.

1959   May 31-June 14: Conservative party guerrillas, led by Pedro Joaquín Chamorro, are defeated and surrender to the GN. President Luis Somoza grants them amnesty the following December.

1959   June 27: A leftist guerrilla unit led by Carlos Fonseca is destroyed by the Honduran army while attempting to cross over into Nicaragua. Wounded, Fonseca flees to Cuba.

1960   July 23: Founding of the FSLN in Honduras by Carlos Fonseca, Tomás Borge and Silvio Mayorga.

1963   Feb. 2: Rene Schick, candidate of Somoza's Liberal Party is elected president in a race with a "mosquito" candidate from a splinter branch of the Nicaraguan Conservative Party. Schick, widely regarded by his opponents as a Somoza puppet, introduces further liberalization into the Nicaraguan political process.

1963   Mar.-Oct.: FSLN launches its first armed actions.

1964   Jun. and Dec.: Leaders of the FSLN, including Fonseca and Daniel Ortega, are arrested and later released or exiled.

1965   Fonseca establishes links with the Guatemalan guerrillas led by Luis Turcios.

1965   Fr. Ernesto Cardenal founds a lay community on the Solentiname Islands in Lake Nicaragua.

1966   Jan.: The FSLN sends a delegate to the first Tricontinental Conference in Havana.

1966   Oscar Turcios and Daniel Ortega participate in joint operations with Guatemalan guerrillas.

1967   Feb. 6: Anastasio Somoza Debayle, brother of Luis, wins in presidential election regarded by the major Nicaraguan opposition parties as fraudulent.

1967   Apr.: Luis Somoza dies of a heart attack.

1967   May-Aug.: FSLN's unsuccessful attempt to establish a guerrilla 'foco' in Pancasan fails leaving the Frente decimated.

1967   Oct.: Daniel Ortega, Turcios and a third guerrilla ambush and murder GN sergeant Gonzalo Lacayo. The ensuing repression leads to the killing of some leaders of the FSLN and to the imprisonment of Ortega (Nov).

1968   Latin American bishops conference at Medellin, Colombia, calls Christians to be active in the struggle for human rights and social justice.

1969   FSLN issues its first public program of government.

1969   Tomás Borge has his first secret meeting with Fr. Ernesto Cardenal.

1969   Patricio Arguello, member of the FSLN, is killed in a hijack attempt in Europe carried out in coordination with PLO guerrillas.

1970   Fr. Miguel Obando is ordained Catholic Archbishop of Managua.

1971   May 14: The Nicaraguan bishops conference, headed by Archbishop Obando, issues a pastoral letter criticizing the Somoza regime.

1971   Tomás Borge has his first secret meeting with Fr. Uriel Molina.

1971   Still small, the FSLN numbers only 10-15 full time underground militants, and 50-70 legal members.

1972   Fr. Uriel Molina launches the Christian Revolutionary Movement (MCR) and establishes the first radical base community with middle- and upper-class students.

1972   Mar. 19: In light of criticism from within Nicaragua, the Catholic hierarchy reasserts its right to raise its voice on socio-political matters.

1972   José Miguel Torres, a Baptist pastor, travels to Cuba where he receives his first lessons in "dialectical materialism" from FSLN leader Humberto Ortega.

1972   Dec. 23: An earthquake destroys Managua. Ten thousand or more people are killed. In the ensuing process of reconstruction Somoza and his associates make handsome profits.

1973   The Evangelical Committee for Development Assistance (CEPAD) is formed.

1974   The Nicaraguan opposition, led by Pedro Joaquín Chamorro, announces its decision not to participate in the upcoming presidential elections. As in the past, Somoza gets some lesser political opponents (the "mosquito" candidates) to participate in the race.

1974   Aug. 6: The Bishops Conference issues a new statement about the government and questions the validity of the upcoming elections.

1974   Sep. 1: Somoza reelected carrying roughly 60% of the vote.

1974   Nov.: The Democratic Union of Liberation (UDEL), a coalition of democratic political parties and labor unions, is formed under the leadership of Pedro Joaquín Chamorro.

1974   Dec. 27: An FSLN commando unit kidnaps several Somocistas at a Christmas party and exacts from the government the release of several political prisoners, one million dollars in ransom, and the publication of two FSLN communiques. Archbishop Obando acts as mediator. The commando unit escapes to Cuba where it receives a hero's reception. Somoza declares martial law.

1975   FSLN intensifies guerrilla operations in the countryside. Dozens of peasants begin to disappear as National Guard steps up repression. The guerrillas systematically murder "informers" of the regime.

1975   Oct.: First split in the FSLN: Jaime Wheelock and Luis Carrion form the "Tendencia Proletaria Marxista Leninista."

1975   Feb.: Tomás Borge is captured.

1976   Jun.: Fr. Fernando Cardenal testifies before the U.S. Congress on human rights violations by the Somoza regime. He returns to Nicaragua to work within the MCR giving seminars on liberation theology.

1976   Nov.: Carlos Fonseca Amador, founder and top leader of the FSLN, is killed in combat.

1977   The Nicaraguan Permanent Commission for Human Rights (CPDH) is founded by José Esteban González. The Commission became famous for its denunciations of the government's human rights abuses.

1977   Jan. 8: The Nicaraguan Bishops Conference denounces the "state of terror" imposed on peasants in the mountains of Matagalpa, Zelaya and the Segovias.

1977   Second split in the FSLN. The Tercerista faction, led by the Ortega brothers, is created. It favors urban-based insurrections and a "strategic" alliance with the "bourgeois" anti-Somoza forces.

1977   May.: The Terceristas issue their political-military platform, identifying their cause with the "sacred and historical cause of Marx, Engels, Lenin and Sandino."

1977   June: The "Group of the Twelve" is created by the Tercerista tendency of the FSLN as a front group to win international support for the movement.

1977   June 23: The Carter administration cuts off military and economic aid to the Somoza regime.

1977   June: A Sandinista mob sabotages a meeting led by Pedro Joaquín Chamorro in Matagalpa.

1977   Aug.: Eden Pastora joins the outer circle of the Terceristas.

1977   Sep.: Pressured by the United States, Somoza lifts the state of emergency. The newspaper *La Prensa* and several independent radio stations are able to openly criticize the government.

1977   Oct.: The FSLN (Tercerista) launches ambushes on the army in various parts of the country. An insurrection in Masaya fails.

1977   Oct.: Archbishop Obando creates the Committee of Patriotic Reflection to seek dialogue and a peaceful solution to the deepening crisis in the country.

1977   Dec.: A Jesuit priest, Fr. Pedro Miguel, is physically attacked by a Somocista mob. The archdiocese of Managua excommunicates the aggressors.

1978   Jan. 10: Pedro Joaquín Chamorro is assassinated by a hit squad apparently connected with some Somocistas living in Miami. From this point, Nicaragua explodes in turmoil.

1978   Jan. 23: The first general strike is called by the business community and the independent labor unions.

1978   Feb.: The Indian community of Monimbó, near Managua, stages a spontaneous insurrection against the regime. The FSLN moves quickly to take the lead in these outbursts and gain control of the rebellion.

1978   July 25: Archbishop Obando publicly asks Somoza to resign.

1978   Aug.: A Sandinista commando unit led by Eden Pastora seizes the Nicaraguan National Palace taking hundreds of hostages. Somoza is forced to meet the guerrillas' demands.

1978   Sep. 9-20: Massive insurrections take place in Leon, Masaya, Chinandega, Managua and Esteli. The revolt is crushed by the National Guard, but the FSLN retreats with hundreds of new recruits.

1978   Dec.: The three factions of the FSLN begin to unite under pressure from Fidel Castro to do so.

1979   Mar. 7: Unification of the FSLN is made official. Military supplies for the guerrillas begin to flow freely into Nicaragua from Costa Rica and Cuba.

1979   May: the Sandinistas and their supporters launch a final offensive. Most important cities are eventually taken over.

1979   June 2: The bishops conference, meeting in Leon, accepts the legitimacy of armed insurrection.

1979   June 23: The OAS asks for the resignation of Somoza, supports the opposition forces, and calls for early free elections after a change of government.

1979   July 17: Somoza resigns and flees the country.

1979   July 18: The National Guard disbands.

1979   July 19: The guerrillas enter Managua and take over headquarters of the former regime without opposition.

1979   July 20: The new government junta is installed in Managua.

1979   July: All television stations are confiscated and placed in the hands of the FSLN.

1979   July 31: The Nicaraguan bishops issue a pastoral letter welcoming the revolution.

1979   Aug.: Sandinista Defense Committees (CDS) are created on most blocks in all cities. They are given various state prerogatives to carry out their function of being "the eyes and ears of the revolution."

1979   Aug.: The government refuses to recognize the Miskito Indians' traditional authorities (the elders' council). The Indians are instructed to submit to the CDS's.

1979   Aug.: Moravian and other Protestant schoolteachers in Miskito territory begin to be replaced by Cuban teachers.

1979   Aug.: The Sandinista Confederation of Labor (CST) is created. The FSLN insists that all workers should join it.

1979   Sep. 13: The Nicaraguan army, as well as the police and the television networks, are officially established as branches of the Sandinista Party. The melding of state and party is made legal.

1979   Sep.: Daniel Ortega, in Havana, express his solidarity with the Communist countries and his condemnation of U.S. imperialism.

1979   Sep.: Unrest and anti-Cuban demonstrations in the Atlantic region of Nicaragua. Many Miskito leaders are arrested. Elders' council leader Lyster Athders is arrested and murdered.

1979   Oct. 3: José E. González of the CPDH discovers a burial site near the town of Granada containing bodies of people executed by the Sandinista army shortly after the revolutionary victory.

1979   Nov. 17: The Nicaraguan bishops issue a pastoral letter stating their position on socialism and their support of an authentic effort to build a new Nicaragua.

1979   Dec.: The Nicaraguan Confederation of Labor's (CTN) headquarters in Managua are shot up by Sandinista troops.

1979   Dec.: Daniel Ortega turns down the request of anti-Somoza democratic leader Fabio Gadea to open an independent television station. Television is declared a monopoly of the Sandinista party.

1980   Jan.: The government orders the suspension of a radio program directed by anti-Somoza journalist Oscar L. Montalvan.

1980   Jan.-Mar.: The government expropriates the lands of the Indian communities of Yulo, Taswapowne and Wulkiamp.

1980   Mar.: The FSLN changes the composition of the State Council giving itself and its organizations two thirds of the seats. This measure prompts the resignation of democratic junta members Alfonso Robelo and Violeta Chamorro.

1980   Mar. 20: The leaders of the revolutionary Christians sign a document stating that it is a duty of all Christians to support the Revolution and the FSLN.

1980   Mar. 22: The Nicaraguan government signs a joint declaration in Moscow with the Soviet Union supporting the latter's foreign policy.

1980   Apr.: Nicaragua abstains from condemning the Soviet invasion of Afghanistan at the UN, in contrast with 119 other officially non-aligned nations who did.

1980   Apr.: An internal conflict at *La Prensa* leads to the Marxist-dominated union withdrawing to create the pro-Sandinista newspaper *El Nuevo Diario*. *La Prensa* begins to publish as an independent newspaper.

1980   Apr.: Radio newsman Guillermo Treminio is sentenced to six months of imprisonment for broadcasting information "detrimental to the revolution."

1980   May.: Evangelical preacher Morris Cerullo is expelled from Nicaragua upon landing at Managua's airport.

1980   Aug.: The International Commission of Jurists of the United Nations condemns the Special Courts created by the Sandinistas to judge the Somocistas.

1980   Aug.: Commander Humberto Ortega, chief of the army, announces that elections in Nicaragua shall be to strengthen revolutionary power. They are announced for 1985. He also threatens *La Prensa*.

1980   Aug. 27: Bishop Pablo Vega denounces the harassment of the church in his diocese of Juigalpa.

1980   Sep.: Mass demonstrations take place in the Atlantic Coast region demanding the removal of Cuban teachers.

1980   Sep. 10: First decree limiting freedom of expression is enacted.

1980   Oct. 7: FSLN publishes a communique on religion. The bishops conference responds questioning the government's intentions.

1980   Nov. 20: Jorge Salazar, leader of a strong union of coffee growers, is murdered by a squad of Sandinista police led by Commander Omar Cabezas.

1981   Feb.: Roger Suarez, leader of the Puerto Cabezas workers union, is murdered after arrest. Thirty-three leaders of the Indian organization MISURASATA are jailed.

1981   Feb. 14: Government mobs make their first appearance, attacking a group of friends of human rights activist José E. González.

1981   Feb.: A clash in the town of Prinzapolka between Sandinista soldiers and Miskito civilians leaves four soldiers and four Indians dead.

1981   Mar. 16: Mobs break up a legal rally of the MDN and terrorize dissidents all over the country. Two independent radio stations are destroyed.

1981   Mar.: The first Miskito exodus to Honduras takes place after mass arrests are made by the government in the towns of Gaspin, Puerto Cabezas and Minerales.

1981   Mar.-Apr.: The Sandinista government dissolves the Miskito workers union of Sandy Bay North.

1981   June: Sixteen prisoners are killed and twenty-seven wounded in a riot at the Zona Franca prison. The government reports no casualties among prison officials.

1981   June 4: The bishops conference asks the priests occupying government office to return to their pastoral duties. The government and the revolutionary Christians launch a campaign against the bishops.

1981   July 7: Archbishop Obando's televised Sunday mass is put off the air by government decree.

1981   July 7: Unidentified hands destroy and deface religious billboards in Managua. Reporting this destruction brings the first government shutdown of *La Prensa* a day later.

1981   July: Mass arrests of Moravian pastors in the Atlantic Coast region are made.

1981   Aug.: Commander Humberto Ortega delivers a speech to the officers of the Sandinista army in which he states plainly that Marxist-Leninism is the doctrine of the Revolution.

1981   Aug.: Miskito leaders Alfredo Stland and Leonel Stone disappear after capture. Stedman Fagoth, another Miskito leader, is arrested. He is subsequently released and escapes to Honduras.

1981   Sep. 9: Worker strikes are banned in the whole country.

1981   Oct. 19: Revolutionary Christians attempt to show their strength at a public liturgy in Managua. According to official estimates, five hundred attend.

1981   Nov.: Bishop Vega first, and then Archbishop Obando, are physically attacked by Sandinista mobs.

1981   Dec.: Massacre at Cruce de las Balsas: thirty-five Miskito Indians are killed by Sandinista soldiers; many of them buried alive.

1982   Jan.: The forced relocation of more than ten thousand Miskito Indians begins. Over forty-nine Indian villages are completely destroyed including crops and livestock. The Sandinistas defend their action claiming that the relocations are to protect the Miskitos from counterrevolutionary attacks.

1982   Jan.: Moravian church leaders Norman Bent and Fernando Colomes are expelled from the Atlantic Coast region.

1982   Jan. 13: Five North American religious (three nuns and two priests) are expelled from the country.

1982   Jan. 17: Dissident radio newsman Manuel Jiron, director of the Mi Preferida radio station, is attacked by three gunmen in an attempt to kidnap him.

1982   Feb. 18: The Nicaraguan Catholic bishops issue a communique condemning the violation of human rights of the Miskitos.

1982   Feb.: CEPAD, Centro Antonio Valdivieso and other organizations of the revolutionary Christians go on record justifying the forced relocations of the Miskito Indians.

1982   Mar. 3: The official newspaper *Barricada* starts a propaganda campaign against Protestant denominations.

1982   Mar.-Apr.: Forty CTN activists are arrested.

1982   Mar. 15: The government decrees a state of emergency, suspending personal rights and imposing complete censorship on the media.

1982   May: The Committee of Social Action of the Moravian Church is closed down by government orders.

1982   May 17: Armed attacks are made on the headquarters of the CTN.

1982   May: All churches in the Atlantic Coast region are required to submit all sermons and publications to state security for approval.

1982   June: *La Prensa's* co-editor Horacio Ruiz is kidnapped and brutally beaten by three armed militiamen.

1982   June: The Sandinista government denies the Catholic Church authorization to receive a grant from the Agency for International Development (AID).

1982   July 20: The Catholic bishops issue an open letter decrying the harassment of the church and the several expellings of Bishop Schlaefer of Bluefields.

1982   July 21: Sandinista mobs take over several Catholic churches. The auxiliary bishop of Managua, Bosco Vivas, is severely beaten.

1982   July 31: The Ministry of the Interior bans the publication of a letter from Pope John Paul II to the Nicaraguan bishops. *La Prensa* closes down in protest.

1982   Aug.: Catholic Radio is taken off the air for one month for broadcasting "inaccurate information."

1982   Aug. 9: More than twenty churches are taken over by Sandinista mobs. The mobs claim that the pastors of the churches are involved in counterrevolutionary propaganda.

1982   Aug. 11: The government stages a public defamation of Archbishop of Managua spokesman Fr. Bismarck Carballo. The incident sets off a chain of anti-government riots involving high school students and the Monimbó Indians. Three people are killed.

1982   Aug.: Two Salesian priests are expelled from the country. A Salesian high school is confiscated (later returned) by the state. Episcopal conferences from around the world protest the treatment of the Salesians.

1982   Aug. 30: The government lifts the ban on the publication of the pope's letter. Some of the churches taken over on August 9 are returned.

1982   Nov. 4: A military emergency zone is imposed on 24 Miskito municipalities depriving the Indians in these areas of freedom of movement.

1982   Dec.: A second massive relocation of Miskito Indians begins in the province of Jinotega.

1982   Dec. 8: The bishops conference issues a pastoral letter praising progress made in the field of education but criticizing its increasingly atheistic contents. The government responds with a new round of verbal attacks against the Catholic hierarchy.

1982   Mar.: Dock workers at the port of Corinto are harassed and jailed because of their decision to join the independent labor organization CUS rather than the Sandinista CST.

1983   Mar. 4: The Pope visits Nicaragua and is rudely treated by Sandinista agitators during his outdoor liturgy in Managua.

1983   Mar.: Anti-Sandinista rebel forces stage their first large-scale offensive in the northern provinces of Nicaragua.

1983   Apr.: A government decree requires sermons by church leaders to be censored by the Ministry of the Interior prior to broadcast. Live broadcasts are prohibited.

1983   May: Thirty-four theologians from around the world express their support for the revolutionary Christians in Nicaragua and criticize the Pope for the way he handled his visit.

1983   May: A Catholic priest, Fr. Timoteo Merino, is expelled from Nicaragua.

1983   Aug. 29: The bishops conference issues a pastoral letter criticizing the military law enacted by the government on the grounds that it forces young men to join an essentially partisan army.

1983   Oct. 30: Twenty-six Catholic churches are attacked by Sandinista mobs. Many parishioners and some priests are beaten.

1983   Nov. 1: Two Salesian priests are expelled.

1983   Nov.: Bishop Pablo Vega, president of the Nicaraguan bishops conference, denounces the murder after arrest of lay Catholic leaders in the diocese of Juigalpa.

1983   Dec. 22: Daniel Ortega announces that a *contra* unit has kidnapped the Indians of the relocation camp "Francia Sirpe," killing the Atlantic Coast region's Catholic bishop

Salvador Schlaefer. The Bishop arrives in Honduras unharmed and declares that the Indians had willingly left.

1984   Jan.: Sandinista soldiers kill eight Miskitos in Honduras. Fr. D'Escoto, Nicaraguan Minister of Foreign Affairs, accuses the Honduran army of having massacred two hundred Nicaraguan Indian refugees.

1984   Jan.: The Ministry of Education does not allow the Catholic La Salle High School to hire its own teachers. Strikes and negotiations follow. The government does not yield.

1984   Jan.: Argentinian evangelist Alberto Montessi faces last-minute obstacles to his crusade in Managua two days after he refused to publicly condemn "U.S. imperialism."

1984   Jan.-Feb.: The government cracks down on the National Council of Evangelical Pastors, a Protestant umbrella organization representing most Nicaraguan evangelicals. Unlike CEPAD, the National Council has sought to remain independent of the regime.

1984   Apr.: The bishops conference issues a pastoral letter calling for reconciliation and dialogue between all Nicaraguans, including the armed rebels. Sandinista spokesmen call it "criminal."

1984   Apr.: *La Prensa* journalist Luis Mora arrested.

1984   June: Vocational school of the labor organization CUS attacked by mobs.

1984   June 17: A Sandinista mob attacks participants at a service in El Sauce concelebrated by the Nicaraguan bishops.

1984   June 19: Sandinista police chief Lenín Cerna announces that the government has uncovered a conspiracy against the state involving a Catholic priest, Fr. Amado Peña. The Catholic hierarchy denies the charges and supports Fr. Peña. A few days later a Sandinista mob attacks Fr. Peña's church forcing him to seek refuge at a seminary.

1984   July: Ten Catholic priests holding important leadership positions in the church are expelled. The government charges that they have been involved in counterrevolutionary propaganda.

1984   Aug.: The Sandinista government fails in an attempt to setup and discredit Bishop Baltasar Porras of Venezuela on a visit to Nicaragua.

1984   Aug. 25: The headquarters of the labor organization CUS is occupied and vandalized by the Sandinista police.

1984   Sep.: An evangelical-sponsored Month of the Bible is carried through in spite of government obstacles.

1984   Oct.: The Coordinadora Democratica, a coalition of democratic parties and labor unions led by Arturo Cruz, refuses to participate in the national presidential election claiming that the minimum conditions for a free election have not been met.

1984   Nov. 4: Amidst intense controversy, a national presidential election is held in Nicaragua. After the election, all criticisms of election procedures and results is censored.

1984   Jan.-Mar.: Forced relocation of more than fifty thousand peasants takes place in five Nicaraguan provinces.

1985   Apr.: A Catholic priest, Fr. Gregorio Raya, is expelled.

1985   Apr.: The Vatican appoints Archbishop Obando y Bravo of Managua a cardinal of the Catholic Church.

1985   May 1: The Sandinista police break up a march by the workers of the CTN and CUS labor organizations.

1985   May 2: One hundred Cuban military advisors leave Nicaragua. Present at the farewell ceremony is Cuban General Arnaldo Ochoa, former top commander of the Cuban forces in Angola, and currently stationed in Nicaragua.

1985   May: The president of the Union of Catholic Parents (UNAPAFACC), Sofonías Cisneros, is arrested and tortured by Sandinista police chief Lenin Cerna after he denounces the Marxist and overpoliticized nature of official education programs.

INDEX

This index does not include citations for Somoza or the Somoza regime, the Sandinistas, Somocistas, etc., as these are discussed throughout the book.

178, 180, 191, 194, 200,
230, 233, 246
Central America, 2
Centro Antonio Valdivieso
(CAV), 155, 171, 173, 178,
179, 193, 194, 195, 196,
223, 234
CEPAD see *Center for
Promotion and
Development*
Cerna, Lenín, 199, 225, 226
Cerullo, Morris, 192
César, Alfredo, 96
Chamorro, Pedro (son), 37,
91
Chamorro, Pedro Joaquín, 8,
10, 36, 37, 38, 39, 85, 154
Chamorro, Violeta, 38, 43,
51, 57, 85, 89
Chile, 133
Christian Democrats, 7, 15,
79
*Christian Faith and
Sandinista Revolution in
Nicaragua,* 159
Christian Revolutionary
Movement (MCR), 23, 24,
28, 32
Christianity, Christians,
and Marxism, ix, x, xiii, 1,
12, 24, 25
and revolution, x, xii, 2,
12, 20, 21, 22, 25, 26, 30,
40, 139, 140, 143, 150,
154, 155, 156, 157, 158,
159, 160, 162, 163, 164,
169, 173, 177, 189, 195,
214, 215, 216, 241, 242,
243
persecution of, 138, 154,
161, 191, 202, 233, 242,
245

Christianity and Crisis, 161
CIA, 43, 82, 86, 92, 109,
110, 111, 130, 192, 193,
194, 195, 214, 222, 225
Cisneros, Sofonías, 208
Class struggle, 17
Clevban, Rev. Santos, 201
Colombia, 21
Colomes, Fernando, 201
Comintern (Communist
International), 17
Communists, communism, x,
xi, 1, 2, 7, 8, 9, 17, 20,
23, 34, 36, 37, 53, 64, 72,
73, 75, 134, 154, 160,
161, 169, 170, 195, 197,
220, 234, 235, 247
Contras, the, 113, 128, 129,
131, 178, 216, 218, 220,
223, 224, 225, 227, 246
Contreras, Eduardo, 27
Corsi, Carlos, 131, 190
Cortés, Benjamin, 155, 158,
161, 177
Costa Rica, x, xi, 42, 63, 77,
201, 220
*Cristianos en la Revolucion
Nicaragüense* (Margaret
Randall), 23
Cristo Campesino, 179
Cruz, Arturo, 31, 65, 66, 91,
95, 98, 130
Cuadernos Garcia Laviana,
179
Cuadernos Rutilio Grande,
179
Cuadra, Joaquín, 23, 31, 236
Cuadra, Pablo Antonio, 85,
110, 122
Cuba, xii, 8, 9, 10, 15, 16,
20, 21, 36, 42, 53, 62, 71,
74, 76, 77, 78, 102, 108,

ABOUT THE AUTHOR

Humberto Belli is a native Nicaraguan who was a Marxist and a member of the Sandinista movement before becoming a Christian in 1977. He is trained as a lawyer (University of Madrid) and a sociologist (University of Pennsylvania).

After the Sandinista revolution in 1979, Belli worked as editorial page editor of the independent daily newspaper, *La Prensa,* often exploring the theme of church and state interaction. The imposition of total censorship on the press in March 1982 made this work impossible. He moved to the United States to continue communicating about the difficulties that Christians in Nicaragua are facing. His articles have appeared in numerous religious and secular publications, such as *America* magazine, *Catholicism in Crisis,* and *Pastoral Renewal.* In 1984, he published **Nicaragua: Christians Under Fire,** which formed the base for **Breaking Faith.**

Belli is founder of The Puebla Institute, a non–profit organization concerned with fostering a Christian understanding of theological and socio–political issues affecting Latin America.

He and his wife, Rosario have four daughters.